NORTH SEA HEROES
True Stories from a Scottish Shore

Mike Shepherd

Mike Shepherd

A Wild Wolf Publication

Published by Wild Wolf Publishing in 2022

First print

ISBN: 978-1-907954-82-5
Also available as an E-Book

www.wildwolfpublishing.com

CONTENTS

1. The Men of the Armada
2. Sir George Bruce
3. Jacobites in Rebellion
4. The Men of the Bass
5. The Glorious Frances Wright
6. Nashoba
7. Cincinnati
8. James Croll
9. The Ice Age
10. James Croll's Big Ideas
11. Tryggve Gran and Captain Scott
12. Tryggve Gran Flies the North Sea
13. Tryggve Gran Goes to War
14. Mary Pratt

References

THANKS TO:

Gordon Casely
Gordon Findlay
Colin Johnston
Elizabeth Oates
Elizabeth Park
Aud Lise Rosland
John Ross
Nora Simpson
Aberdeenshire Libraries
The Port Erroll Heritage Group

INTRODUCTION

The stories in this book are sourced from primary historical documents and nothing is made up. Because they are narrated as they happened the text resembles a work of historical fiction, although it is not. The aim is to make the stories more immediate and vivid, not the least because their heroes deserve this treatment.

1. THE MEN OF THE ARMADA

November 26, 1588
James Melville, the minister of Anstruther-Wester Parish Church, awoke at the break of day to find one of the village bailiffs at his bedside, 'I have news to tell you, sir. A ship full of Spaniards arrived at our harbour this morning, asking for mercy.'

The ship held 250 soldiers and crew who sailed with the Spanish Armada. Nobody in Anstruther had any idea why they had arrived in their village on the Fife coast.

The chapter to follow is the story of these men. Many heroes emerge from its telling, although two stand out: Juan Gómez de Medina, the Catholic commander of the Squadron of Hulks, and James Melville, Protestant minister of the church in Anstruther. Based on eyewitness accounts, it includes excerpts translated from the diary of a Spaniard who sailed with the Squadron of Hulks.

May 30, 1588
The Spanish Armada has set sail from Lisbon on a mission to invade England - a mission likely to succeed, because Queen Elizabeth's tiny army must surely be overwhelmed by the military might coming its way. Sailing in the wake of Gómez de Medina's flagship *El Gran Grifón* as it leaves Lisbon is his squadron of twenty-two hulks, huge ships carrying troops, equipment, and supplies. And this squadron is but a small part of an invasion fleet of 129 ships filled with 26,170 men; a fleet so large that when it sails in battle formation it stretches across six miles of sea.

Once the Armada arrives in the English Channel, the intention is to link up with the main invasion force of 26,000 men in the Spanish Netherlands; an army that will then cross over to England in 300 flat-bottomed barges under the protection of the Armada's warships.

A successful invasion would see Philip II, King of Spain, seize the English throne from Queen Elizabeth of England, the Catholic faith restored in the country, and will put a stop to the exasperating behaviour of the English, who are helping the Protestant rebels in the Spanish Netherlands. Not only that, English privateers led by Francis Drake had recently plundered Spanish treasure ships off the coast of South America.

The Armada will take two months to sail from Lisbon to the English Channel.

July 31, 1588

The Spanish ships have arrived off England, and are met by the English navy. The English tactics impress the diarist: 'They won the windward [sailing behind the Armada] and began to fire their cannons, being careful not to get too close. We did not have ships as fast as theirs.'

When the English do engage with the Spanish ships, they fire their cannons at a rapid and effective rate: 'I suspect they did more harm than they received.'

These skirmishes mark a new phase in the history of naval warfare. The Spanish employ old tactics: the use of ships as floating barracks of soldiers that will be brought alongside an enemy vessel to board and seize it by hand-to-hand fighting. Confronting them today are English ships kitted out with rows of heavyweight cannons – ships that are small, highly manoeuvrable, and sailed by expert seamen. They are in effect floating artillery batteries. The naval strategy employed by the English sailors is to keep a safe distance from the enemy to avoid being boarded, and then crash out cannonball after cannonball into wooden ships crowded with men. This proves highly effective.

And if this was not a bad enough start for their campaign, the Spanish then suffer two disasters.

The *Nuestra Señora del Rosario* breaks her bowsprit and foresail when she accidentally collides with another Spanish ship. Worse follows, her foremast collapses making her unsteerable. Although an attempt is made to attach a line to tow the *Nuestra Señora del Rosario*, which has 464 men on board, the effort is quickly abandoned when the English approach to attack. The ship, its sailors, and soldiers are now left to the mercy of the enemy, that is, if they show any at all. The incident causes much bad feeling amongst the Spanish, not the least because it reminds everyone they are expendable. Many believe that not enough effort had been made to rescue the men.

And then another calamity happens at four o'clock in the afternoon when an explosion rips apart the *San Salvador*, 'blowing up half or most of the ship,' writes the diarist. Another eyewitness reported the events. The *San Salvador* 'caught fire in the powder magazine, two decks and the poop castle being blown up. In this ship was the Paymaster-general of the Armada, with a part of his Majesty's treasure.' What is left of the ship still floats, so assistance is given, the fires put out, and the ship towed.

In the darkness of night, when it is safe to do so, the Spanish launch a rescue operation. The officers are amongst those taken off in four boats, including the paymaster, together with his papers and some of the money. Fifty burnt and severely wounded men are left behind on the shattered shell of a ship. It lumbers along hopefully in the wake of the rest of the fleet, before being swallowed up by the murky gloom.

Rumours spread as to what caused the explosion. Our diarist has heard that an English gunner was responsible; he was one of the foreign contingent of Catholics who had shipped with the Armada. Another wrote that the captain of the *San Salvador* had beaten a German gunner, who then went below decks and threw a lighted match into a barrel of gunpowder, 'killing over 200 men'.

In a melancholy frame of mind, the diarist writes that these disasters are '*the announcement of our doom*' and foretell an '*ill omen*' for the navy.

August 3, 1588

The history books record that the *Revenge*, captained by Francis Drake, attacked *El Gran Grifón* today. Two broadsides, forty cannonballs or more, crashed into the ship causing much damage and sending deadly wood splinters whistling through the air. Sixty men are killed and seventy are wounded. Gómez de Medina's flagship is saved from destruction when two Spanish ships sail back to fight off the *Revenge*, many cannonballs having been fired on both sides.

August 6, 1588

'With a favourable wind we arrived at Calais, a city of the King of France, at four in the afternoon. We set anchor [four miles offshore] and the opposing navy arrived, laying off just beyond cannon shot,' writes the diarist.

The ships of the Armada are here to link up with the invasion force of 26,000 soldiers camped in Dunkirk, twenty-four miles from Calais. However, the soldiers are nowhere near ready to set off yet, and are unlikely to do so for at least a week. The Armada will have to wait for them in an exposed position off the coast with hostile ships lurking nearby. It is a parlous situation because the English navy will almost certainly not allow the Spanish time to combine their forces.

August 7 - 8, 1588

As could be expected, the English take the initiative. The diarist writes: 'At about twelve o'clock at night, a little more or less, the current and the wind coming against where we were at anchor, the English let loose eight ships, which they then set on fire, and these were aimed at the middle of our fleet.'

Another eyewitness provides more details. The fireships 'advanced in line at a distance of a couple of pikes' length between them. Wind and tide were in their favour.' Lurching towards the Spanish, one fireship 'flared up with such fierceness and great noise as were frightful, and at this the ships of the Armada cut their cables at once'. And from someone else who was there: The fireships 'burnt with such fierceness that it was believed they were "artificial machines" [ships loaded with gunpowder or explosive mines], and as the Armada was in close order, the admiral of the fleet, fearing the damage that might be caused by them, gave orders for the cables to be cut, and the whole of our ships spread their sails, leaving nearly 300 anchors behind them.'

That the Spanish panicked is no surprise. 'Artificial machines', sometimes known as 'hellburners', had been used against them by the Dutch during the Siege of Antwerp three years earlier. The hellburners were sent in to attack the pontoon barrier blocking the River Scheldt and denying hostile forces access to the heart of the city. Much devastation was caused and many died when the 'artificial machines' exploded.

Our diarist notes that the English 'were so fortunate with their efforts, because they evicted us with eight ships, which they could not and did not dare to do with 130 ships.'

And now the direction the wind is blowing compels the ships of the Armada to sail north; the English navy in chase. Catching up with the Spanish ships on the morning of August 8, the English 'attacked with the greatest fury, firing great loads of cannon fire, trying to throw us thoroughly and to make us hit the sandbanks on the shore to finish off our entire navy'. History books describe this as the Battle of Gravelines.

Here is another account of the battle:

> At seven o'clock on Monday morning, at about two leagues from here [Calais], both fleets came into action, the firing on both sides being the greatest ever seen or imagined... The cannonade was heard with the same fury the whole of that day, until at last it died away in the

distance. Since then we have no news except for a fisherman who came in yesterday.'

The fisherman had witnessed the battle: 'He saw some ships broken into bits, others without masts or sails, from which they were throwing overboard artillery, trunks, and many other things whilst men were striving to save themselves by escaping in boats, with such lamentations as can be imagined.'

A Spaniard captured by the English told them what he knew about the battle. A ship had ran ashore at Calais, 'two galleons, one called *St Philip of the Brando*, the other called the *San Mateo* with 800 men, a Biscay ship with about 500 men, and a Castile ship with about 400 men, all sunk... After this fight ended, he had heard from the admiral that there were 120 ships left of the Spanish fleet, and those were very sore beaten, and the admiral's ship was many times shot through. The mast was so weak because of the shot in it, they dare not abide any storm.'

August 11, 1588

Today, the Spanish receive the only piece of good luck so far in their campaign. A strong wind had been blowing their damaged ships relentlessly towards the sand banks off the Dutch coast, but just as they are on the verge of grounding on the sand to be then shot apart by English cannons, the wind changes direction, allowing the ships to escape to the open sea.

It is a miracle. Even so, the diarist notes that the ships of the Armada have been left in a desperate situation: 'With the enemy following us, they had the wind, we were short of powder and ammunition, food and water were running out, and not having a port to repair the damage to the ships, the admiral decided to return to Spain.'

Because of the way the wind is blowing, to get to Spain the fleet has no choice but to sail around the Scottish mainland and then down the west coast of Ireland. Yet, the planks on their ships' hulls are loose, with water leaking through the gaps between them; the masts, rigging, and sails have suffered much damage; and their anchors have gone. What's more, the autumn gales have started to blow for the season.

Worst of all, the Armada had set out from Lisbon with barely enough food and water to get to the English Channel. The Spanish expected to restock their supplies on arriving onshore, but this had not been possible. The situation is dire because their ships are packed full of men - jam-packed full - only the officers have bunks; no hammocks are provided, the men having to sleep where they can, some in makeshift shelters on the top deck. That is altogether too many men and not enough food.

The diarist records that, 'the daily rations were reduced; each person to get half a pound of biscuit, half a quart of wine and a quart of water.'

And in a letter to Philip II, King of Spain, the admiral of the fleet, the Duke of Medina Sidonia, wrote: 'Our provisions are so scanty that, in order to make them and the water last a month, the rations of every person on the fleet without exception has been reduced; just enough being served out to keep them alive.' It's a calamity. 'Your Majesty may imagine what suffering this entails in the midst of the discomfort of so long a voyage. We have consequently over 3,000 sick without counting the wounded, who are numerous on the fleet.'

Here are two snapshots taken from witness accounts highlighting the problems facing the Armada:

'The troubles and miseries we have suffered cannot be described... On board some of the ships there was not one drop of water to drink for a fortnight. On the flagship 180 men died of sickness, three out of the four pilots on board having succumbed, and all of the rest of the people on the ship are ill, many of typhus and other contagious maladies.'

Disease spreads rapidly in the crowded ships. And because the men are starving, the natural response of their bodies is to conserve energy by minimising the activity of its immune system. The men will die of disease before they starve to death.

And another account: 'There is in this ship left but 25 pipes of wine, and very little bread; and no water, but what they brought out of Spain, which stinketh marvellously.'

August 12-14, 1588

The Armada is sailing up the North Sea on their long and roundabout journey home. On August 12, the men on board the *El Gran Grifón* 'woke up within a cannon shot of the enemy navy, and at noon we saw how the enemy navy was getting close. It was all very sad, so that no one spoke to each other, not even the admiral responded when we came to greet him.

On the 13th of that month, the admiral sent an order to throw all the horses and mules into the sea to save the drinking water on board.'

The diarist does not mention how many animals went overboard, although the Armada is known to have set out with approximately 300 horses and 40 mules.

'On the 14th of that month we saw many horses and mules swimming past us after they had been thrown out, which was a great pity, because they were all approaching the ships to get help.'

According to an English intelligence report, this happened in the middle of the North Sea offshore from Newcastle.

So why did the Spaniards throw the horses and mules overboard when they could have butchered them for meat? An eyewitness mentions that 'their flesh meat they cannot eat, their thirst is so great'. Without fresh water to drink, it is only safe to eat food rich in carbohydrates such as biscuits. Meat contains protein and fat, and because these require water for digestion, eating meat will quickly kill a dehydrated man.

The diarist also notes that, 'This day was when we woke up without seeing the enemy's army.'

The English navy had chased them as far as the Firth of Forth, and then sailed home because their supplies were running out.

What now ensues is a desperate act of survival under extreme conditions. The Spanish ships, many badly damaged by cannon shot, are struggling through slashing North Sea gales around an unfamiliar rocky coast.

August 18 – September 2, 1588
The diary continues:

> 'We woke up without the Navy or the Admiral, and there were only four ships in our group. We continued sailing together up until the end of August, when one of the hulks asked for help. They were shipping water and the pumps were choked with ballast. The 180 men on board were taken off and distributed around the other three ships. It was not possible to take food or anything else out of the ship because of the bad weather, although it was badly needed.
>
> From August 18 to September 2, we made a determined effort to see if we could double the Cape of Clare on the coast of Ireland [probably the Galway coastline]. It was God's will that he would not allow it. On September 2, we lost the other ships and we ran alone.

We then spent the next three days in great danger from a horrendous storm.

We were given respite from the storm on the 5th, which encouraged us to go back to Spain. We slept until eleven o'clock, and then made another attempt to round the cape. We tacked back and forth until the 17th to see if we could get past it but the winds were not in our favour.' And then:

'A great storm damaged our ship, opening up gaps in the planks of our hull. Even with two pumps and all the men helping we could barely cope with the water flooding in.'

September 18-23, 1588

'We will have to go to Norway to get the ship repaired. After tacking for three days, we discovered an island of Scotland at $57^{1/2}$ degrees latitude. And after sailing for ten leagues during the morning, the wind veered, giving us a north-west wind. This gave us the courage to try for dear Spain again.

And for three days we sailed until we reached the same place as before, only to face a wind so strong and a sea so wild that the waves blocked the sky and the ship was being torn apart.

Water is still flooding in through the hull. God served us with a calm day, and we went below to stuff the leaks with cow hides and boards, which allowed us to pump the water out.'

September 24-26, 1588

'The wind rose again and contrary to the direction which would take us home. We decided to turn around and make for Scotland. Late on the 25th, we discovered some islands, which our pilot said were Scottish and inhabited by wild people.

We sailed to the north-east until the 26th when we discovered other islands. We would try to get away from them in case we were shipwrecked there. We were now resolved to find the nearest part of the mainland of Scotland, ramming the ship onland should we have to, because the sea was turning rough and the hull was filling with water again. We must finish this tonight, because the sea is so rough it is as if it fills the sky.

13

At four o'clock in the afternoon, we discovered an island to our windward side, which gave us much grief to see because the night was coming and we would find ourselves caught between islands [A perilous situation in a storm], although we had thought they were behind us.'

September 27, 1588

'At two o'clock at night the rain stopped, revealing another island on our prow. Those who have experienced such a situation will understand the confusion we felt. God had helped us at this moment by giving us enough light to see so that we could flee from this peril. As it became lighter, in two hours, more or less, we came upon a very large island which looked impossible to get round. This was the island they call Creane [the Mainland of Orkney?], which was where we would land should we not make the Scottish mainland. We wanted to get close to her but we feared the sea and its fierceness.'

The Spaniards sail along the coast of this island for three or four hours but cannot find anywhere to land:

'The sea was crashing into us with huge waves and our only thought was that our lives were now at an end. We beseeched God to show us the true path before our ship fell apart. If we are to stay in the ship any longer we will die.'

It is looking hopeless for the Spaniards - their ship has filled with water to a level of eight feet inside the hull, and most of the men are too weak and dispirited to operate the pumps. It does not help that the work appears pointless anyway because water is filling the ship faster than it can be removed:

'The men are in despair, 230 soldiers from our ship and forty more who were rescued, didn't lift a finger, and each one so disheartened they are calling to the Virgin Mary, bewailing their lot that they had come on such a bitter journey.'

Those who are still working with pumps and buckets to remove the water pray that they will be judged favourably by God for having made

14

the effort. Only God could help them now, a deity 'who never lacked anyone to call him,' writes the diarist. And then, at two o'clock in the afternoon, they spot Fair Isle, a rocky island, five miles long and one and half miles wide, which lies between Orkney and Shetland.

The diarist does not discuss what happened next, and the following is a guess.

With the sun setting and the light dimming, Juan Gómez de Medina knows he must take action, *desperate action*. As he rounds the south-east shore of Fair Isle, he spots a deep rocky inlet, which today is named Stroms Hellier. This inlet offers hope because he might be able to ram his ship into it.

Taking immediate action, Juan Gómez de Medina points the 650-ton *El Gran Grifón* directly towards the inlet. His men are screaming, the wind is howling, and the waves buffeting the ship make his task near impossible. The ship closes in - this will be a tight fit. The timbers of the hull forcibly meet both the rock bottom of the shoaling inlet and a reef to one side, and as they do so, the sounds of shearing timber are to be heard even above the roaring of the storm. The great mass of the *El Gran Grifón* grinds forward until it shudders to a stop largely intact and wedged fast inside the inlet. Not only that, a ledge on the cliffs, accessible from the ship's masts, provides a fortuitous route to safety and the island beyond.

This is a huge feat of seamanship - Juan Gómez de Medina has deftly sailed his enormous flagship *El Gran Grifón* into a rocky inlet through high seas, and then rammed the ship onshore in such a way that his men can escape to safety. Three hundred men are now alive because of his efforts. *Heroic efforts.*

September 28 – November 14, 1588

The diarist picks up the story again:

> Fair Isle is populated by seventeen households living in shacks; they are wild people. They eat mostly fish and they do not have bread, except for cakes baked from barley. They cook these over fires fed with fuel taken from the earth, which they call *turba* [peat]. They have cattle, quite a lot for them because they seldom eat meat. They herd cows, sheep, and pigs; the cows are the most productive supplying them with milk and butter. They get wool from the sheep for their clothes.

15

They are very dirty people. They are not Christian but not quite heretics either. Their minister comes from an island to preach to them once a year. They do not like this but cannot do anything about it. It is a shame.

Three hundred men landed on this island without any food. From September 28th to November 14th fifty men have died. Most of them from hunger. *It is the biggest sorrow in the world.*

We decided to send messengers to the neighbouring island to get boats to Scotland. However, because the weather was so bad, this was not possible until October 27th, which was a pleasant day. They have not returned yet because the seas have been so rough.

The diary ends here on November 14. We know from another source that Juan Gómez de Medina and his men arrived in Anstruther on November 26: William Asheby, the English Ambassador to Scotland, reported this at the time.

Extra information is available about the six or seven weeks the men of the Armada were resident on Fair Isle. The Reverend John Brand visited Orkney, Shetland, and Northern Scotland in 1701, writing a book about his travels. Bear in mind that what he describes took place 113 years before his visit. He recounts what must have been the family memories of ageing great-grandchildren on Fair Isle. Although the events were dramatic enough to be recalled by them years later, it is inevitable that errors, distortions, and exaggerations have crept into the narrative. For example, John Brand reports that it was the admiral of the fleet, the Duke of Medina Sidonia, who had been stranded on Fair Isle, not Juan Gómez de Medina. And that the Spanish overwintered there, whereas they left the island in November.

Even so, some of what follows feels authentic given that 300 starving Spaniards had descended on an island with a population of perhaps a hundred or more subsistence farmers and fishermen; islanders who had been scraping through in a year beset by much bad weather:

They wintered here in great misery, for the Spaniards at first eating up all they could find, not only meat, sheep, fishes and fowls, but also horses; the islanders in the night carried off their beasts and victuals to places in the isle

16

where the Spaniards might not find them. The officers also strictly commanded the soldiers to take nothing but what they paid for, which they did very largely, so that the people were not great losers by them, having a great deal of Spanish *reals* for the victuals they gave them.

But now the people fearing a famine amongst themselves, kept their victuals from the Spaniards; thus all supply from the isle failing them, they took their own bread (which they had preserved), which being dipped in fish oil, they did eat, which being also spent, it came to pass that many of them died of hunger, and the rest were so weakened, that one or two of the islanders finding a few of them together, could easily throw them over the banks, by which many of them died [a highly unlikely story].

At length all sustenance failing, not only to the Spaniards, but also to the islanders, they sent a small boat to Shetland, desiring a ship to carry them out, less all the inhabitants of the isle should be famished.

Notice came to Andrew Umphrey of Burra (then proprietor of the isle), who having a ship of his own, instantly went to the isle, and brought them to Shetland, where for the space of twenty days or a month, they met with better entertainment. The Duke stayed at Quendale till the ship was ready... From Shetland Andrew Umphrey carried them in his little ship to Dunkirk, for which the Duke rewarded him with three thousand Merks [Another inaccuracy: William Asheby, the English Ambassador, wrote that the Spaniards intended to head for the Scottish mainland, 'meaning to hire a couple of ships to take them into the Low Countries'].

November 26, 1588

Today the Spaniards arrive in Anstruther. James Melville, Minister of the Anstruther-Wester Parish Church, takes up the story in his diary. He has just been woken up and informed about the 250 Spanish men at the harbour: 'The officers had landed, and [the bailiff] told them to get back on their ship again until the magistrates of the town had given their advice. The Spaniards had humbly obeyed. He wanted me to rise and to negotiate with them.'

17

James Melville is a linguist, having studied Greek and Hebrew. He was appointed Professor of Hebrew and Oriental Languages at St Andrews University, only to resign after six years to take up his present job: one that brought in a better income to support his family.

He continues, 'I quickly got up, and assembling the honest men of the town, came to the Tolbooth; and was taken to meet their commander.'

In 1588, everyone in Scotland knew that Spain had launched a great fleet of ships to invade England (some even believing that they would land in Scotland first). Nothing more was then heard after it had left Lisbon, whereupon the rumours abounded for months. Reports variously came in that the Spanish had landed at Dunbar, or St Andrews, in the Tay, 'and now and then at Aberdeen and Cromarty'.

James Melville had written in his diary about the 'the prayers, the sighs and sobs, and the abounding tears' of the Protestant ministers and elders who had met at the extraordinary meeting of the General Assembly of the Kirk in February 1588. It had been organised when news came through that the Spanish were preparing their Armada. Panic set in because it was widely believed that following the successful invasion of England, as thought inevitable, the Spanish would then march into Scotland, whereby the Catholic faith would be restored and all those refusing to conform persecuted. The Protestant ministers would most likely be declared heretics, tortured, and perhaps executed.

James's uncle, Andrew Melville, had given the opening speech at the extraordinary meeting of the Church. In it, he urged King James VI to lock up all the Jesuits and Roman Catholic sympathisers in Scotland who were likely to aid the invaders. The King, unwilling to provoke the Spanish by doing this, took the lesser course of issuing a proclamation in May 1588, declaring that all able-bodied men between the age of sixteen and sixty should take up arms and be in readiness at six hours warning. Although Scotland was neutral in the war between England and Spain, the threat was real that Spanish troops would cross the border, and that the many Catholics living in the North of Scotland would rise up in support of them.

Then, just the month before the Spanish landed in Anstruther, the great news arrived that the Armada had been defeated. Churches throughout Scotland held public fasts to celebrate. And so, on this day, November 26, 1588, the men and women of Anstruther must have

18

asked each other, 'why, then, if the Armada has been defeated, has a ship full of Spanish sailors and soldiers turned up in our harbour?'

James Melville continues the story, having arrived at the Tolbooth:

> Facing me was a very respectable man of big stature, and grave and stout countenance, grey-haired, and very humble like, who, after much courtesy, bowed down with his face near the ground, and touching my shoe with his hand, began talking quickly in Spanish, of which I understood the substance; and just as I was about to reply in Latin, a young man, who was his interpreter, talked to me in good English.
>
> In summary, King Philip, his master, had rigged out a navy and army to land in England to avenge many wrongs which he had received from that nation; but God for their sins had been against them, and stormy weather had driven the navy up the coast of England. He was the commander of a squadron of twenty ships in the fleet. His flagship had been wrecked on a Scottish island called Fair Isle; and although many had survived the merciless seas, they then had to endure six or seven weeks of great hunger and cold on the island, until a ship took them from Orkney to the mainland where they intend to make obeisance to the King of Scotland, and to find relief for his officers and men, whose condition was for the present most pitiful and miserable.
>
> This is a summary of what I said to him at length: 'That how be it, our friendship cannot be great, seeing their King and his friends in war, the greatest enemy of Christ, the Pope of Rome, have been defied by our King; nor yet their cause against our neighbours and special friends in England could procure any benefit at our hands for their relief and comfort; nevertheless, they should know by experience that we were men, and so moved by human compassion, and Christians of better religion than they... For whereas our people, resorting amongst them in peaceable and lawful affairs of merchandise, were violently taken and cast in prison, their goods and property confiscated, and their bodies committed to the cruel flaming fire for the cause of religion, they should find nothing on our side but Christian pride and works of mercy and alms, leaving God to work in their hearts concerning religion as it pleased him.

After the translator had reported these words to Juan Gómez de Medina, the Spaniard 'with great reverence gave thanks, and said that he could not answer for the Catholic Church, only for himself, that there were several Scotsmen who knew him, and to whom he had shown favour at Calais, and as he supposed, some from Anstruther.'

Juan Gómez de Medina and his captains are told they will be fed and given lodgings in the town, but that none of their men should land until King James has been informed and his opinion on the matter known. 'Thus with great courtesy he departed.'

The men of Anstruther have a choice to make. What is to be done with these Spaniards from this despised Catholic nation? The countryside will have to be scoured for food, and quickly too if the men are not to die of hunger. Such will require a huge effort to be made by people who hate the Spanish with a passion, and will be most reluctant to help.

That evening the Laird of Anstruther arrives to see the situation for himself, and asks James Melville for advice about what to do with the Spanish men.

'Give them bread and water.'

James later wrote in his diary that 'my advice was that of the Prophet Elijah to the King of Israel, in Samaria'. Here is the relevant text from the Bible:

> And the king of Israel said unto Elisha, when he saw them, My father, shall I smite them? shall I smite them? And he answered, Thou shalt not smite them: wouldest thou smite those whom thou hast taken captive with thy sword and with thy bow? set bread and water before them, that they may eat and drink, and go to their master.
>
> And he prepared great provision for them: and when they had eaten and drunk, he sent them away, and they went to their master. So the bands of Syria came no more into the land of Israel. [2 Kings 6.]

The next morning, the Laird of Anstruther gives Juan Gómez de Medina and his captains much the same speech as they had received from James Melville the day before. He then 'received them in his house, and entertained them humanely, and suffered the soldiers to come on land and lie altogether, to the number of thirteen score, for the most part young beardless men, enfeebled, hardly able to move, and hungered, to which kail, porridge, and fish was given.' It takes between one and two days to feed them all.

James Melville provides more details about the Spanish visitors in his diary:

> The names of the officers were Jan Gomes de Medina, General of twenty hulks, Captain Patricio, Captain de Legoretto, Captain de Luffera, Captain Mauritio, and Senor Serrano.
>
> But verily all the while my heart melted within me for desire of thankfulness to God, when I remembered the prideful and cruel nature of these people with their forces amongst us; and saw the wonderful work of God's mercy and justice in making us see them, the chief commanders of them to make such thanks-to-God salutations and courtesy to pure seamen, and their soldiers so abjectly to beg alms at our doors and in our streets.
>
> In the mean time, they knew nothing of the wreck of the rest [of their ships], but supposed that the rest of the army was safely returned, until one day I got in St Andrews in print *The Wreck of the Galleons* in particular, with the name of the principal men, and [what happened to them] in Ireland and our Highlands, in Wales, and other parts of England; which I read to Jan Gomes by particular and special names. *O then he cried out for grief, burst, and wept.*
>
> This Jan Gomes showed great kindness to a ship of our town, which he discovered had been seized at Calais on his home-coming, got the ship released, and made great praise of Scotland to his king, took the sailors to his house in Calais, and inquired after the Laird of Anstruther, for the minister, and his host, and sent home many commendations.
>
> But we thanked God with our hearts, that we had seen them amongst us in that form.

2. SIR GEORGE BRUCE

1575

Twenty-five-year old George Bruce has been given *a challenge*: his cousin has granted him the lease to mine coal at the Castlehill Colliery near Culross on the northern shore of the Firth of Forth, but, as the lease document explains, the colliery 'has been long in desuetude, insomuch, that we have neither large nor small coal for our own house fire'. The colliery is indeed in 'desuetude', an old-fashioned word for disuse. It was abandoned years ago once all the accessible coal had been dug out by the Cistercian monks from nearby Culross Abbey. Nevertheless, the lease document strikes a hopeful note - George is the ideal man to bring the colliery back to life because he has shown 'great knowledge and skill in machinery, such like as no other man has in these days; and for his being the likeliest person to re-establish' the coal pits. *But what can George Bruce do at Culross that the monks have not already done?*

Those monks were innovative and dynamic. They established the Scottish coal industry in the early part of thirteenth century when they opened collieries at Blackness and Tranent near Edinburgh. The holy men used coal to forge iron, and shovelled it into furnaces to produce lime for building material.

Coal extraction by the monks at Castlehill probably started not long after Culross Abbey was founded in 1217. Located on a long ridge of land overlooking the coast of the Firth of Forth, their colliery targeted a coal seam at ground level just over a metre thick. Once the surface coal had been picked out, it took a bit more effort to get at the buried coal. That is because the seam dips into the ground at a gentle angle, requiring successively deeper pits to be dug through the overlying rock to reach it. A pit, bell pits they were called, was dug vertically, and on reaching the coal seam the pit was widened out to recover as much coal as could be had without causing the overlying rock to collapse. To help haul the coal up to the top, a wooden platform was constructed across the narrow neck of the bell, and connected by ladders to the pit floor below and to the ground surface above.

Dug up to ten metres below ground level, sometimes deeper, the bell pits were prone to flooding when it rained and because water was forever seeping out the pit from pores and fractures in the rock.

Yes, water, the coal-miner's enemy. Much of the history of the advances in coal-mining technology has involved the search to find better ways to remove huge volumes of water from mines. The most basic technique employed deep sloping trenches dug outwards from the floor of the pit to drain water downhill – this was the method used by the monks. Ultimately, there came a limit as to how deep the monks could dig them without the trench walls collapsing, or because the trenches had been excavated to the lowest practical depth allowing drainage to take place. Overall, a depth of about ten metres proved to be the limit for bell pits at Castlehill.

The demand for coal had been increasing in Scotland since the thirteenth century, and the monks were supplying that demand. Back then, coal was exclusively used in industry - it was not burnt in houses because the smoke was widely believed to be unhealthy - fuel for domestic use was wood, peat, and turf. But then trees became scarce in Scotland, and coal started to be used in the home. Thereafter, domestic use accelerated when it became customary for chimneys to be built on houses.

Demand from overseas started in the sixteenth century once the effectiveness of coal as a fuel for furnaces became widely known in continental Europe, thus creating a thriving export market. Coal had not been commonly used on the continent before then. When the papal legate who later became Pope Pius II visited Scotland in 1435, he was surprised to see stones given to the poor people begging for alms outside churches, and was even more surprised to see their delight at getting them. 'This kind of stone', he explained, 'being impregnated with sulphur or some fatty matter, is burnt instead of wood, of which the country is destitute.'

And now, in 1575, the problems facing George Bruce are that all the easy coal has gone and the Castlehill Colliery is waterlogged. Not only is finding new coal resources a challenge for George Bruce at Culross, it is also an issue nationwide. Scotland is undergoing an energy crisis because the easy coal has been fast disappearing everywhere in the country.

The demand for coal and the problems supplying it has caused the price to soar. It has not helped that the export of Scottish coal abroad has contributed to 'a maist exorbitant dearth and scantinesse of fewall' in the country. This is why in 1563 an Act was passed in the Scottish

Parliament prohibiting the export of coal. The punishment for breaking this law is the confiscation of both the coal-carrying ship and its cargo.

If George Bruce can find a way to resurrect the Culross coal industry, a fortune will come his way. Perhaps at this stage he imagined what success would look like should he succeed – he could be a very rich man at a time in Scotland when only the landed aristocracy were wealthy. He would then become someone important to reckon with.

So George sets out to investigate where the exploitable coal is to be found at Culross. Perhaps the monks had overlooked coal resources amenable to exploitation. Failing that, the remaining coal is either under the sea, or deeper than ten metres below the land surface where the monks could not get at it.

He carries out a survey of the rock strata onland, and probably made a geological map of the area around Culross: a map showing where the various rock beds crop out at the surface. This would have confirmed that no easy coal has been left behind on land and, what's more, a large bald spot extends along the shore where the coal seam has been completely removed by erosion. The coal reappears again south of the bald spot at a location just inside the low tide mark, and where for much of the day it is covered by the sea when the tide comes in. A geological map would have shown George Bruce that the coal seam dips from here towards the waters of the Firth of Forth, thus taking it deeper underground in this direction. Here, then, is where the remaining coal is to be found in Culross: it dives under the sea from the very edge of the coast.

But is it possible to dig a coal mine under the sea? No one had ever tried this before, not even in the thriving coalfields of North East England. Yet, if this could be done then a huge resource of coal will become available for exploitation.

Drainage is the first problem to solve should a scheme for an undersea mine be put into operation. Another issue to be dealt with is ventilation – the miners will need to breathe air inside the mine. In addition, should coal gas (methane) seep out of the rock in large quantities and not be removed by ventilation it will asphyxiate the miners or might even explode, killing them outright. Onshore, ventilation shafts can be driven from the surface to provide air circulation underground, but this is obviously impractical under water.

So assuming a mine can be dug below the sea, its entrance would have to be on land close to the coast, and a ventilation shaft could be provided there. But if only one ventilation shaft is dug, how then can air circulate around the mine? At least two shafts will be required, and these should be sited some distance apart to get enough air moving through.

George Bruce finds a solution. How about digging a shaft on the rocks of the shore near the low-tide mark? This will provide a second ventilation shaft about 400 metres from the one to be sited on the coast. To protect the entrance of the shaft from the sea, a stone tower will need to be built to a sufficient height, which is not only above the level of the sea at high tide, but to a height whereby storm-generated waves cannot drive water into the open top.

That setup will work, and with it, the concept of an undersea coal mine. So George builds this tower on a low-lying rock crag near the low tide mark on the shore. The tower is referred to as the 'Moat', a term used in Scotland for a stonework construction in a mining operation. His new mine will be called the 'Moat Pit'. [We do not know the height of the tower – a guess is that this was between eight and ten metres.]

Two ventilation shafts having been provided – one beneath the moat and the other at the entrance to the mine onshore, George now builds a third shaft between them. Located at the high-tide mark, it will provide drainage, as will be explained later in the chapter.

1618

Forty-three years have passed since George Bruce was given the lease for coal mining at Culross, and his mine has proved a huge success. Widely considered throughout Scotland to be a man-made wonder, the profits from the mine have made George wealthy. He has branched out into other moneymaking schemes including merchant shipping and the import of Spanish wine into Scotland.

His small town house in Culross has been substantially extended and decorated with painted ceilings. Today it is known as Culross Palace, although it was not called this in George Bruce's time; the name came later when someone misinterpreted the wording of the title deeds for the property, and then assumed the house had been built as a royal residence.

George Bruce's wealth has also brought him influence. He represents the newly-created burgh of Culross in the Scottish Parliament, and following the Union of the Crowns in 1603 when James VI of Scotland also became King of England, George was asked to sit on a commission to investigate what changes would have to be made to tax and customs legislation should Scotland and England come together as one nation. In recognition of these services, King James knighted him in 1604. He is now Sir George Bruce.

In 1618, Sir George Bruce receives an unusual visitor: namely, the English poet and writer John Taylor. Taylor describes himself as the 'Water-Poet' because he once worked as a waterman in London, ferrying passengers along the River Thames. John Taylor writes travel books as well as poetry.

One of Taylor's books gives an account of his travels around Scotland, and bears the bizarre title *The Pennyless Pilgrimage, or the Moneylesse Perambulation of John Taylor, Alias, The King's Majesties Water-Poet: How he Travailed on Foot From London to Edenborough in Scotland, Not Carrying Any Money to or Fro, Neither Begging, Borrowing, or Asking Meate, Drinke, or Lodging.* The following includes excerpts from his book (the prose has been modernised to make it more readable).

John Taylor visits 'the truly noble knight Sir George Bruce, at a town called Culross. There he made me right welcome, both with variety of fare, and after, he commanded three of his men to direct me to see his most admirable coal-mines, which (if man can or could work wonders) is a wonder: for myself neither in any travels that I have been in, nor any history that I have read, or any discourse that I have heard, did never see, read, or hear of any work of man that might parallel or be equivalent with this... unmatchable work.'

The Water Poet describes the Moat Pit:

> The mine has two ways into it, the one by sea and the other by land; but a man may go into it by land, and return the same way if he please, and so he may enter into it by sea, and by sea he may come forth of it: but I for varieties sake went in by sea, and out by land. Now men may object, how can a man go into a mine, the entrance of it being into the sea, but that the sea will follow him and so drown the mine? To which objection thus I answer, that at low water, the sea being ebbed away, and a great part of the sand bare; upon this same sand (being mixed with rocks and crags) did the master of this great work build a round circular frame of stone, very thick, strong, and joined together with glutinous and bituminous matter, so high withall, that the sea at the highest flood, or the greatest rage of storm or tempest, can

neither dissolve the stones so well compacted in the building, or yet overflow the height of it.

This is the moat tower. The water-poet continues:
Within this round frame he did set workmen to dig with mattocks, pick-axes, and other instruments fit for such purposes. They did dig forty foot down right, into and through a rock. At last they found that which they expected, which was sea-coal, they following the vein of the mine, did dig forward still: so that in the space of eight and twenty, or nine and twenty years, they have dug more than an English mile under the sea, that when men are at work below, a hundred of the greatest ships in Britain may sail over their heads.

One other advantage of building the tower near the high-water mark is that ships can moor alongside a jetty built next to the tower and load coal directly from the mine head.
John Taylor goes down the Moat Pit:
The mine is... cut like an arch or a vault, all that great length, with many nooks and by-ways; and it is so made, that a man may walk upright in the most places, both in and out... But when I had seen the mine, and was come forth of it again, after my thanks given to Sir George Bruce, I told him, that if the plotters of the Powder Treason in England had seen this mine, they would [not have tried to blow up Parliament], and undermined the Thames...

Taylor's comment at the end here provides historical context to Bruce's engineering accomplishment. When he refers to the Gunpowder Plot, the attempt by Guy Fawkes and his associates to blow up King James VI and the Houses of Parliament on November 5, 1605, it had only taken place thirteen years before his visit. And when George Bruce set out in 1575 to investigate the coal resources at Culross, Mary, Queen of Scots, was still alive.

John Taylor explains how George solved the drainage problem: 'The sea at certain places doth leak, or soak into the mine, which, by the industry of Sir George Bruce, is all conveyed to one well near the land.'

The floor of the mine probably follows the coal seam so that it climbs slightly upwards, thus ensuring water drains down the inclined floor to the well.

Above the well is 'a device like a horse-mill, that with three horses and a great chain of iron, going downward many fathoms, with thirty-six buckets fastened to the chain; of the which eighteen go down still to be filled; and eighteen ascend up to be emptied, which do empty themselves (without any man's labour) into a trough that conveys the water into the sea again; by which means he saves his mine, which otherwise would be destroyed with the sea.'

The device is known as an Egyptian Wheel because the Ancient Egyptians invented it four centuries before Christ. The contraption was later employed to drain mines in Germany, which is probably how George Bruce became aware of the technique. He will undoubtedly have read a copy of Georgius Agricola's textbook on mining and mineralogy *De Re Metallica* (On the Nature of Minerals) published in 1556. Agricola's book gives an account of German mining technology, then the most advanced in the world, and it discusses the use of Egyptian Wheels for drainage in mines.

Horses currently drive the Egyptian Wheel, although previously a water mill powered the contraption. Evidence survives suggesting that George Bruce considered tidal energy as an alternative source of power: a letter sent to Bruce's grandson in 1658 refers to 'tide mills' at Culross, and the sender asks if he was aware whether they worked or not.

Back then tidal energy was harnessed either by a water wheel held between two boats or pontoons, which turned in response to tidal currents passing through it; or by the operation of a reservoir which filled with water at high tide, and was then opened at low tide to let the water drain and turn a wheel. At a later date, experiments were made with windmills as the motive power to drain mines, although this ran into the obvious disadvantage that they did not work in calm weather. The huge breakthrough in pit drainage came with the invention of the steam engine in the eighteenth century.

The water-poet also wrote about Sir George Bruce's mine that: 'Many poor people are there set on work, which otherwise through the want of employment would perish.' What John Taylor does not mention were the harsh conditions experienced by coal-miners in Scotland at this time – they were extreme, even by the standards of the day.

In 1606, a government Act was passed in Scotland, which effectively gave miners and their families the status of serfs. As such, the only difference from slavery was that the miners and their families could not be bought and sold as individuals. It must be emphasised that this was a new law enacted at the time by the Scottish Parliament and was not an ancient social custom that had survived from before medieval times.

The Act came about because mine owners were incensed that their experienced colliers were being enticed away to work elsewhere. In response to the rising demand for coal, new entrepreneurs had stepped in to open mines, all of which required to be staffed up, and by preference, with colliers who knew what they were doing. And once men had left a mine to work elsewhere it was difficult to replace them. Nobody would willingly do a job, which was filthy, backbreaking, dangerous, and unhealthy. As a telling example of what this work did to the men, Daniel Defoe, author of *Robinson Crusoe*, described the appearance of the miners he saw in Fife – he noted the 'dejected countenances of the men, occassion'd by their poverty and hard labour, and ... the colouring or discolouring which comes from the coal, both to their clothes and complexions... they are indeed frightful fellows at first sight'.

The obvious solution was for the mine owners either to pay their experienced miners more money or to give them a retention bonus. However, this would have eaten into their profits, and they considered this unacceptable. Therefore, the owners made an application to Parliament to stop others from enticing away their miners, and the 1606 Act was the result.

Once put in place, no person could take on colliers, coal bearers (and those working in the salt pan industry in Scotland) without a testimonial from their previous employee that allowed them to be released. And should a testimonial not be given, the workers remained legally bound to their place of employment. Any mine owner hiring experienced workers without a testimonial was required under challenge by their previous owner to return them or else be fined £100 for each person employed. And should the workers leave their employer of their own accord they were deemed to have committed an act of theft – they were stealing themselves, the property of the mine owner.

Although the intent of the Act was to prevent workers from being lured away, the new law effectively created serfdom in all but name in

Scotland. A worker was bound to a coal pit as long as it was in operation and that could be for life, as it often was. And although the law did not apply to the children of miners, the way the law was loosely interpreted in the courts by legal officers sympathetic to the mine owners meant in practice that sons and daughters were also bound to the mine.

Once the 1606 law was in place, further amendments were made. An Act passed in 1672 allowed 'coal-masters, salt-masters, and others, who have manufactories in this kingdom, to seize upon any vagabonds or beggars wherever they can find them, and to put them to work in the coal-heughs or other manufactories...'

The miners' unfortunate legal status persisted until 1775, when they were set free by a British Act of Parliament. The opening words of the new Act was clear about what was to be revoked: 'Whereas by the Statute Law of Scotland... many Colliers, Coal-bearers, and Salters are in a state of slavery or bondage, bound to the Collieries and Salt-works where they work for life, transferable with the Collieries and Salt-works, when their original masters have no further use for them...' This situation is astonishing to us now: it is a sad fact that a class of serfs was emancipated in Scotland only forty-four years before Queen Victoria was born.

Even though miners from 1775 onwards had been freed from bondage, women continued to be exploited in Scottish mines up until 1842; at which date the employment of woman and girls in mines was prohibited. Before then, the wives and daughters of the miners were required to haul the coal from the coalface where their menfolk worked to the foot of the entrance shaft, and from there, the women climbed a series of ladders or steps to bring the coal to the surface.

James Bald, a mining engineer, gave a graphic account in 1808 of the life of woman coal-bearers - women at this time were still being employed in coal mines in Midlothian and around the Forth estuary:

> The mother... descends the pit with her older daughters, when each, having a basket of suitable form, lays it down, and into it the large coals are rolled; and as is the weight carried, that it frequently takes two men to lift the burden upon their backs: the girls are loaded according to their strength. The mother sets out first, carrying a lighted candle in her teeth; the girls follow, and in this manner they proceed to the pit bottom, and with weary steps, ascend the stairs, halting occasionally to draw breath, till they arrive at

the hill or pit top, where the coals are laid down for sale; and in this manner they go for eight or ten hours almost without resting. It is no uncommon thing to see them, when ascending the pit, weeping most bitterly from the excessive severity of the labour...

Bald records the lament made by a woman coal-bearer as she climbed up from the depths of a Scottish pit with her heavy load: 'Oh sir, this is sore, sore work. I wish to God that the first woman who tried to bear coals had broke her back. And none would have tried it again.'

He adds that, 'The wages paid them for this work are eight pence per day! – a circumstance as surprising almost as the work performed.' The alternative to employing women was to use pit ponies to carry the coal, although this would have entailed far more expense for the mine owner compared to the tiny wages paid to the women: the expense of buying the ponies, providing oats to feed them, and employing men to look after them.

Sir George Bruce appears to have treated his mine workers better than most. In 1793 Archibald Cochrane, the 9th Earl of Dundonald, wrote a sales brochure advertising the sale of the lease for the Culross mining property. In writing about 'the colliers formerly employed at Culross' he records that 'their wives were exempted from the drudgery of bearing coals in the pits; and by staying at home, contracted a habit of domestic attention and care of their families.'

Coal brought great riches to George Bruce. The good quality coal was exported to Europe; the poorer-quality coal was used for producing salt. George owned forty-four salt pans, huge metal pans which were filled with sea water and then heated with coal to make the water evaporate, thus leaving behind a salt residue. John Taylor, the water-poet, mentions that 'he makes every week ninety or a hundred tons of salt, which serves most parts of Scotland; some he sends into England, and very much into Germany.' The salt, although low quality, was in demand everywhere to preserve meat and fish for domestic use. And because the coal was mined at the coast, it was readily available for heating the saltpans.

The extent of Sir George Bruce's property and business has been described: 'Seven different baronies near Culross; three other estates in Fife and Clackmannanshire; had three going collieries, including the Colliery of Culross; 175 pickmen and 44 salt pans.'

1625

This year the Moat Pit was destroyed.

In his book *History of the Sutherlands*, Robert Gordon mentions the death of King James VI on March 27, 1625. He also writes that, 'About that very day of his death, there were such storms and inundations in Scotland, that the sea passing the accustomed limits, drowned a number of persons in various sea towns, and destroyed most of the salt-pans upon the coast of Fife and Lothian, together with the curious coal-pit of Culross, which had entry within the sea...'

Sir George Bruce died six weeks after his mine was flooded.

Bruce's remarkable engineering achievement makes him the first engineer listed on 'The Scottish Engineering Hall of Fame' website. The early entry comes about because his engineering marvel was in operation fifty years before the Industrial Revolution started in Britain. Way ahead of its time, the Moat Pit was the first mine to have been dug under the sea in the British Isles, and it may even have been the first example of its kind anywhere in the world.

Such ingenuity is to be recorded and celebrated because, as John Taylor the water poet reminded us, should we not, '*the memory of so rare an enterprise, and so accomplished a profit to the common-wealth shall be raked and smothered in the dust of oblivion*'.

3. JACOBITES IN REBELLION

The Bass Rock, a block of volcanic stone 400 metres long, 200 metres wide, 107 metres high, and skirted by cliffs, soars out of the sea near the Firth of Forth's southern shore. Every minute of every day, waves crash against this rugged crag – and the waves are resisted.

Although not deemed desirable living space by human standards, the island is much sought after by the thousands of screaming seabirds that roost there every year. Even so, men once lived on this bleak and barren spot. At the end of the seventeenth century, the Bass Rock held a prison: it was a place where the rebellious were brought, the rebellious were jailed, and the rebellious were *forgotten*.

Four men were sent here in 1689; men whose names have *not* been lost to memory – they are Captain Michael Middleton, Lieutenant James Hallyburton, Ensign Patrick Roy, and Ensign David Dunbar - defiant men - as defiant as the rock they were imprisoned on.

The spotlight of history will not land on them until close to the end of the first Jacobite rebellion. Although it is not known when the four men joined the fighting, for the purpose of completeness and context, the story to follow starts from the beginning of the conflict.

1688

The separate countries of Scotland and England share a monarch whose royal title is King James VII in Scotland and James II in England. James, a Catholic, appears to be edging both nations towards the restoration of the Catholic faith. His actions have thus aroused fury amongst the Protestant majority, making him numerous enemies.

The anger reaches breaking point, whereby a group of English politicians and grandees take action by inviting William of Orange, a Protestant, to cross over from his native Netherlands to take over the English throne.

Events happen rapidly in November when William lands in the south of England with a large army: James's soldiers desert him, and rather than fight on, King James flees to France. His enemies in England now argue that he has abandoned the throne and can thus be replaced.

1689

William of Orange and his wife Mary jointly take over the crown of England in February 1689. Both the new king and queen are relatives of the now exiled James: William is James's nephew and Mary is James's daughter. Such illustrates the complexities of the interbreeding extant within the royal families of Europe. William's father, the Prince of Orange (a tiny Dutch principality embedded within the South of France), had married Mary, Princess Royal, the daughter of King Charles I (Charles I was also the father of James VII). With William and Mary on the throne, the royal bloodline is thus considered to have continued. More importantly for the English, both William and Mary are Protestants.

The English, more than happy that their Catholic-leaning monarch has gone, refer to these events as 'The Glorious Revolution'. Although William and Mary are now joint head of state in England, their influence has been curtailed. Power in the land has passed over to a Parliament under a constitutional monarchy. The outcome of this is that the aristocracy have taken charge and *they* make the laws, not the king or queen. The aristocrats harbour a vision for the continued stability of the nation they now control: one based on tradition, the rule of law, and the ownership of landed property (much of which is theirs).

A new king and queen have arrived in England - yes - but for the time being James VII is still King of Scotland. Affairs come to a head in March when the Scottish Convention of the Estates meets in Edinburgh. Comprising nobles, bishops, and burgh representatives, the Estates will figure out what to do next in Scotland now that their king has gone abroad and William and Mary are on the throne of England.

The question they face is this: should James be retained as king or should the throne be offered to William and Mary? That is not an easy decision. There is a certain reluctance to remove James as king; yet, he has annoyed many in Scotland by his over-bearing behaviour and his pro-Catholic stance.

Given what we know now, that for the next fifty-seven years Scotland will be convulsed by rebellion because of the actions of King James VII, his son, and his grandson ('Bonnie Prince Charlie'), the attitude prevailing in the country in 1689 may surprise the reader. Most Scots show sullen indifference as to who is on the throne, that is, with two exceptions: James is hated by the Presbyterians in South West Scotland, and is supported by several clan chiefs in the Highlands.

Here is why James is in favour with the clansmen - a partiality to his family line that will persist in the Highlands for years to come. When the ninth Earl of Argyll, the head of Clan Campbell and a Presbyterian, launched a rebellion against King James VII four years earlier and failed in the attempt, he was executed. James then gave Argyll's estates to the Highland chiefs who had remained loyal to him.

Argyll's son, who under normal circumstances would have inherited his father's property, intends to get it back. Knowing where to get help, he left for the Netherlands to seek favour with William of Orange. Now that William is likely to get the throne in Scotland, the young duke confidently expects that his father's estate will be returned to him. The clan chiefs who currently own the land will be most aggrieved should their recently gained property be taken away from them. It is easy to anticipate the outcome should this happen: *a rebellion in the Highlands*.

The clansmen, held fast by fierce loyalty to their chiefs, have taken up James's cause with great fervour. Iain Lom MacDonald, the Bard of Lochaber, expresses the anger they feel:
'Tis not William that I prefer,
But King James and his seed,
Whom God ordained for our defence,
No borrowed King is worthy of our homage.

William and his followers are hated:
'Tis Prince William and his men
Steeped this country in woe,
When they banished o'er seas King James from us.

Let me invoke ruin and plague,
Famine, malice, and death
On their race, as on the children of Egypt.

Each day that doth pass
May swords gnaw through their skin,
And dogs devout their remains on the hillside.

Such violent passions will make men risk death by taking to the field of battle. They will become known as Jacobites, a word derived from the Latin word for James – *Jacobus*.

Back in Edinburgh, the Convention of Estates is still deliberating, and, after a month, finally comes to a decision. The Scottish throne is declared vacant and then offered to William and Mary, which they accept. The Convention will go on to become the Parliament of Scotland within a constitutional monarchy, similar to the setup in England.

Having made their decision, there is one man in Scotland who the Estates do not trust to abide by it: and that man is John Graham of Claverhouse, Viscount Dundee. John Graham, the Bonnie Dundee of popular history, is a man who is dynamic, headstrong, and determinedly loyal to King James VII. He *is trouble* wrapped up in one person. James, just before he left for France, told John Graham that once he was settled overseas he would send Graham instructions 'to command my troops in Scotland'. John Graham is steeped with a sense of duty: duty to God; duty to his King; and duty to his military calling. He will do what he is told.

As an illustration of his obedience to royal authority, John Graham committed atrocities three years earlier at the behest of King James VII. His soldiers roamed the countryside of South West Scotland seeking out Presbyterians and summarily executing them without trial if found to be carrying arms or they had refused when challenged to pledge an oath of loyalty to King James. The Presbyterians bitterly referred to these actions as 'The Killing Time'.

Yet there are many sides to John Graham. A portrait, now in the possession of the University of Aberdeen, shows Graham in body armour with a long brown curly wig reaching down to chest level. The wig frames a long face, which is open, friendly, and lit by a half-smile. Looking most unlike that of a warrior, the portrait depicts someone eager to please. It hints that you would like John Graham should you meet him.

Having gained his military experience in European wars, Graham proved himself an exceptional leader. One of his many admirers wrote that, 'the vivacity of his parts, and the delicacy and justness of his understanding, joined with a certain vigour of mind and activity of body' distinguished him 'from all others of his rank'. Yet, in spite of his manifest superiority as a human being, he had gained 'the love and esteem of all his equals, as well as those who had the advantage of him in dignity and estate'.

And the Earl of Balcarres wrote, 'none had more the ability to insinuate and persuade; he was extremely affable, and, although a good manager of his private fortune, yet had no reserve when your service and his own reputation required him to be liberal, which gained him the hearts of all who followed him...'

The Convention of Estates passes judgment on John Graham, well aware of his unquestioning loyalty to King James VII. Too dangerous to leave at large, orders are given to proclaim 'the said Viscount of Dundee fugitive and rebel, and ordains the heralds with sound of trumpet to denounce him at the Mercat cross of the head burgh of the shire of Forfar where he lives'.

The trouble now starts.

The first Jacobite rebellion in 1689 was not yet the popular movement it would become later: the Jacobites were only a tiny minority in the country at the time. According to the historian Bruce Lenman, the Jacobite movement only gained traction in Scotland after 1690. From then on, a series of economic calamities including a famine, all of which coincided with heavy-handed English dealings on Scottish matters, led to the widespread belief that the woes of the Scots people had been inflicted on them by a God angered at the deposition of King James. The logic went like this: James had been granted God's divine right to rule and to pass on that rule to his successors: as such, it was not up to mere men to decide who should be King. And given that almost everyone believed in God at the time, the perception became widespread that God had been roused to fury because his will had been obstructed by mortal human beings. By taking revenge, God had made the Scottish people suffer for it.

All of this is ahead of our story, which we now return to. Graham has gathered a small Jacobite army, mostly Highlanders. A number of followers from the Lowlands are also with him, but not many - King James's cause has not excited much passion there.

King William takes immediate action to counter the threat of rebellion in Scotland. He brings over General Hugh Mackay from the Netherlands together with three Scots regiments that had been fighting there. General Mackay will now seek the permission of the Convention of Estates to go after the rebels in Scotland. He tells them his desire is 'to act in concert with the said Convention, in so far as their commands should agree with their Majesties interests'. That is not a problem, and Hugh Mackay is made the commander-in-chief of the army in Scotland.

A strategic tussle now ensues to take control of Blair Castle in Perthshire. The importance of this castle for the Jacobites is that it controls a route connecting their heartland in the Highlands down to the Lowlands; the latter is an objective that must be seized to gain total control of Scotland. Thus, the Jacobites cannot allow the castle to fall into the hands of Mackay's soldiers. Military strategy at the time frequently revolved around which castle was held where within a theatre of war. That is because a large army requires a vast quantity of supplies to be sent to it from their heartland, food in particular. Should a castle guarding a vital supply route be captured by the enemy this creates a huge problem. The enemy soldiers in the castle can then mount raids to capture any baggage trains passing by. That route is now effectively blocked to troops and no further initiative can be taken in the war unless the castle is captured by siege, a procedure that can take many months to bring about.

July 27, 1689

General Hugh Mackay is leading a government army of between 3,500 and 5,000 men north through Perthshire towards Blair Castle. Comprising both battle-hardened veterans and raw recruits, they make for a colourful display. Some wear the traditional red coats, others the uniforms they brought over from the Netherlands, which are scarlet with yellow trimmings. The men in the cavalry corps sit on their horses wearing buff-coloured coats and caps of polished steel.

Trailing behind them is a team of 1,200 horses, which transports their baggage of food, military supplies, and equipment. This is their 'baggage train', and a long train it is. Last of all comes a troop of horsemen and a regiment of soldiers tasked with defending the baggage against enemy raids and opportunistic bandits.

At noon, the government army reaches the Pass of Killiecrankie, a narrow gap in the mountains where the River Garry has incised a mile-long gorge into ancient Highland rock. They are three miles from Blair Castle.

General Mackay, an experienced soldier, believes there is every chance that the Jacobite army will aim to block his advance on Blair Castle by taking up a position somewhere near the pass. He guesses right - Jacobites soldiers are spotted ahead. The general now orders his men to take arms, and ammunition is distributed amongst them. Looking around to locate the Jacobite main body, he spots a force of about 1,800 men on the high ground at the northern end of the pass. With them are 120 horsemen. The sun is shining brightly on the

Highlanders; and they too present a colourful display: a kaleidoscope of tartan cloth and glittering steel.

Mackay marches his men through the pass and up to a terrace of rough ground lying below the Jacobite army, which is positioned on the slope of a hill. The Highlanders are being organised for the battle to come, and this will take some time. The soldiers opposing them are at least double their number, and their ranks stretch over a long continuous line below. John Graham will have to dispose his army in such a way that it will not be out-flanked at its margins by the redcoats, because this would lead to certain defeat. His solution is to arrange his army in three divisions with large gaps between them, such that its left and right edges match those of the enemy below.

'The afternoon was well advanced before Dundee got his army formed...' While this is underway, the Jacobites are under constant fire from below, so much so, that the government army is covered 'by a thick cloud of smoke' from their muskets. Some of the bullets hit their mark, Jacobite soldiers 'dropping from time to time, and many being wounded, they grew impatient for action. But the sun then shining full in their faces, the General [Dundee] would not allow them to engage till it was nearer its decline.'

For two hours, the Jacobites waited. General Mackay, looking on from below, believes that the Jacobites' intention is to wait until dusk when the approaching darkness will add 'fright and disorder' to the terror of a Highland charge. He knew what to expect from such a charge:

> Dundee had already got possession before we could be well up, and had his back to a very high hill, which is the ordinary maxim of Highlanders, who never fight against regular forces upon anything of equal terms, without a sure retreat at their back, particularly if their enemies be provided of horse; and to be sure of their escape, in case of a repulse, they attack bare footed, without any clothing but their shirts, and a little Highland doublet, whereby they are certain to outrun any foot [soldiers], and will not readily engage where horse can follow the chase any distance.
>
> Their way of fighting is to divide themselves by clans, the chief or principal man being at their heads with some distance to distinguish betwixt them. They come on slowly till they be within distance of firing, which, because they keep no rank or file, doth ordinarily little harm. When their

fire is over, they throw away their firelocks, and every one drawing a long broad sword, with his targe (such as have them) on his left hand, they fall a running toward the enemy, who, if he stand firm, they never fail of running with much more speed back again to the hills...

All our officers and soldiers were strangers to the Highlanders' way of fighting and embattling, which mainly occasioned the consternation many of them were in.

He remarks that 'the Highlanders are of such a quick motion, that if a battalion' keeps up its fire once the enemy is close enough 'to make sure of them,' the Highlanders are upon then before 'our men can come to their second defence, which is the bayonet in the muzzle of the musket'.

His men's morale will require boosting to face such a charge; so General Mackay gives a speech to the soldiers close by him. He appeals to their religious faith - their cause is not only that of the 'Protestant interest in Britain, but in all the world'. They are also defending the maintenance of law, and owe an obligation of 'honour and conscience' to 'their master's service'.

Moreover, he insist that he has their self preservation at heart, because they alone can guarantee 'their own safety; assuring them that if they kept firm and close they should quickly see their enemies take the hills for their refuge: for which reason more than the hopes of pursuing the chase they stripped themselves almost naked'.

The worse thing they can do is panic and run for it, and should they do so, 'few or none of them should escape those naked pursuers far speedier of foot than they; besides that all the men of Atholl were in arms ready to strip and knock in the head all runaways'. To yield will be certain death; they must 'stand to it, like men fighting for their religion...'

At about 8 p.m. the order is finally given for the Highlanders to charge. Fury is unleashed, and the air is split by raucous Highland battle cries. Down they come, the clansman carrying loaded muskets to fire at their foe, which they will then throw away, leaving their hands free to wield their broadswords and targes (round shields).

The soldiers facing the Jacobites form a long line, three men deep, with the intention of firing a 'volley'. When the running Highlanders come into range at about a hundred paces, the first line of Redcoats will fire, drop to their knees, the second line will open fire, crouch, and then the third line will fire. A continuous hail of bullets will fly out to kill huge numbers of the approaching enemy in anticipation that the survivors will be stunned to a standstill. Should this happen, the Redcoats will be given time to reload their muskets and will then fire another volley.

And should this not happen, only one volley will be possible, because hundreds of screaming Highlanders will be immediately upon the redcoats with murderous intent. The soldiers will then plug bayonets into the muzzles of their muskets to defend themselves. Such will have to be done at great speed and with no fumbling – yes, no fumbling... that is the idea anyway.

Ewen Cameron of Locheill, Chief of the Clan Cameron, gave an eyewitness account from the Jacobite side of the momentous clash:

> It is incredible with what intrepidity the Highlanders endured the enemy's fire; and though it grew more terrible upon their nearer approach, yet they, with a wonderful resolution, kept up their own, as they were commanded, till they came up to their very bosoms, and then pouring it in upon them all at once, like one great clap of thunder, they threw away their guns, and fell in pell-mell among the thickest of them with their broad swords.
>
> After this the noise seemed hushed; and the fire ceasing on both sides, nothing was heard for some moments but the sullen and hollow clashes of broad swords, with the dismal groans and cries of dying and wounded men.

The killing is savage; the Highlanders' swords chop the government soldiers apart. The evidence of this was seen the next day when the Highlanders returned to the field of battle,

> where the dreadful effects of their fury appeared in many horrible figures. The enemy lay in heaps almost in the order they were posted; but so disfigured with wounds, and so hashed and mangled, that even the victors could not look upon the amazing proofs of their own agility and strength without surprise or horror. Many had their heads divided into two halves by one blow; others had their skulls cut off above the ears... The thick buffe belts [shoulder belts which support a scabbard and sword suspended at the waist] were not sufficient to defend their shoulders from such deep gashes as almost disclosed their entrails. Several picks

41

[pikes], small swords, and the like weapons, were cut quite through, and some that had skull-caps [helmets] had them so beat into their brains that they died on the spot.

Panic ensues on the left wing of the government army. Many soldiers flee, some without firing a shot. Mackay turns around 'to see how matters stood', only to see the men fleeing out of the fight 'in the twinkling of an eye', The Highlanders pursue the Redcoats but not relentlessly; they are tempted and then distracted by the sight of the government's baggage train where rich pickings are to be found. What had turned out a rout will not now be a massacre, and several hundred Redcoats, among them General Mackay, are given the chance to escape.

A soldier, who fled, Donald McBane, gave his account:

...the sun going down caused the Highlandmen to advance on us like madmen without shoe or stocking; covering themselves from our fire with their targes. At last, they cast away their muskets, drew their broadswords and advanced furiously upon us, and were in the middle of us before we could fire three shots apiece, broke us and obliged us to retreat. Some fled to the water, and some another way (we were for the most part new men). I fled to the baggage, and took a horse in order to ride the water; there follows a Highlandman with sword and targe, in order to take the horse and kill myself. You'd laugh to see how he and I scampered about; I kept always the horse between him and me, at length he drew his pistol and I fled. He fired after me. I went above the pass, where I met with another water very deep; it was about eighteen feet over between two rocks. I resolved to jump it, so I laid down my gun and hat and jumped, and lost one of my shoes in the jump. Many of our men were lost in that water and at the pass.

The spot where Donald McBane jumped for his life across the gorge of the River Garry is known today as 'The Soldier's Leap'.

The left and centre of Mackay's army stood firm, only to withdraw later. The Highlanders here, on being halted in their attack by these soldiers, retreat, and, by doing so, discover the wounded body of John Graham lying on the ground. He is 'breathing out his last'.

Dundee had been leading a small horse brigade into battle when he was shot off his horse. 'The fatal shot, that occasioned his death, was about two hand-breadths within his armour, on the lower part of his left side; from which [it was] concluded that he had received it while he raised himself upon his stirrups, and stretched his body in order to hasten up his horse.'

And now: 'The Highlanders had an absolute and complete victory. The pursuit was so warm that few of the enemy escaped; nor was it cheap bought to the victors, for they lost very nearly a third of their number, which did not amount fully to two thousand before they engaged.'

Although the Jacobites have won the Battle of Killiecrankie, albeit with substantial casualties, it is the death of their commander that dashes any hopes of succeeding with their rebellion. This was fully appreciated at the time: '...the true reason the victory became ineffectual was the unseasonable death of the great Dundee. He seemed formed by Heaven for great undertakings, and was in an eminent degree possessed of all the qualities that accomplish the gentleman, the statesman and the soldier.'

The Jacobites' remaining commanders are second rate, and this will show. A disastrous attack on the village of Dunkeld in August was repelled by the defenders, even though they had been vastly outnumbered by the Highlanders.

Winter 1689 / 1690

As winter takes hold at the end of 1689, some of the clansmen desert the Jacobite cause, returning home to their families and homesteads. The hardy men who remain have been moving around North East Scotland; men requiring sustenance in a sparsely populated and impoverished area. They resort to grabbing cattle and grain from the local inhabitants, who have barely enough to feed themselves in the winter months. And if the locals are much angered by that, they are also subjected to bullying and harassment to join the Jacobites, with many having reluctantly done so.

In April, the Jacobites arrive in the Strathspey area of North East Scotland. Most of the locals here oppose the Jacobite cause, amongst them the Laird of Grant. He sends one of his men to Sir Thomas Livingstone, commander of the government army garrisoned in Inverness, with the news that Jacobite soldiers are in the area of

Cromdale, thirty miles to the south-east of the town and close by Castle Grant, the laird's castle.

Livingstone loses no time in going after the Jacobites, writing that the 'Highland Army, having for a while marched up and down this country' was increasing 'as a snowball daily'. Immediate action was required: 'I resolved to march out of Inverness, with a detachment of four hundred men of Sir James Leslies, six companies of Grants, the Highland Company of Captain Mackay, three troops of my dragoons, and my Lord Yester's Troop of Horse, and camped that night near Brodie, where I was forced to stay two days, for my baggage horses coming in very slow from the country, as likewise for the three other troops of dragoons from Elgin, and Captain Burnets of Horse.'

April 30 –May 1, 1690

Livingstone gets confirmation that 1,500 Jacobites are camped at Cromdale. 'The enemy threatening to slay and burn all that would not join; whereupon I resolved the thirtieth of April, about twelve a clock in the day, having then got certain intelligence where they camped, and what number they were, to march towards them...'

He sets off from Brodie with his horsemen and soldiers, 1,200 in number, marching over difficult terrain, and only arriving at his destination at 2 a.m. on the first of May. When he gets there, Livingstone looks around: 'I informed myself of the nature of the ground and the depth of the river, and notwithstanding they told me, the ground was somewhat boggish. I formed a design to attack [the Jacobites] by surprise, for they did not know of my being arrived.'

To avoid any risk that the rebels will be warned, the gates of Castle Grant are locked, 'permitting none of the gentlemen of the country which came in to avoid the enemy, to go out again, least [the Jacobites] be advertised of our forces approach'.

The captain of the castle Captain Grant takes Livingstone to a hill nearby and points out the fires of the Jacobite camp on the other side of the River Spey. The commander, aware that his men are 'extremely weary' after their march, wants to know if they have enough energy left to fight a battle that night. Sir Thomas Livingstone gives his men 'about half an hour to refresh themselves, after which time, I called the officers together, and told them my resolution, so that they might examine their soldiers, if they were able to do it, who unanimously told me, they would stand by me to the last man, and desired earnestly to go on'.

The first task is for Livingstone to get his men across the River Spey where the Jacobites are camped on the opposite bank at a mile distant: 'I having got guides by this time in readiness, we passed the river by three o' clock in the morning, at one ford, where there was a church [Cromdale Church]. The enemy kept a strong guard [100 men], where I sent some foot and a few dragoons to fire upon them, and amuse them.'

The remaining troops pass to the second ford, a quarter of a mile south of the church where they cross the river. When they reach the camp, Livingstone 'seeing the enemy take the alarm as moving confusedly as irresolute men, he sent orders to the rest of his regiment... to join.'

The surprise is complete. The 1,500 Jacobite men are camped on 'a plain a great mile and a half from any strong ground, just as if they had been led thither by the hand, as an ox to the slaughter'. Much alarmed by the ambush, the men from the camp ran up and down not knowing which way to turn - some of them are naked.

Livingstone described what happened next, 'I commanded all the horse and dragoons to join, and pursued them, which affrighted them, so that they took themselves to the hills, and at the foot of Cromdale we overtook them, attacked them, killing betwixt three and four hundred upon the place, and took about hundred prisoners, the greater part of them officers. The rest got off by a mist, that came just at that time upon the top of the hill, so that we could scarcely see one another, otherwise the slaughter would have been greater...' By this stage, it is reported that seven or eight horses were killed on the government side, although no men had died.

The horses are exhausted, 'being ready to fall down'. Leaving them behind on the low ground, the soldiers go off on foot and bring in more prisoners. The Jacobite commander, Thomas Buchan, is not amongst them; he escaped without his hat, coat, or sword, fleeing to a cousin's house in Glenlivet, where he rests 'very much fatigued'.

The action is not quite over yet. Some of the Jacobites have taken over Lethendry Castle nearby: 'About fifty of them made their retreat, most of them gentlemen, resolving there to defend themselves to the last. Sir Thomas sent a messenger to them, with an offer of mercy, if they would surrender.' The offer is refused, whereupon the Jacobites 'fired upon our men, killing two of our grenadiers and wounding another'.

Lieutenant George Carleton of Leslie's Foot knows what to do. He has experience in the use of grenades from the war in Holland. This early version of a grenade is a hollow ball, typically made from iron and filled with fine gunpowder. Lit by a slow-burning fuse, it is ideally thrown into crowded enclosed spaces for maximum effect; the iron splinters causing most of the injuries.

Having learned to throw a grenade, I took three or four in a bag, and crept down the side of a ditch to an old thatched house near the castle... The castle wanting a cover, I threw in a grenade, which put the enemy immediately into confusion. The second had not so good success, falling short; and the third burst as soon as it was out of my hand, though without damage to myself. But throwing the fourth in at a window, it so increased the confusion, which the first had put them into, that they immediately called out to me, upon their parole of safety to come to them.

Accordingly, I went up to the great door, which they had barricaded and made up with great stones; when they told me they were ready to surrender, upon condition of obtaining mercy. I returned to Sir Thomas, and telling him what I had done, and the consequences of it, and the message they had desired me to deliver. Sir Thomas, in a high voice and broad Scotch, best to be heard and understood, ordered me back to tell them, 'He would cut them all to pieces for their murder of two of his grenadiers after his offer of quarter.'

I was returning, full of these melancholy tidings, when Sir Thomas, advancing after me a little distance from the rest of the company, 'Hark ye, sir,' says he, 'I believe there may be among them some old acquaintance (for we had served together in the service of the States in Flanders), therefore tell them they shall have good quarter.'

I very willingly carried back a message so much changed to my mind; and upon delivering it, without the least hesitation, they threw down the barricade, opened the door and out came one Brody, who as he told me then, had had a piece of his nose taken off by one of my grenades. I carried him to Sir Thomas, who, confirming my message, they all came out, and surrendered themselves for prisoners. This happened on Mayday, in the morning; for which reason we returned to Inverness with our prisoners and boughs in our

46

hats; and the Highlanders never held up their heads so high after this defeat.'

Amongst the prisoners are the four Jacobite officers mentioned at the start of the chapter: Captain Michael Middleton, Ensign Patrick Roy, and Ensign David Dunbar were captured inside the castle; James Hallyburton was taken on the field of Cromdale.

These men have given no first-hand accounts of the battle, although it is not too difficult to guess how they felt after such a miserable defeat. With their bodies slumped and their heads in their hands, all is hopelessness and misery. These are men who had given their utmost to help restore the 'true king', yet their brave efforts have come to nothing. James will remain in France while the man and wife who replaced him on the throne in 1689 - those imposters William and Mary - will continue in place. Such is an outrage against God and Scotland.

The four Jacobite officers will now be locked up on the Bass Rock.

4. THE MEN OF THE BASS

The Bass Rock prison was built in 1672 to hold covenanters, religious dissenters who opposed the attempts by the Stuart Kings to interfere with the Presbyterian Church in Scotland. A large number of the 'rebels' held on the rock had been Church ministers.

A jailed covenanters gave a description of the prison:

> The Bass... is covered with grass on the uppermost parts, where is a garden, where herbs grow, with some cherry trees that bear fruit. Below the garden, there is a chapel for divine service; but, in regard no minister was allowed for it, the ammunition of the garrison was kept therein.
>
> Landing here is very difficult and dangerous; for if any storm blow you cannot enter, because of the swelling waves which beat with a wonderful noise upon the rock, and sometimes in such a violent manner, that the broken waves, reverberating upon the rock with a mighty force, come up with a mighty force on the court before the prisoners' chambers... and with a full sea must you land; or, if it be ebb, you must either be craned up, or climb with hands and feet up some steps artificially cut into the rock, and must have help of those who are on the top, who will pull you up by the hand; nor is there any place of landing but one about the whole rock...
>
> On the south side, where the rock falls a little level, you come first to the governor's house, and from that, some steps higher, you ascend to a level court, where a house for prisoners and soldiers is... On the higher parts, there is grass sufficient to feed twenty or twenty-four sheep... The accessible places are defended by several walls, and cannon placed on them. The rest of the rock is defended by nature, by its huge height and steepness...

The crane at the landing point is guarded by three cannons. Three flights of steps ascend from here to the prison buildings, with each flight protected by strong gates at the top and base.

Let's also mention that the island is home to 250,000 gannets in the summer months: large white seabirds with a yellowish tinge to the head, long beaks, and black tips on their wings. So many of these birds are crowded onto the Bass Rock or are seen flying around the cliffs, they are said to resemble a swarm of bees. A human living on the rock will be continuously aware that the gannets are around; the ever-present sensations to be experienced are the acid stink of the birdlime covering everything, and a continuous and deafening honking sound. These birds are not good neighbours.

Such discomforts are no longer the lot of the covenanters. James VII having fled, the Presbyterian Church is now in royal favour because its members support William and Mary. The covenanters have been freed from the Bass and a new governor installed: the prison will now hold Jacobites.

June 15, 1691

The four Jacobite officers captured at Cromdale have been locked up on the rock for over a year now. That is long enough for a regular routine to have set in; the high points of which are the arrival of supplies by boat from the mainland. Today, the coal boat is here, and the men of the garrison know they will have a laborious job ahead of them to drag the coal up the three flights of stairs from the landing platform - a task requiring the efforts of most of the soldiers on the rock. While they are doing this, guards stay behind, 'two or three' in number, to keep an eye on the prisoners. A sentry is also on duty.

What the soldiers hauling the coal do not know is that one of the guards, Sergeant La Fosse, has been converted to the Jacobite cause. A struggle now ensues inside the jailhouse, the remaining guards are seized, tied up, and their keys taken. A shot is fired at the sentry on duty, which passes through his shoulder.

The soldiers down below turn around to discover that the freed prisoners are pointing muskets at them and are making threats to shoot. No choice remains should the soldiers want to live: they now depart for the shore on the coal boat, having taken the wounded sentry on board. The Jacobites are left behind in charge of the Bass Rock: *a small part of Scotland having become loyal once more to King James.*

June 16, 1691

Friends of the rebels landed on the island tonight to reinforce the garrison. They are Crawford, Laird of Ardmillan, his servant, and two Irish seamen who had stolen the boat. The boat had been hired on the pretence that the Irishmen were carrying provisions and household furniture from the port of Leith to the village of Elie on the south coast of Fife. The owners who were manning the boat, on being ordered to sail to the Bass, protested loudly, only to be beaten around the face. They will be kept imprisoned on the rock for several days before being taken onshore again.

Meanwhile, Lieutenant Wood, who had been in charge of the prisoners before he was ejected by them, has been arrested in Edinburgh and charged with negligence.

The Privy Council, the body handling Scottish affairs on behalf of William and Mary, including law and order, have wasted no time in issuing instructions to remove the Jacobite rebels by any means possible:

> The Lords of their Majesties' Privy Council being informed that, through the negligence or rather knavery of the sergeant [La Fosse] in the Bass, that island is now fallen in [to] the hands of James Hallyburton, Michael Middleton, Patrick Roy, and David Dunbar, persons who were prisoners there. They hereby recommend to Sir Thomas Livingstone, commander-in-chief of their Majesties' forces within this kingdom, to take such effectual course for reducing the said island.

June / July / August 1691

The news arrives in France that the Bass Rock has been taken by the Jacobite officers. King James VII responds by sending a ship from Dunkirk with provisions for them. When the ship arrives at the rock, the provisions are unloaded together with two small cannons, twelve muskets, and two small boats, one with twelve oars. The boats will be used to sneak out from the island at night to get supplies from the shore.

In anticipation of such an action, Sir Thomas Livingstone sends three officers and a detachment of soldiers to the coast opposite the Bass, where they will be stationed at the harbour at Castleton. The men are ordered to hinder any contact between the coast and the island, and to prevent the escape of the Jacobites from the Bass. Every night from now on, two boats will be sent out, each with twelve men and an officer; their task to hunt down any suspicious ships approaching the rock. And during the day, men are posted along the coast to warn off any boat that gets too close to the island.

This setup does not work - two ships are not enough to cover the wide expanse of open sea around the Bass Rock, more so at night. Supplies are still getting through to the rebels.

In August, a ship called *The Janet* left the port of Leith carrying provisions to Fife. Unbeknown to the sailors, two of the passengers onboard are rebels from the Bass. They order the crew to sail to the Jacobite island; an argument starts, the sailors are beaten, and then threatened with death should they refuse to do as they are told. Just to make sure, a gun is held to the helmsman's head, compelling him to sail to the rock. Once the boat gets there, the men unload the provisions, which include oatmeal, butter, biscuit, and brandy. The boatmen are kept on the rock for six days before being allowed to leave.

August 15, 1691
Something more will be required if the Government is to retake the Bass Rock, so a raid is organised to grab the boats from the island. On the night of August 15, nine soldiers land on the Bass, removing the large boat that had been taken to the island back in June. This is a huge blow to the Jacobites. They are now in despair – the boat was needed to transport their provisions from shore, and they will not be able to live on the rock without it.

Three days later, having drawn up proposals to surrender, Ensign Dunbar is sent off to the mainland to negotiate terms with the authorities. The Laird of Ardmillan leaves with one of the smaller boats, drops Dunbar onshore, and somehow is able to return with a larger boat carrying eight men and much-needed provisions. The negotiations to surrender are now abandoned. Also abandoned is Ensign Dunbar, who is taken prisoner onshore.

September 3-4, 1691
Today, the Privy Council dispatched a boat to the Bass with two men, Sergeant John Sloan and drummer James Wishart. Sergeant Sloan meets with Michael Middleton, telling him that that the rebels will be set free should they surrender. A document is handed over to confirm this. Middleton reads it, makes huffing noises, and appears 'very dissatisfied'. He confers with the others - they are overheard expressing 'their detestation against the present government' and that they will 'receive command from none but King James', the rightful

king. James Wishart will tell later how they were put under duress to drink King James's health before being seized as prisoners.

The government sends out another boat late the next day, which wisely stays well clear of the cannons near the crane. Indeed, Michael Middleton had issued orders to fire a cannon at it, but had been talked out of it by the others. Shouts are heard from the government boat demanding the return of the men and the boat they came with. Sergeant John Sloan and James Wishart are set free, although the rebels keep the boat.

And the day after this episode, a Danish ship passes by the Bass Rock - its crew oblivious to the situation there. Firing a cannon to signal the ship to heave to, the Jacobites board the ship, take all of the seamen's provisions, and then allow the Danish ship to sail off.

Undated 1691 / early 1692

Sixteen men are now on the Bass. To defend themselves they have fourteen cannons, ten barrels of gunpowder, numerous cannonballs, and sixty muskets. Fresh water is not a problem - a spring flows on the Bass - and they now have several months of food in store. This includes thirteen sheep, a large quantity of oatmeal, two-hundred weight of biscuit, two barrels of butter, a barrel of peas, a barrel of salt, a barrel of vinegar, and a hogshead of brandy. The supplies seized from the Danish ship are also stored away: three dozen hard fish, half a barrel of beef, and two barrels of beer.

Nevertheless, as the months go by, the food runs short. The large rowing boat is now sent off to get provisions from land, but runs into trouble: the soldiers detailed to keep watch ambush the landing crew. History does not record what happened next, although it appears that the men escaped.

Getting provisions from onshore has now been shown to be risky. Therefore, the Jacobites resort to piracy as the safer option, a lesson learned when they boarded the Danish ship in September. Piracy proves to be a chancy affair however. On one occasion, they board a ship carrying a cargo of wheat, with the intention of diverting it to the Bass. But then, annoyingly, the wind started blowing in the wrong direction for the men to return home. So they sail the ship forty miles to the north and run it aground on the sands near Montrose. The men escape, avoiding capture.

March 22, 1692

The Jacobites come up with another scheme to get provisions. The Scottish Privy Council explains how in their minutes: 'Last week the rebels in the Bass seized three fishing boats from Fisherrow while fishing, took all their fish from them and forced them to go the Isle of May [offshore from Crail in Fife], where they loaded them with coals and brought them to the Bass, another boat strongly armed attending them all the while...' They also grabbed the sheep from the Isle of May, which will now be put out to pasture on the grassy slopes high up the Bass Rock.

And now, 'the government being enraged at their repeated boldness, King William ordered the whole revenue of the kingdom [Scotland] to be expended on their reduction'. The English navy will now help.

April 14, 1692

The London Gazette. Edinburgh. April 15, 1692.

On Thursday last, the *Sheerness* frigate, commanded by Captain Anthony Roope, with another frigate of thirty guns anchored within less than musket shot of the Bass, and fired upon it both great and small shot from eight in the morning till two in the afternoon, which beat those within from their low works, made a breach in the upper wall, and broke down their crane, by which they drew up everything that was brought into the place. What other damage they suffered we do not know. Their men appeared but little, lying on the top of the hill in hollow places, and to save their boats they had buried them in the ground near the low fort, so that they could not be seen. They fired some shot upon the frigates, the biggest guns they have being two nine-pounders, and wounded four or five of our men. There are about twenty men in the Bass, [the commander] and the sergeant that betrayed it.

Further details are provided from the captain's log for the *London Merchant*, the thirty-gun frigate accompanying the *Sheerness*. The two ships anchored four miles from the Bass: 'Captain Roope sent his boat to know if they would surrender it to King William and Queen Mary.'

The reply came back from Michael Middleton: 'We will not surrender the Bass, and neither care for all the shipping or [illegible] or what other damage we could do them.'

The next day:

At 6 a.m. we anchored to the southward of the island abreast of the fortifications about a cable's length astern of the *Sheerness* three-quarters of a mile distant, with our stream anchor astern and kedge anchor on our starboard bow to keep our broadside to the batteries, which done, we both began to play our cannon on their fortification and crane, and continued battering of them and they at us...

We continued battering and they at us till three in the afternoon; then the *Sheerness* making the signal for cutting away, we hauled up our stream anchor and roused in as much of our hedge anchor as we could, then cut him and made sail after the *Sheerness* for Leith road. In this action four of our men were wounded. We received one shot in the steerage, and one through the rail on the quarter-deck, and one that splintered the after part of our main topmast, and likewise the comings of our hatches shattered apieces, and the larboard side of our [illegible] in the waist shattered apieces, about 70 foot.

Although the crane and the masonry had been damaged during the assault, the Jacobites can still live on the island. The damage was less than it might have been because it is difficult for conventional navy ships to fire their cannons at a fortified position high up on a cliff or a rock. And neither had it been possible to bombard the Bass Rock from cannons onshore as an alternative, because the rock was too far away to hit it.

The naval bombardment has been an expensive operation. The Privy Council reports that the two English frigates had 'consumed great quantity of powder and spent a great number of cannon ball, and these ships of war being to sail as convoys with some transport ships carrying forces from this kingdom to Flanders, necessary it is that they be supplied of powder and ball from the magazine in their Majesties' Castle of Edinburgh before they enter upon their voyage'. It is also reported that the ships 'cost the treasury of Scotland about £500 to repair them'.

July 21, 1692

Because the French are still getting supplies to the Bass, Sir Thomas Livingstone sends Major Monro to investigate. He confirms 'that by what he could know there was a French ship come to the Bass on

Tuesday at 7 p.m. and went away on Wednesday at 8 a.m. after delivering some things in three great boats...'

August 1693

The Jacobites have now been on the Bass Rock for two years and two months; what's more, French ships are still landing supplies there unopposed. It is a huge embarrassment for the Scottish Privy Council.

For example, during August a twelve-gun French frigate came up the Firth of Forth to drop off supplies, whereby none of the Scottish ships detailed to blockade the Jacobite isle dared to come anywhere near the French ship because they would have been blown to pieces had they done so.

The ship also brought a letter from James VII in France:

> **James VII to Captain Michael Middleton, Governor of the Bass. August 21st, 1693.**
> We have received your message by W. Henderson, and are perfectly satisfied with the zeal you have shown all along for our service in the management of that command. We have sent you some provisions with this occasion and shall from time to time send you more, and you may assure all our subjects there under your command that we are sensible of their loyalty, and that, if they shall persist in their duty, they shall receive their due reward. We expect accounts from you from time to time of the condition of the place and behaviour of the garrison, that, if there be any disorders, measures may be taken to remedy them... and that you will continue to keep the garrison in good order, encouraging them to stand out, managing the provisions, and doing all for the best for our service.

The mayhem continues:

> **The London Gazette. Edinburgh. February 22, 1694.**
> On Sunday last the rebels in the Bass perceiving a barque sailing by from Dunbar laden with corn for Leith, they manned out their boat with eighteen of their number and seized the said barque, which the garrison at Castletown having notice, they sent off about twenty soldiers in boats, upon which those of the Bass quitted their own boat, and

betook themselves to the laden barque, but a violent storm arising, they could not get back to the Bass and were forced out to sea and have not since been heard of, so that there now remain but seven or eight men in the Bass.

This day John Trotter and Marklif were found guilty by the Justice Court of furnishing provisions to and keeping correspondence with the rebels in the Bass, and were condemned as traitors.

The London Gazette. **Edinburgh. February 24, 1694.**
By letters of yesterday from Dundee we are told that the vessel laden with corn which was lately seized by the rebels, who went off in their boat from the Bass, was by stress of weather forced into Dundee, and that the men who were in her got ashore in the night, of whom three were apprehended, and the rest were skulking in the country, though 'twas not doubted but they would be likewise taken.

The loss of these men will cause problems for the rebels left behind on the Bass. They were needed to help get provisions off boats arriving at the rock - a task that will be more arduous and time-consuming from now on.

March 19, 1694
The members of the Privy Council 'ordain that John Trotter, prisoner in the Tolbooth of Edinburgh under sentence of execution at the Cross of Edinburgh on 28 March instant, be taken to the town of Castletown by a strong guard of horse and hanged by the Sheriff of Haddington thereupon a gallows at a spot where he can be best seen by the rebels in the Bass. Sir Thomas Livingstone is appointed to transport the prisoner and not to do so until the day of execution.' John Trotter's crime is cited as 'treasonably' supplying the Bass with food and provisions.

And the same day, James VII writes again to Captain Middleton.

James VII to Captain Michael Middleton, Governor of the Bass. March 19, 1694. Saint-Germain, France.
We are informed of the scarcity of provisions our garrison under your command is reduced to, and have ordered it to be supplied. We have likewise sent Major Middleton to assist you with his advice in all things relating to our

service in the said garrison, not doubting but his experience will be both a help and comfort to you, and that you will conjointly manage all things to the best for our service by keeping the garrison in union and discipline and encouraging all our subjects under your command to stand firm to their duty, letting them know they may assure themselves of a due reward of their services and sufferings whenever we shall be in a condition to do it.

In the meantime we shall send you from time to time what supplies can be conveniently transported to you from this place, which you are to manage with all the economy possible, as likewise to do your endeavours, when a favourable occasion offers, to purchase provisions for yourselves by making incursions on our rebel subjects, whenever you can without endangering the loss or ruin of the garrison. That all our Catholic subjects with you may have the comfort of the exercise of their religion we have likewise sent you - Nichols, to perform the duty of a priest to the garrison by administering to the Catholics all the spiritual assistance that is incumbent to his function.

The afore-mentioned Captain Robert Middleton is Michael Middleton's brother. He has been ordered by James to sail from Dunkirk to the Bass where his role will be to assist his brother as governor or, if necessary, to take over from him in case of sickness or death.

March 28, 1694

The following anecdote appears in *The small and rarer collection of Jacobitical tracts (memoirs of Lord Viscount Dundee & co.) published in London, 1714*. Readers are told that: 'The day of Mr Trotter's execution being come, the gibbet was erected at Castletown, and he being brought to the place a gun was fired from the Bass amongst the crowd, which terrified them, and obliged them to remove the gibbet to a further distance, where he was hanged.' The cannonball would not have made it that far, although it is credible that a cannon was fired from the Bass with the intention of giving everyone a scare.

April 5, 1694

Finally, the Scottish government gets in heavyweight warships. About time too – and should the French now brazenly send in a warship to resupply the Bass, it will be challenged by a warship of similar strength.

Letter from the Privy Council to King William. Edinburgh.

May it please your Majesty - We had good information weeks ago that the garrison of the Bass was in great straits, and they having at that time made some attempts with their Iona boat upon some small vessels passing and repassing in the Firth, we thought fit to give an order and commission for providing and outrigging a frigate of twenty-four guns to cruise upon them and hinder both their supplies and excursions.

And immediately after the frigate was set out there came a privateer to have supplied the Bass but was repulsed and forced back to sea, having only had the time to land a few men upon the rock, which must prove rather a further straitening than relief to the place; but having good reason to apprehend that the beating back of this privateer may occasion the sending of a greater force we thought it necessary to order out another frigate of twenty guns with a fireship, that we may neither expose our first ship to so visible a hazard nor lose so probable an advantage. These things we have done in the easiest manner we could, and have recommended the defraying of the charge to the Lords of your Majesties' Treasury, whose concurrence we also had in this matter.

More details have been provided about the aborted privateer mission. The ship arrived from Dunkirk with a cargo of rusk (twice-baked bread with the consistency of hard, dry biscuit) and other provisions. However, there had not been enough men on the island to unload the ship. So ten sailors came out of the French ship to help them. They had only unloaded seven bags of rusk on the island when the largest of the government surveillance ships, a frigate, sails into view. Time for a rapid exit - the French ship cuts its anchor and immediately departs, leaving the ten sailors behind on the Bass. The ship will have no problem making an escape: a French privateer is the fastest vessel on the sea, and this one will outrun the navy ship to get back home. The incident is telling however. It shows that the rebels on the Bass are now struggling, and may not be able to hold out much longer.

The Jacobites are left with no more than five or six days of provisions. In desperation, they fly a flag of truce from the island, whereby the government asks them what they want, and are told in return that the Jacobites will now discuss surrender. Two members of the Privy Council will be sent to the Bass Rock to negotiate. The Jacobites now prepare their surrender terms.

And here is one of these fables that frequently appear in old books about the Jacobites – and like many such stories, this one makes them out to be smarter than their foes even though the Jacobites lost their cause in the end. Even so, this anecdote might be plausible.

The canny Jacobites aim to finesse the meeting with the Privy Council members. They have saved some bottles of the best French wine and brandy, tasty biscuits too. On arriving, the visitors receive a friendly welcome. The talks are held with much conviviality, and the guests are beseeched to drink as much as they want. Yes, they are told, we Jacobites are not short of supplies on the island and can easily hold out longer should this be necessary. Suffice it to say, we will not give up the Bass unless it is our surrender terms that are agreed to.

And when the government men left by boat, they would have looked back to see a long line of Jacobites watching them go. That was also a ruse - the men standing in line had been joined by 'soldiers' - muskets stood upright and dressed with all the coats and hats to be found within the garrison.

The Privy Council agree to the Jacobite conditions: everyone will be pardoned; nobody involved with the Jacobites at any time in the past will be questioned or troubled; and 'every person of the Bass shall have the liberty to go for France, together with such of them that are in prison, or out of prison belonging to the Bass; and those that are not willing to go for France, may have protection to stay in the kingdoms'.

April 21, 1694

The London Gazette. Edinburgh. April 22, 1694.

The Bass was surrendered yesterday in the evening upon articles, by which those that were in it are indemnified, and such as were under sentence of death for holding correspondence with them pardoned. There came out of the Bass sixteen men with their baggage and swords, and at the same time Major Reid with a party of men took possession of it by order of the Privy Council.

The occupation of the Bass Rock is over - it had lasted almost three years.

April 24, 1694

Minutes of the Privy Council of Scotland. Edinburgh. Item: Warrant to Hire a Ship for Transporting the Rebels that were in the Bass.

The Lords of their Majesties' Privy Council do hereby appoint George Baillie of Jerviswood, general receiver of their Majesties' crown rents, to make search and try out for and conduce a sufficient well-conditioned ship, well furnished and provided with all necessaries, for transporting to Havre de Grace in France the persons lately come out of the Bass at the time of its surrender and others who have corresponded with them; and for that effect to conduce and agree with a skipper and seamen for sailing the said ship at an easy and reasonable a rate as he can, and to condescend upon a fixed day for the ship's sailing between and the fifteenth day of May next, and to make report of his diligence in the afternoon to the committee of Council appointed in this affair.

1701

King William orders all the buildings and fortifications on the Bass to be destroyed and all the cannon and ammunition to be removed. The Isle of Bass will now be left for the birds.

The following was said at an earlier date, and provides a fitting farewell to the prison on the Bass:

This bleak sequestered isle, seems not to have been destined for the habitation of human beings, but for those winged tribes, whose element is waves and storms, who shun the society of man, and claim not his protection. Nature has instructed these tenants of the rocks to seize the cliff and promontory, - to choose these inaccessible retreats, where no enemy can approach, and where they may lodge and breed their young in safety. She appears to have given them undisputed possession of these formidable mansions, and to

60

have provided for their security, by raising barriers of defence that repel the most daring adventurer.

5. THE GLORIOUS FRANCES WRIGHT

1844

Frances Wright, sometimes known as Fanny Wright, is visiting her native Dundee where she has family legal matters to deal with. Now 49 years old, Frances is famous - and the news of her arrival 'soon spread through the town'. Because of her celebrity, local bookseller James Myles is eager to secure an interview, describing her as 'a woman whose eloquence has gone so far as to effect a revolution in the mind of America'. He intends to publish her biography, knowing it will sell many copies.

Myles finds Frances 'among the tallest of woman; being about 5 feet 10 inches high; she walks erect, and is remarkably handsome. Her brow is broad, and phrenologically speaking magnificent; her eyes are large, her face is masculine, but well formed.' He might also have mentioned her distinctive short curly hair, mostly grey now, having once been reddish-brown in colour.

Here in Dundee is one of the most extraordinary human beings ever to have walked the planet. She is 'the glorious Frances Wright' according to the American poet Walt Whitman: 'I never felt so glowingly toward any woman... she possessed herself of my body and soul.' Whitman saw her in his childhood when he was taken to a lecture theatre in New York: 'It was there that I heard Fanny Wright; the noblest Roman of them all, though not of them, except for a time a woman of the noblest make-up whose orbit was a great deal larger than theirs – too large to be tolerated for long by them: a most maligned, lied-about character – one of the best in history though one of the least understood.'

1795 – 1818

Frances Wright wrote with openness and candour about what shaped her outlook on life. So much so, that not only do we get to understand this astonishing woman, we are also given the rare opportunity to satisfy our endless curiosity about how another human being handles this mysterious thing called life.

Her father, James Wright Junior, made his living as senior partner of the Dundee Tanwork Company, a workshop where animal hides were tanned to make leather. And according to his daughter, he 'took a lively and deeply sympathising interest in the great events and the greater principles which agitated the French Revolution'. These events took place between 1789 and 1799, an interval of time extending either side of the date of Frances's birth on September 6, 1795. Frances mentions that her father 'was instrumental in spreading thro' his own city and neighbourhood, popular translations of French treatises, political and philosophical'.

The French Revolution transformed political debate in Scotland from almost non-existent to a boiling cauldron of fervour, such that 'everything rung and was connected with the Revolution in France; which for above twenty years was, or was made, the all in all. Everything, not this or that thing, but literally everything, was soaked in this one event.'

What happened in France was seen as extraordinary in Scotland and elsewhere: a European country had dispensed with its king and nobles, and in their place had arisen a republic based on liberty, fraternity, and equality for all. This stunned everyone in a way that is difficult for us to understand today. Before the French Revolution, it had been taken for granted by everyone that the power wielded by a king in combination with the extended network of a landed gentry provided the only means to maintain peace and stability within a large country. But now, a large nation, France, is being run without a king or nobles, and has coped.

This turn of events horrifies the ruling aristocracy in Britain. Frances mentions that her father's activities 'brought him to the attention of the authorities', who were anxious to suppress a popular revolt against them. 'Nevertheless, they left him alone, because of his high standing as a scholar and a gentleman.'

Perhaps James Wright was not the fearless man his daughter thought he was. Yes, he made a medallion celebrating the French Revolution and had brought Thomas Payne's radical book *The Rights of Man* to Dundee, but had then taken fright when the authorities noticed his activities.

Thomas Payne's subversive tome was a dangerous item to have in your possession at the time; nevertheless, it was circulated everywhere in Britain, and not only by James Wright. Its views appalled the government; for example, statements such as this one must have shaken them to the core: 'When it shall be said in any country in the world, my poor are happy; neither ignorance nor distress is to be found among them; my jails are empty of prisoners, my streets of beggars; the aged are not in want, the taxes are not oppressive; the rational world is my friend because I am a friend of its happiness; when these things can be said, then may the country boast of its constitution and government.' Such sentiments were too much to bear for the British ruling class, and they now took action to suppress radical opinion in the country.

James Wright was terrified at what might happen to him now, undoubtedly aware that two Dundee men had recently been sentenced to transportation to Australia for handling seditious documents. So 'one night about twelve o'clock [he] got into a small boat at the harbour, with all his radical medals beside him, crossed about half-way over to Fife, and deposited the suspicious cargo at the bottom of the Tay, after which he returned, burned a large quantity of objectionable papers and books, then retired to bed, and no doubt slept sounder than he did the night before'.

Alas, both James and his wife Camilla die young, Camilla on February 18, 1798, to be followed to the grave by James on April 17, three months later. James was only twenty-nine years old, and Camilla was probably a similar age. Frances is a two-and-a-half-year-old infant when this tragedy happens.

Now orphans, Frances, her younger sister Camilla, and her older brother Richard are separated from one another: Frances moves to London at the request of her maternal grandfather General Duncan Campbell where she will be put in the care of his daughter Frances Campbell. Richard is given over to his granduncle in Glasgow, and Camilla is looked after by foster parents in Dundee. She will be allowed to join her sister in England a few years later.

And in 1803, the three children come into a large inheritance when their uncle is killed in India, having made his fortune there. This matters for our story because Frances Wright has now become independently wealthy. She can pursue her aims later in life without having to worry about money. Such is a gleam of good fortune in an otherwise miserable childhood.

The family tragedy continues when, in 1809, Richard is killed while travelling to India. Only the two sisters now remain.

Believing 'orphanship' to have formed and strengthened her character, Frances told James Myles that this was due to the 'absence of all sympathy with the views and characters of those among whom her childhood was thrown' and 'to the presence of a sister who looked to her for guidance, and leaned upon her for support'. Frances endures the 'solitude of orphanship', which lingers for hours on end, desolate

64

hours... Frances finds a solution: endowed with rampant curiosity and the need to make sense of the world, she takes to books and learning as a distraction.

But this is not passive learning, she truly wants to understand everything inside and out – to dig deep. Thus, 'at an early age' Frances is 'surprised at the inability of masters to answer her questions... Being checked on one occasion by a deep and shrewd mathematician and physician, who observed that her question was dangerous, she replied – "Can truth be dangerous?"

"It is thought so," was the answer.

She learned on this occasion two things: the one, that truth had still to be found; the other, *that men were afraid of it.'*

These are insights that are hard-wired into her brain from this moment on. More thoughts spiral off from them: if there is no common agreement between human beings about anything in the world then she must somehow establish her own version of the truth. But where can she find it? And if men are afraid of finding the truth, then it is probably hidden beneath the surface.

The 'truth' is not to be found in the drawing rooms of her despised aunt, her relatives, or their friends, where only approval of the status quo is to be heard and 'little was to be learned'. Such experiences of aimless socialising 'inspired her with a disgust for frivolous reading, conversation, and occupation'. Frances, highly intelligent and self-possessed, can see through all the adult sham - 'every kind of quackery and pretension, literary, scientific, and, more than all, political and philanthropic'. Intellectually severe for one so young, this distancing from her aunt has now 'driven her into all but seclusion'. And because Frances is approaching adulthood, a time when a young person normally makes choices about who they are and how they see adulthood, one thing is for sure – her life choices will not be guided by anyone around her.

A huge moment arrives at the age of fifteen when she witnesses how the working men and women in the rural areas of England are treated with great cruelty by the landed gentry. Frances tells James Myles about 'the painful labour of the aged among the English peasantry; and, again, when she saw that peasantry ejected, under various pretexts, from the estates of the wealthy proprietors of the soil among whom she moved: "has man, then, no home upon the earth; and are age and infirmity entitled to no care or consideration?"'

65

The misery she witnesses in 1810 is a consequence of the ongoing Enclosures Acts, a series of measures enacted by the British Parliament since 1760. The Acts brought about changes in how agricultural land was used in England and Wales. In the old system, practised since medieval times, large numbers of tenant farmers grew crops on scattered strips in large open fields, and the communal grazing of their livestock on rough round was allowed as a long-standing tradition. Following enclosure, the local lord hedged or fenced in this land, essentially forcing the poorer farmers off it to create agricultural fields much as we see today. By doing so, agricultural efficiency has been significantly improved, thus making more money for the aristocrats. Meanwhile, having lost their livelihood, the peasants are impoverished. To add to their miseries, the price of bread has increased substantially since the start of the Napoleonic wars because Napoleon has imposed a trade embargo on Britain, thus blocking the import of grain from Europe.

The Enclosures Acts have led to changes in the countryside: 'In all the really agricultural villages and parts of the kingdom, there is a shocking decay; a great dilapidation and constant pulling down or falling down of houses... To cultivate and ornament these villainous spots [enclosures] the produce and the population are drawn away from the good lands. There all manner of schemes have been resorted to get rid of the necessity of hands...' Whereas the landed gentry live in huge mansions filled with the best furnishings and artworks, the dispossessed peasants have drifted away to slum districts in the towns and cities, or have built hovels on road-side verges, the only land now available to them.

These Acts have been made by a Parliament that is largely controlled by the landed aristocracy. The two dominant political parties are the Tories and the Whigs. The way they govern the country illustrates a point Frances will make in her later years: 'Much of history were only so many skirmishes between wings of the same army... a mock battle between those who equally lived off working people.'

The misery she witnesses baffles Frances. How can rich people be so cruel when it is clear they have more than sufficient resources to live in comfort? Life holds a 'strange secret', she concludes, 'some extraordinary vice lay at the foundation of the whole of human practice'. She ponders whether she should 'devote her whole energies to its discovery'.

On further contemplation, she makes 'a solemn oath, *to wear ever in her heart the cause of the poor and the helpless; and to aid in all that she could in redressing the grievous wrongs which seemed to prevail in society.*' Frances Wright has thus nailed down her life's purpose at the age of sixteen - one she will stick to resolutely and unflinchingly.

Years later, in a letter to a close friend, Frances explained the motive force that acts to drive her along her chosen path. She has rejected a life of luxurious repose and the common route that many women follow, whereby the diamonds of friendship, love, conviviality, and amusement turn up every now and again intermixed with the coarse grit that usually trickles through the hourglass of life. She knows that an unfocussed day-to-day existence like this, one of expectance, can lead to a life much 'disquieted' by vague yet undefined yearnings. She has made a hard-edged decision to apply her abundant physical and mental energies in the pursuit of a fixed aim, thus consistently directing her actions. Not that her chosen path is easy: those female yearnings for sympathy and nurture by a 'strong and understanding spirit' surface every now and again to distract her.

From now on, Frances Wright's devotion to the 'cause of the poor and the helpless' will be hard-chained to her formidable personality. Such will transform her being into the human equivalent of a Second World War tank. Having defined a clear objective for her life's work, she will pursue it relentlessly. Perhaps her behaviour is similar to those orphans who have written in their biographies about the intensity of the pain they experienced at an early age; a horrendous pain that lingers into adulthood where it can only be forgotten by deliberate second-to-second absorption in a chosen task. She hints at this: 'I can truly declare that I have never enjoyed tranquillity but when my time has been steadily employed.'

At the age of seventeen, Frances makes a huge discovery - one that changes the trajectory of her life: 'It was while engrossed, perplexed, and often depressed with silent and unsuccessful attempts to arrive at a satisfactory view of the truth in anything; to unravel the complications and evident contradictions existing alike in the opinions and practice of men...' that, on a whim, she opened the book *History of the War of Independence of the United States of America* by the Italian historian Carlo Botta.

Frances 'awoke to a new existence. Life was full of promise; the world a theatre of interesting observation and useful exertion. There existed a country consecrated to freedom, and in which man might awake to the full knowledge and full exercise of his powers.' Here is a vast area of land with no king or landed aristocrats mercilessly exploiting the peasants - a republic where the perfectibility of human beings is possible through the application of rational thought by rational leaders.

Her discovery 'kindled a new life of hope in her soul'. Now obsessed with the idea of America, Frances is desperate to find out more. But therein lay a problem.

Although the American Declaration of Independence had been issued thirty-six years prior to Frances's discovery of Carlo Botta's book, very little has been published in Britain about this young upstart nation. Frances has great difficulties finding out anything at all, to the extent that doubts have surfaced: 'A panic terror seized upon her...Was the whole a romance? Was the story she had read a true one?' She feverishly searches for any book that might reassure her, and then discovers Belsham's *History of George III*. In this book are the details she seeks: 'Her heroes were true men, and her land of promise had a local habitation and a name.'

And while the rest of the British nation frets over the war and the fortunes or otherwise of Napoleon and the allies ranged against him, Frances's thoughts 'dwelt with unceasing interest, frequent alarm, and unsatisfied curiosity on the fate and history' of the United States, about which 'the papers of the day scarcely vouchsafed an intelligible notice'.

She is desperate for news about her American utopia, in particular about 'the actual condition and point of progress of the American population'. Alas, 'she could obtain little information'.

All that changes in 1813 when Frances and Camilla leave behind their unloved aunt in the south of England to take up residence in Glasgow with their granduncle, James Mylne, a philosophy professor. Frances is now eighteen years old. Her quest to find out more about the recently established American republic takes her to the library at the University of Glasgow. On asking for documents on the subject, 'she was led to a remote and little frequented compartment of the gallery... filled with volumes and pamphlets from floor to ceiling... there she would find all that had ever appeared in print respecting the American colonies'. Heaven...

Frances's investigation into the new American republic is not her only source of intellectual stimulation at the time. Her uncle introduces her to a social circle of like-minded people in Glasgow who share his delight in philosophy and learning. Through their influence, Frances becomes steeped in the ideals of the European Enlightenment: namely, the ideals of equality, liberty, tolerance, and the power of the rational mind to bring about the improvement of man's condition on earth.

A mind of great clarity has formed in this young woman. Frances will accept no received wisdom unless she agrees with it. 'The first and last thing I would say to man,' she once wrote, 'is think for yourself.'

Frances Wright will go on to hold unswerving views about life and how the world should be organised - views that make sense to her, although differing substantially from almost everyone around her. Such views will never be dislodged through the persuasion of others. Not ever. The display of her rigid self-belief will unnerve many who come to cross Frances's path from now on.

Robert Dale Owen, a close friend in her later years, although admiring her 'courageous independence of thought', is of the opinion that her mind 'had not been submitted to early discipline, the courage was not tempered prudence, the philanthropy had little of common-sense to give it practical form and efficiency. Her enthusiasm, eager but fitful, lacked the guiding check of sound judgment.' He added that, 'an inordinate estimate of her own mental powers and an obstinate adherence to opinions once adopted detracted seriously from the influence which her talents and eloquence might have exerted.'

Perhaps this is a valid assessment of Frances Wright's character, but then again, had she been a different person your author would not have a story to tell here. That is because people like Frances create huge waves in this world of ours.

The expression of her views in public will bring down dog's abuse from others when she dares to challenge the *status quo* in society; nevertheless, Frances's armour plating cannot be dented. This woman is fearless: 'I know of none, from the modest Socrates and gentle Jesus, down to the least or greatest reformers of our own time, who have remembered the poor, the ignorant, or the oppressed, raised their voice in favour of more equal distributions of knowledge and liberty, or dared to investigate the cause of vice and wretchedness, with a view to their remedy; I know of none, I say who have not been the mark of persecution, drank the poison of calumny, or borne the cross of martyrdom.'

If that is the way it is, well so be it. 'What better and wiser have endured, I shall not lack the courage to meet. Having put my hand to the plough, I will not draw back, nor, having met the challenge so long

69

cast at human nature and human reason, alike by privilege and superstition, will I refuse to meet all hazards in their cause.'

The armour-plated tank that is Frances Wright moves relentlessly forward...

She now writes her first book, *A Few Days in Athens*, although it will not be published until eight years later. Within its pages is an imagined dialogue between Greek philosophers focussing on the philosophy of Epicureanism, which she summarises as follows: 'Our senses then being the judges of all things, the aim of all men is to gratify their senses; in other words, their aim is pleasure or happiness...' Enlightenment ideas also creep in to her tome, such as the value of science for explaining the world, and the view that religion has perverted human progress.

When the book came out in 1822 it impressed two famous men. Thomas Jefferson, author of the American Declaration of Independence, wrote in a letter that *A Few Days in Athens* 'had been a treat to me of the highest order' and 'may we not hope more from the same pen?' And the poet Walt Whitman said that her book 'was daily food to me: I kept it about me for years...' *A Few Days in Athens* influenced Whitman by pointing out the logic of taking a joyous approach to life (as opposed to the Biblical belief that we are all sinners). And from then on, Walt Whitman cheerfully sang songs of himself and relentlessly celebrated his existence on earth - Frances's book having 'set him free in a flood of light'. Whitman even adapted some lines from *A Few Days in Athens* for a poem, although he never published it.

Frances will spend the next three years in Scotland, employing 'her summers in visiting its Highlands and Lowlands; and her winters in closet study', thereafter returning to England. And throughout all this time, she has been mulling over her secret ambition – one kept close to her heart – *to visit the United States*.

1818 - 1824

And so in 1818, at the age of twenty-three, Frances Wright together with her sister Camilla travels to Liverpool, where they will board the steamship *Amity*, their destination: New York. But not without drama beforehand; their uncle James Mylne rushed from Glasgow on hearing about his nieces' plans to tour American unaccompanied. Arriving at the quayside, he pleads with them not to go, but to no avail; Frances is headstrong and determined, no matter what the personal risk.

This woman fervently wants America to be her special place, recognising that: 'An awful responsibility has devolved on the American nation; the liberties of mankind are entrusted to their guardianship; the honour of freedom is identified with the honour of their republic; the agents of tyranny are active in one hemisphere; may the children of liberty be equally active in the other.'

Once the sisters get there, they will stay in the United States for twenty months.

First impressions as the ship approaches New York do not disappoint: 'Everything in the neighbourhood of this city exhibits the appearance of life and cheerfulness. The purity of the air, the brilliance of the unspotted heavens...' And as the ship closes in on the shore, 'it was with pleasure that I observed the number of smiling dwellings that studded the shores of Staten and Long Islands. Here was seen no great proprietor, his mighty domains stretching in silent and solitary grandeur for uninterrupted miles, but thousands of little villas or thriving farms, bespeaking the residence of the easy citizen or tiller of the soil.'

In contrast to Britain, here are 'no dark alleys, whose confined and noisome atmosphere marks the presence of a dense and suffering population; no hovels, in whose ruined garrets, or dank and gloomy cellars, crowd the wretched victims of vice and disease, whom penury drives to despair, ere she opens to them the grave.'

Later, Frances will admit that her first impressions had been somewhat naive, having seen America with what she describes as a 'Claude-Lorrain tint' (Claude Lorrain was a French artist who specialised in painting peaceful pastoral scenes). She explained that she had mistaken for 'enlightened liberty what was, perhaps, rather the restlessness of commercial enterprise'.

Yet, despite her eagerness on this trip to confirm her dream of America as a paradise for all, Frances will soon discover that the United States shares a feature in common with the sun – a display of surface brilliance marred by spots. Slavery is the biggest spot of all, 'the most atrocious of all the sins that deface the annals of modern history'. She expresses her reaction to this: 'The sight of slavery is revolting everywhere, but to inhale the impure breath of its pestilence in the free winds of America is odious beyond all that the imagination can conceive.'

Yet, Frances will come to believe with astounding naivety that most Americans support the abolishment of slavery should a way be found

71

to do so. This attitude is widely held in the north, where slavery had been prohibited by legislation in 1819, but is not commonly supported in the south, where large profits are made by land owners using slave labour. Only a civil war will eventually end slavery in the United States.

Frances Wright returns to Britain in 1820, and writes a book about her travels - *Views on Society and Manners in America*. Published the following year, it brings her much attention in Britain, Europe, and America.

In particular, two men who read it will help her to enlarge her world view. She met them both in 1821.

The social reformer Jeremy Bentham invites her to dinner on two successive evenings in July. He has been enchanted by the libertarian views expressed in her book; a sense of delight further reinforced when the pro-government newspapers damn the book in their reviews - one newspaper describing it as 'a tissue of impertinence, and injustice, and falsehood'.

Bentham, enthused by the spirit of the French Revolution, believes there is a better way to govern society in Britain – a much better way. Forget the establishment idea that the rigid imposition of power by a privileged aristocracy is the way to provide stability in a nation – 'we rule and you are safe' – that sort of thing. Bentham is part of a group of philosophers and reformers who advocate an approach to government they call 'utilitarianism'. It employs science as the means to find the better way of running a country. And because science needs data and measurements to come up with hypotheses – then what in society is to be measured here? The answer: you measure the happiness of all the people in the nation. This is because the ideal government policy is the one that creates the greatest happiness for the greatest number. Unsurprisingly, the Parliament of the day finds this proposal subversive because they only believe in the greatest happiness for the privileged few.

Frances is influenced by Jeremy Bentham; he has shown her that it is always possible to think up better and more enlightened ways to organise human society.

And in the autumn of 1821, she visits France, where she falls under the spell of the Marquis de Lafayette, an extraordinary man who had taken a key role in not one but two revolutions, both of which helped to create the modern world. So how did Lafayette become involved with making revolutions?

In 1777, at the age of nineteen, Lafayette sailed to America to take part in the revolutionary war being fought there against the British. Attracting the attention of George Washington, he was put in charge of a division of the American continental army, which went on to play a key role in the Siege of Yorktown. The siege ended with the British conceding defeat, a pivotal moment eventually leading to their withdrawal from the American colonies.

Lafayette returned to France a hero. And then in 1789, the rumblings at the start of French Revolution were heard. Lafayette favoured the formation of a constitutional monarchy as a solution to the crisis now enveloping the country. When the Bastille fell that July, the revolutionaries took control of Paris and put Lafayette in charge of the National Guard, asking him to keep order in the city. He designed a new 'cockade' for the Guard, a cloth rosette sewn onto a hat as an emblem. Its colours were red, white, and blue: the red and blue taken from the colours of the coat of arms of Paris, the white representing the monarchy. These are now the colours of the French flag.

That same year, Lafayette with the help of Thomas Jefferson produced the first draft of the *Declaration of the Rights of Man and of the Citizen*. A landmark document for human rights, it guaranteed individual rights to liberty, security, property, and freedom of speech. Within its pages are ideas that will serve to guide the newly proclaimed citizens of France. Rather than blindly rioting with passion but not direction, the public having been informed by this document can now strive for specific aims with a specific purpose; aims worth risking their lives for. Should they succeed, they will be living in a nation where equality of all is guaranteed; where they can say whatever it is they want to say; and will be safe from arbitrary arrest without trial. Such demonstrates the power of *ideas* in human affairs.

Frances Wright and the Marquis de Lafayette have now become close friends, perhaps more. Her pet name for Lafayette is 'the general'. Although Lafayette has been widowed for fourteen years, the attention Frances gets from him causes tension within Lafayette's family. Frances spends much time with Lafayette at his chateau forty miles outside Paris, an old French castle, which is surrounded by a moat, and looks out onto park designed by an English landscape gardener. Beyond the garden lies Lafayette's four-hundred acre farm. Frances more or less moves in with Lafayette for the better part of two to three years.

Lafayette is an important influence on her. He is in one person the demonstration of how to make a revolution happen. Above all, *action* and an unswerving determination to win through are essential. And if Lafayette can help bring about a revolution *then so could she.*

1824

Lafayette has been invited on an official visit to the United States where he is to be feted as a national hero. He asks Frances and Camilla to come with him. They say yes, although the sisters will arrange to leave on a separate ship not wanting to excite any hints of scandal - nevertheless, they will often be seen in his company for the early part of their visit.

'The general' introduces them to the important American politicians of the time, most notably Thomas Jefferson. The two sisters visit his Monticello estate in Virginia, arriving there two days after Lafayette. This is a poignant meeting for both men – they have not seen each other for thirty-five years. Back then Jefferson had been based in Paris as the United States Minister to France, and they had worked together to draft the *Declaration of the Rights of Man* while the French Revolution raged around them.

Increasingly during her second visit to America, Frances frets about slavery. An excerpt from a letter to a friend reveals her state of mind: 'This plague spot so spoils the beauty of the robe of American liberty that I often turn in disgust from the freest country in the world...'

She has yet to see slaves sold at a market, although she had observed them manacled onboard a steamboat bound for New Orleans. Fortunately, the steamboat passed by quickly, preventing the enraged Frances Wright from 'committing what could only have been folly'.

Meanwhile, yet another big name from Frances's era crosses her path in America - Robert Owen, a Welshman, an industrialist, and social reformer. He believes that it is possible to run a factory at a profit while still treating the workers humanely, having demonstrated this at his textile mill in New Lanark, Scotland.

Robert Owen moved to America in 1824 with the intent of setting up a community run on communitarian lines. He believes that when human beings live in an environment based on cooperation with one each other they will live happier and more productive lives. This, in contrast to the prevailing economic system whereby one person vies against another. In Owen's view a competitive society is one that destroys basic human decencies.

1825

Frances Wright is in Washington in March when Robert Owen gives two addresses to the House of Representatives with the title a 'Discourse on a New System of Society'. It is not known whether Frances listened to any of the speeches he gave in the Unites States Capitol building, although this was likely because she talked about them later.

Robert Owen tells the politicians in Washington that a study of history demonstrates that the 'great object' of human institutions is, 'or ought to be, to secure happiness for the greatest number of human beings'. This can be brought about, 'first, by a proper training and education from birth of the physical and mental powers of *each* individual; second, by arrangements to enable *each* individual to procure in the manner at all times, a full supply of those things which are necessary and the most beneficial for human nature; and third, that *all* individuals should be so united and combined in a social system, as to give to each the greatest benefit from society.'

Owen is here because he sees the United States as the land of the future. A dynamic man full of purpose, someone who consistently translates thought into action, he has bought the town of Harmonie in the state of Indiana together with the twenty thousand acres surrounding it. The town had been set up as a Christian community by German immigrants under the leadership of George Rapp. George explained to Robert Owen the reason for selling up - the community moved every ten years to find somewhere else to spread their Christian message, and were now close to doing so.

The Welshman intends to set up a new community here to be renamed New Harmony. It will mark a great new beginning for human beings - one where selfishness is eradicated as a driver for economic relations and is replaced with a system of cooperation and mutual benefit for all.

Frances takes a journey west, and visits Harmonie in March 1825. Rapp and his German Christians are still there, and are getting ready to move out prior to Robert Owen's takeover. She will visit Harmonie a second time in May at the time of the handover.

She is impressed with how Harmonie is run as a self-contained, self-sufficient community. But that insight is nothing as yet. Once she witnesses what has clearly been a highly efficient and rapid effort by the German Christians to build their new home, she is astounded. She 'twice visited her German acquaintances in their new Settlement of Economie, below Pittsburg, on the Ohio; and as it were, a new village – with its fields, orchards, gardens, vineyards, flouring-mills, manufactures – [had risen] out of the earth beneath the hands of some eight hundred trained labourers.'

A new vision has been revealed to her: 'Upon inspecting all the departments of industry, and more especially the agricultural, which formed necessarily the large base of the growing wealth and prosperity of the property, she was forcibly struck... with the advantages of united and organised labour...'

This prompts Frances to muse about the psychological drivers that make people work, and how these can be leveraged to produce a well-run and happy community. She believes that what she has seen in Harmonie and Economie clearly demonstrates that a business run as a cooperative will on every occasion outperform private businesses run by individuals seeking a profit.

Because of her prejudice against religion, she has failed to recognise what is really happening in Harmonie; that this is a community of like-minded individuals with a common purpose that lies beyond themselves: and that purpose is to show their devotion to God and a Christian way of life. As such, they have bonded together as a coherent group. Frances sees things differently: 'Christian fanaticism and subjection were the means employed to stultify the intelligence, and hold the physical man submitted to the will of others.' And the labour undertaken by the community is 'the regular and unvarying occupation of the mass, broken only by psalm-singing and other tedious, and sometimes ludicrous ceremonies'. She is right about one thing - the singing of psalms is forever heard throughout the community – it had given Harmonie its name.

This is not the ideal society as Frances sees it, a view she now shares in common with Robert Owen. The perfect setup is one where free individuals are allowed to strive towards improvement and happiness as guided by the way of thinking of the European Enlightenment. For her, Harmonie and Economie both signify nothing more 'beyond well-cultivated farms and gardens, and well-conducted manufactories. No great or beautiful works of art; no libraries; no laboratories... and no men and women beaming with intelligence and that joy of the soul, the necessary result of worldly independence...' Human beings in her ideal society will see their children benefit by the experience handed down to them, all of which contributes to the 'ever accumulating knowledge and capital of society'. The guiding light for all must be science, not religion.

Nevertheless, George Rapp and his Christian community have shown her that a cooperative movement can be made to work with great efficiency.

These visits have given Frances insight into what will become her big idea: communities like these might provide the solution to the slave problem in America. By following the path taken by George Rapp and Robert Owen, she envisages an experimental community to be built as a cooperative; and one set up with a specific aim - to emancipate the slaves.

Frances is not a dreamer she is a doer. And so, in 1825, this woman from Dundee works out a plan to end slavery in the United States, *and then proceeds to carry it out.*

6. NASHOBA

1825

The October 15th issue of the *Genius of Universal Emancipation and Baltimore Courier*, an anti-slavery newspaper, has set out Frances Wright's 'Plan for the gradual abolition of slavery in the United States, without danger or loss to the citizens of the south'.

The objectives of the plan are to buy two sections of public land 'within the good south-western cotton line', and to establish a community to be run as a farm rather than as a cotton plantation. The farm will employ between 50 and 100 slaves bought from their owners. Each slave is required to spend five years working in the fields, with the money earned from their labour set aside to pay back the cost of buying them and to provide a contribution to the expense of running the community. Once their five-year term is up, the slave will be set free, and then sent abroad rather than be allowed to remain in the United States (a policy in keeping with the wishes of anti-slavery groups at the time).

Readers are informed that the slaves will work under 'a system of cooperative labour, conducted as far as shall be advisable in the given case, on the plan of the German and other communities, holding out, as the great stimulus to exertion, the prospect of liberty, together with the liberty and education of the children'.

Education is a key part of Frances's plan. The slaves 'moral, intellectual, and industrial apprenticeship' will, on completion, set them up as upstanding citizens within the community. One of Frances's friends, Frances Trollope, later commented that: 'Her first object was to show that nature had made no difference between blacks and whites, excepting in complexion; and this she expected to prove, by giving an education perfectly equal to a class of black and white children. Could this fact be once fully established, she conceived that the Negro cause would stand on firmer ground than it had yet done, and the degraded rank which they have ever held amongst civilized nations would be proved to be a gross injustice.'

The anticipated cost of her project is $40,000, with an annual projected net profit of $10,000 per year. To help shape her plan, Frances has used the Harmonie and Economie establishments as her economic model, noting the 'great advantages of united over individual labour'. George Rapp and his Christian community had established

Harmonie with 'a total deficit of any monied capital whatsoever' and are now 'in possession of superabundant wealth.' By comparison to the cooperatives, she believes that slave plantations run as conventional businesses are 'profitless'.

Assuming that 'superabundant wealth' will be generated by her scheme: 'It is hoped that, after one successful experiment, a similar establishment will be placed in each state...'

Frances anticipates that when the owners of slave plantations get to see one of her cooperative communities for themselves, they will come to recognise that an economic powerhouse has arrived in their neighbourhood. In consequence, 'many planters will lease out their property, to be worked in the same way, receiving an interest equal or superior to that returned at present...' Her community, 'which it is proposed to establish by subscription, will... offer an asylum and school of industry for the slaves of benevolent [plantation] masters, anxious to manumit their people, but apprehensive of throwing them unprepared into the world'.

Frances firmly believes that the landowners in the southern states will be enthusiastic about ending slavery should a suitable way be found to do so. She still harbours the naive view that the slave owners run their plantations with great reluctance, having had the evil practice forced upon them by British colonialists in the historic past.

The final part of her plan is *epic* in conception. The expected runaway success of her experiment will lead to the formation of many more Nashoba-type communities throughout the United States. This grand vision forms the basis for what she describes as her calculation: 'Showing at what period the labour of 100 people (doubling itself every five years) might redeem the whole slave population of the United States'.

On this basis, all two million slaves in the country will be freed within 85 years.

In the months leading up to the publication of her plan, Frances wrote a letter to Thomas Jefferson setting out her thoughts. This is Jefferson's reply:

August 7, 1825. Monticello, Virginia. Thomas Jefferson to Frances Wright [extract]
My own health is very low, not having been able to leave the house for three months, and suffering much at times. In

this state of body and mind, your letter could not have found a more inefficient companion, one scarcely able to think or to write. At the age of eighty-two, with one foot in the grave, and the other uplifted to follow it, I do not permit myself to take part in any new enterprises, even for bettering the condition of man, not even in the great one which is the subject of your letter...

The abolition of the evil is not impossible; it ought never to be despaired of. Every plan should be adopted, every experiment tried, which may do something towards the ultimate object. That which you propose is well worthy of trial. It has succeeded with certain portions of our white brethren... and why may it not succeed with the man of colour? An opinion is hazarded by some, but proved by none, that moral urgencies are not sufficient to induce him to labour; that nothing can do this but physical coercion. But this is a problem which the present age alone is to solve by experiment...

You are young, dear Madam, and have powers of mind which may do much in exciting others in this arduous task. I am confident they will be so exerted, and I pray to Heaven for their success, and that you may be rewarded with the blessings which such efforts merit.

Not all the senior statesmen in the United States are convinced that her experiment will work. James Madison, who succeeded Thomas Jefferson to become the fourth President of the United States, wrote to Frances explaining why he is sceptical.

September 1, 1825. Montpelier, Virginia. James Madison to Frances Wright. [Extract]
Your letter to Mrs Madison... [arrived] with a printed copy of your plan for the gradual abolition of slavery in the United States.

The magnitude of this evil among us is so deeply felt, and so universally acknowledged, that no merit could be greater than that of devising a satisfactory remedy for it. [But this will not be easy. The question arises as to who would work on the plantations once the slaves are emancipated and then sent abroad. That is because] there would not be an influx of white labourers, successively taking the place of the exiles, and which, without such an influx, would have an effect distressing in prospect to the proprietors of the soil.

[Questions also arise about] the aptitude and adequacy of the process by which the slaves are... to earn the funds [which are] required for their emancipation and removal; and to be sufficiently educated for a life of freedom and social order.

The degree [by which] discipline will enforce the needed labour, and in which voluntary industry will supply the defect of compulsory labour, are vital points on which it may be safe to be very positive without some light from actual experiment.

[It may be doubted that the expected profits] would sufficiently accumulate in five or even more years for the objects in view. And candour obliges me to say that I am not satisfied either that the prospect of emancipation at a future day will sufficiently overcome the natural and habitual repugnance to labour, or that there is such an advantage of united over individual labour as is taken for granted.

[In this last respect, the outcome of communal labour towards eventual emancipation] could be less relied on in case where each individual would [look out to see whether] the fruit of his exertions [were] shared equally or unequally...by others. Skilful arrangements might palliate this tendency, but it would be difficult to counteract it effectually.

[In cooperative communities such as Georg Rapp's Christians, there is] a religious impulse in the members, and a religious authority in the head, for which there will be no substitutes of equivalent efficacy in the emancipating establishment.

...it may deserve consideration whether the experiment would not be better commenced on a scale smaller than that assumed in the prospectus.

Such, Madam are the general ideas suggested by your interesting communication, if they do not coincide with yours, and imply less of confidence that may be due to the plan you have formed. I hope you will not question either my admiration of the generous philanthropy which dictated it, or my sense of the special regard it evinces for the honour and welfare of our expanding, and I trust rising Republic.

I join Mrs Madison In hoping that we shall not be without the opportunity of again welcoming you and your sister to Montpelier, tendering you in the mean time my respectful salutations.

James Madison has set out to be both helpful and tactful in his letter. Helpful, in that he provides hints about why people are motivated to work: such as where individuals can see the direct benefits for themselves of the work they do, and for those cooperating in a religious community who have committed to a common goal. But for those working for others and are compelled to do so, there will be no great willingness to work hard unless coerced to do so by a supervisor who watches them constantly. And the extreme of this situation is to endure the status of a slave, someone whose willpower has been deliberately broken from birth to better manage them, leaving passive resentment in its place. Is it then possible to induce slaves to work without bullying them?

Good points: nevertheless, nothing will stop Frances from going ahead with her plan.

Lafayette now brokers a meeting between Frances Wright and Andrew Jackson, the state senator for Tennessee (and who will later become the seventh President of the United States). Jackson is favourable to her plans, and suggests she should look at an area of forest on the south bank of the Wolf River located thirteen miles from the old Native American ('Indian') trading centre of Memphis, then a little town on the east bank of the River Mississippi. The land had recently been bought from the local Chickasaw natives by Andrew Jackson, and then sold on to two of his friends.

November 1825
Frances pays $480 for 320 acres of land, and comes up with the name Nashoba for her community to be – the Native American word for the Wolf River, which delineates its northern boundary. The land is not the best in the area, being covered in dense forest requiring to be cleared. Frances chose the property because she wants to establish her

community at a suitable distance from the River Mississippi marshes where malarial mosquitoes are found in large numbers.

At about the same time, Frances buys ten slaves in Nashville for the community - six men and four women - at prices between $400 and $500. She does not record her feelings about the purchase, although one can guess the disgust she felt. The slaves are to be delivered to Nashoba, which is over two hundred miles from Memphis, although it will be some time before they can be shipped there. Winter is approaching and the rivers are starting to ice up.

Frances provides a snapshot of Nashoba in the days before the slaves arrived in a letter written in November to the *Genius of Universal Emancipation* newspaper. She informs their readers that she will need to employ workmen soon, including carpenters and bricklayers. Once 'the necessary buildings' have been 'erected, machinery, for various branches of manufactures will be put in operation.' Additionally, 'a school will be opened as soon as practicable...' Otherwise, 'It is expected that most of the different branches of business will be carried on by the middle of next summer, or sooner.' She finishes the letter by asking 'public spirited individuals' to make contributions. In order to satisfy her aim of starting with an establishment of between fifty and a hundred slaves, she requires either substantial donations of money from the public or the free gift of slaves from their owners.

1826

No donations have come in by the start of the year, except for $550 worth of goods to help stock the community store. The absence of cash donations is a much bigger problem than it should have been, because chance circumstances have made Frances extremely anxious about money. Nashoba's expenses are being paid from the family estate, but she then discovered that the money in it is in peril. She had granted the power of attorney to a bank agent to buy and sell stock in the Louisiana State Bank for the estate, and he had subsequently invested $140,000 in the bank. However, the agent went bankrupt after speculating on the cotton market, which then crashed. Newly impoverished and with the authority granted to him, he could easily have run off with the sisters' money (he did not, but they would not find that out for another six months). To add to the woe, a stock certificate amounting to two-thirds of the sisters' estate has gone missing from Lafayette's chateau near Paris (it too turned up six months later).

Meanwhile, the work of building the community continues, albeit with many minor hassles. For some reason the cattle and sheep bought for Nashoba have not turned up, and this has left the community with only one milk cow, which had been previously bought in Memphis..

Nashoba has acquired some male helpers. Notably, George Flowers, an amiable farmer from England, who has recently been active in campaigning against slavery in the United States. He will provide much-needed practical know-how. Also James Richardson, who had studied medicine at Edinburgh University but does not appear to have gone into practice. He will help Frances to keep the accounts for Nashoba, and will later put his medical knowledge to good use when both Frances and Camilla fall ill. A flawed character, he comes across to others as 'upright, impractable', and a dreamer obsessed by philosophy.

At the end of February / the start of March, Frances's slaves arrive by steamer from Nashville, although for some reason, unexplained, only eight adults are here: five men, three women, together with their three children. The men are Willis, Jacob, Grandison, Redrick and Henry. The women: Nelly, Peggy and Kitty. And not long after, Francis is offered more slaves for Nashoba by a Robert Wilson from South Carolina; their names are Lukey and her six daughters, Maria, Harriet, Elvira, Isabel, Viole and Delilah, who are aged between six and twenty. Robert Wilson had inherited them from a relative but does not want them. They are unsuitable for the heavy work required in Nashoba, although Frances takes them anyway.

May 1826

The following letter published in the *Genius of Universal Emancipation* provides an update on the progress made so far:

Letter: Frances Wright to Reverend Hugh McMillan, Chesterville, South Carolina. May 3, 1826. [Extract]
With respect to the eight slaves brought by Mr Wilson 'With the exception of Maria, who is naturally active and quick of apprehension, we found them, as Mr Wilson had stated, disposed to laziness. Without any harsh measures whatsoever, they already work cheerfully and steadily, and are very useful field hands, all our labour at present being of that nature. Contrary to expectation, therefore, we have found them serviceable, in our outset. The other bad habits,

84

which they only share in common with those generally born in slavery, and which we have still to counteract, are a disposition to petty thieving and lying, and to the use of bad language...

We shall not consider ourselves as stated in our plan, until a school is formed. For this year we must content ourselves with forming our little company into a Sunday evening class.

Our people consist, at present, of the family brought by Mr Wilson, and five men and three women purchased at Nashville. With these we opened our grounds in the woods, on the third of March last. We have had since much wet weather. We have, however, raised buildings for immediate use; cleared and fenced around them; cleared thoroughly, planted and fenced an apple orchard of five acres; planted in potatoes a vegetable garden; opened fifteen acres for corn and planted two of old ground in cotton. For this climate we are too late to expect a good crop, and only consider our farm as having made a start for next year...

Our establishment now comprises a store for the supply of the neighbourhood and a small tavern for the accommodation of visitors.

June – July 1826

Frances, ever ambitious to expand her scheme, buys another 1800 acres of land near Nashoba. But then disaster strikes early in July when she is laid low by a fever contracted during the ride back home from a visit to New Harmony. The fever attacked her brain and affected her sight, lasting for ten days before burning out. But then comes a much more serious relapse, which will leave her weak and 'entirely prostrated' for months to come.

December 1826

It is clear that Frances cannot stay in Nashoba given her weakened state. She will now return to Europe to recover, but first she will have to find someone to run the community with Camilla. A man by the name of Richeson Whitby now arrives from New Harmony (Richeson will later marry Camilla Wright). He had formerly been a Shaker, a member of a Christian sect who believes in the Second Coming and who get their name from the way they shake their bodies with great passion during worship. Richeson is an experienced farmer.

Frances writes a trust document to put the community on a legal footing, stipulating that ten trustees will now run Nashoba. The document describes what has and has not been achieved so far. The positives: a hundred acres of land has been cleared, and on that land are one single and two double cabins, a cabin used as the slaves' dining room, one for a storeroom, and several small cabins for stores. The negatives: no sawmill, steam engine, washhouse or dairy. No cattle or oxen have turned up despite being ordered months ago. And most telling of all, there is no schoolroom, although the education of the slaves had been seen as a priority for the community.

Robert Dale Owen, the son of Robert Owen, describes the community shortly after the trust was set up:

> At Nashoba, Where I remained ten days, I found but three trustees, Richeson Whitby, James Richardson, and the younger Miss Wright. We consulted daily, but ever sanguine I had to admit that the outlook was unpromising.
>
> The land, all second-rate only, and scarcely a hundred acres of it cleared... slaves released from fear of the lash working indolently under the management for Whitby, whose education in an easy-going Shaker village had not at all fitted him for the post of plantation overseer.

He also mentions that Camilla's heath is poor, although she has agreed to stay behind when Frances goes. Whitby had told him that if Camilla was to leave Nashoba with Frances, 'he despaired of being able to manage the slaves'. That is because they would obey either woman 'as their owner, and himself only when he had the authority to back his orders'.

May – June, 1827

Frances finally leaves on May 2, and on arriving at New Orleans is so feeble she has to be lifted on board the steamer for the journey across the Atlantic. Robert Dale Owen goes with her: 'I had fears even for her life, till we got fairly out to sea; but after that she gradually gathered strength, and when I left her in Paris with intimate friends, her health was, in a measure, restored.'

In her absence the Nashoba community quickly falls apart.

July 28, 1827

The extent to which Nashoba has lost its way is revealed in the latest issue of the *Genius of Universal Emancipation*. In it is an article by James Richardson that shocks everyone who reads it.

Written in diary form, it provides snippets of day-to-day life in Nashoba that reveal how the slaves are being treated without the respect due to them. On May 13, the slave children were forcibly removed from their parents and placed under a care manager. The parents were then informed that all communication between them and their children is forbidden except by permission, and only then in the presence of 'the manager of the children'.

On May 26, it was decreed that 'the slaves shall not be permitted to eat, elsewhere than at the public meals'.

And above all, these are the two revelations in the article that caused uproar:

June 1. Isabel had laid a complaint against Redrick, for coming during the night of Wednesday to her bedroom, uninvited; and endeavouring without her consent, to take liberties with her person. Our views of the sexual relations had been repeatedly given to the slaves: Camilla Wright again stated it, and informed the slaves that, as the conduct of Redrick, which he did not deny, was a gross infringement of that view, a repetition of such conduct, by him, or by any other of the men, ought, in her opinion, to be punished by flogging. She repeated that we consider the proper basis of the sexual intercourse to be the unconstrained and unrestricted choice of both parties.

Nelly having requested a lock for the door of the room in which she and Isabel sleep, with the view of preventing the future uninvited entrance of any man; the lock was refused, as being... inconsistent with the doctrine just explained...

And if that was not bad enough, the following passage shocked all who read it: 'June 17. James Richardson informed them that, last night, Mamselle Josephine [a quadroon daughter of Mamselle Lalotte, a free coloured woman hired as a teacher] and he began to live together; and he took this occassion on repeating to them our views on colour, and on the sexual relation.'

What proved so controversial here is the admission that James Richardson had taken Josephine, a quadroon – someone who is one quarter black by descent - as his mistress. Such behaviour echoed the known sexual exploitation of female slaves by owners of the large southern slave plantations. What is being indulged in here is miscegenation, the inter-breeding of whites and blacks, a practice that horrifies those who advocate that the two races should be kept pure (which is almost everybody on both sides of the slavery controversy with the exception of Frances Wright, who sees nothing wrong with it). Additionally, for those adhering to the strict Christian morality of the age, the evidence that sexual relations have happened outside marriage is equally distressing.

The following letter had been sent by an anti-slaver calling himself 'Mentor' to the August 18 issue of *The Genius of Universal Emancipation*. The editor prefaces it with these comments: 'While we view with detestation the "libidinous" practices of slaveholders in the southern states of the Union, and the West Indies, anything that contains a semblance of the same character must be pointedly condemned if tolerated by those who are labouring to destroy the system of African oppression.'

Letter published August 18, 1827. 'For the Genius of Universal Emancipation' [Extract]

> Mr Lundy, No one possessed of moral or religious feelings, can read without horror the publication in your last paper, of the proceedings of what is termed 'Frances Wright's Establishment'... One would have supposed that the wish of those concerned in an establishment so indecent, so libidinous, so repugnant to the safe and honest maxims of Christian life, would have been to veil and conceal their measures from the public eye, instead of ostentatiously exhibiting them to view... And who can read without disgust, that an accomplished young woman (for such Miss C. W. Is known to be) apparently concurs with her co-trustees in giving sanction to the formation of illicit sexual connections, without the obligations of marriage!
>
> What is all this but the creation of one great brothel, disgraceful to its institutors, and most reprehensible as a public example in the vicinity!

James Richardson unwisely replies to this letter, although the editor only publishes a brief extract. The following section was tactfully

88

omitted: 'Mentor thinks we are instituting a Brothel. I have seen a brothel and I never knew a place so unlike it as Nashoba.'

Frances Wright is in Paris when she hears about the scandal. She is very upset and writes a letter to James Richardson, although only reproving him gently. The damage has been done and it cannot be undone.

In her despair and looking for female companionship, Frances seeks out a woman she has never met, but who might be sympathetic to her woes. This is Mary Shelley, the widow of the poet Percy Bysshe Shelley. Mary's mother is Mary Wollstonecraft, an early advocate of woman's rights, and her father is William Godwin, the radical philosopher and political journalist. Mary is best known today as the author of *Frankenstein*. And curiously enough, in her teenage years she lived in Frances Wright's native Dundee for fifteen months.

Frances writes to Mary, offering no apologies for not having met her, and then proceeds to set out her circumstances:

August 22, 1827. Paris. Frances Wright to Mary Shelley. [extract]
I have devoted my time and fortune to laying the foundations of an establishment where affection shall form the only marriage, kind feeling and kind action the only religion, respect for the feelings and liberties of others to the only restraint, and union of interest the bond of peace and security. With the protection of the negro in view, whose cruel sufferings and degradation had attracted my special sympathy, it was necessary to seek the land of his bondage, to study his condition and imagine a means for effecting his liberation; with the emancipation of the human mind in view, from the shackles of moral and religious superstition, it was necessary to seek a country where political institutions should allow free scope for experiment; and with a practice in view in opposition to all the laws of public opinion, it was necessary to seek the seclusion of a new country, and build up a city of refuge in the wilderness itself.

Fifteen months have placed the establishment in a fair way of progress, in the hands of united and firm associates, comprising a family of colour from New Orleans. As might be expected, my health gave way under the continued fatigues of mind and body to the first twelvemonth. A brain fever, followed by a variety of sufferings, seemed to point to a sea-voyage as the only chance of recovery... I am now in an advanced state of convalescence, but still obliged to avoid fatigue either bodily or mental.

Whatever be the fate of this letter, I wish to convey to Mary Wollstonecraft Godwin Shelley my respect and admiration of those from who she holds these names, and my fond desire to connect her with them in my esteem, and in the knowledge of mutual sympathy to sign myself her friend.

Mary writes back, informing Frances 'you do honour to our species, and what perhaps dearer to me, the feminine part of it.' She is keen to meet this extraordinary woman and is curious to find out more about her.

Frances, delighted at getting a reponse, replies in turn.

September 15, 1827. Paris. Frances Wright to Mary Shelley.
[extract]

My Friend, my dear Friend – How sweet are the sentiments with which I write that sacred word – so often prostituted, so seldom bestowed with the glow of satisfaction and delight with which I now employ it...

I too have suffered, and we must have done so perhaps to feel for the suffering. We must have loved and mourned, and felt the chill of disappointment, and sighed over the moral blank of a heartless world, ere we can be moved to sympathy for calamity, or roused to attempt its alleviation. The curiosity you express shall be most willingly answered in (as I trust) our approaching meeting. You will see then that I have greatly pitied and greatly dared, only because I have greatly suffered and widely observed. I have sometimes feared lest too early affliction and too frequent disappointment had blunted my sensibilities, when a rencontre [meeting] with someone of the rare beings dropt amid the dull multitude, likes oases in the desert, has refreshed my better feelings, and reconciled me with others and with myself.

I [will] run back to my forests. And I must return without a bosom intimate? Yes; our little circle has mind, has heart, has right opinions, right feelings, cooperates in an experiment having in view human happiness, yet I do want one of my own sex to commune with, and sometimes to lean upon in all the confidence of equality of friendship. You see I am not so disinterested as you suppose. Delightful indeed it is to aid the progress of human imrovement, and sweet is the peace we derive from aiding the happiness of others. But still the heart craves something more ere it can say – I am satisfied.

I must tell, not write, of the hopes of Nashoba, and of all your sympathising heart wishes to hear.

They meet near Brighton in October, and any hints given by Frances that she would like Mary to return with her to America come to nothing because Mary's priority is the care of her young son Percy.

November 1827 – January 1828
Nevertheless, Frances has found another author to recruit to her cause - Frances Trollope, writer of travel books and novels (she is also the mother of Anthony Trollope, the future novelist). She agrees to visit Nashoba, and will travel there with three of her children (but not Anthony), her maid, and a manservant. Departing November 3, 1827, they arrive at Nashoba in January 1828.

Frances Trollope is somewhat underwhelmed by the community, describing her short visit in her book *Domestic Manners of the Americans*. She will not stay long, even though she had intended to hang around the community for several months:

> ...one glance sufficed to convince me that every idea I had formed of the place was as far as possible from the truth. Desolation was the only feeling - the only word that presented itself: but it was not spoken... Each building consisted of two large rooms furnished in the most simple manner; nor had they as yet collected round them any of those minor comforts which ordinary minds class among the necessaries of life...

> The only white persons we found at Nashoba were [Camilla] Wright, and her husband. I think they had between thirty and forty slaves, including children, but when I was there no school had been established. Books and other materials for the great experiment had been

91

collected, and one or two professors engaged, but nothing was yet organized. I found my friend [Camilla Wright] in very bad health, which she attributed to the climate. This naturally so much alarmed me for my children, that I decided upon leaving the place with as little delay as possible, and did so at the end of ten days.

January 1828

Frances Wright now concedes that Nashoba is a failure. The slaves have not worked hard to earn their freedom, and the outcome is clear, the community cannot be maintained as a paying farm; indeed, it is rapidly draining away the sisters' savings.

And now: 'Once satisfied as to the course to be adopted with a view of forwarding the one object of her life – the advancement of human knowledge and happiness – she abandoned, although not without a struggle, the peaceful shades of Nashoba, leaving the property in the charge of an individual who was to hold the negroes ready for removal to Haiti the year following.'

She writes to a friend and shares her deepest feelings on the matter, 'co-operation has well nigh killed us all...' Adding that 'we have all had our share of sufferings and exertions: 1 have had mine... but they have left me only firmer in my purpose, more flexible in principle, while they have enriched me with experience, dearly; but not too dearly purchased, seeing that it is invaluable.'

Frances Wright will not now give up, because she never gives up. And why should she? *This woman has a world to change.*

7. CINCINNATI

1828

Frances Wright is horrified, disgusted, furious.

She has just discovered that on Independence Day last year, the Reverend Ezra Stiles Ely, Pastor of the Third Presbyterian Church in Philadelphia, had preached a sermon on the subject of 'the duty of Christian freemen to elect Christian rulers'.

Declaring that every politician must be 'an avowed and sincere friend to Christianity', Reverend Ely insisted that once elected, a politician must put in place policies guided by the Bible's teachings. And to make sure this happens, he advocated the formation of the 'Christian Party in Politics', ideally constituting an alliance of Protestant denominations such as Presbyterians, Baptists, Methodists, and Congregationalists. The block vote wielded by such a Christian Party would become a huge influence in all elections held in the United States, and will guarantee that only Christians gain office, whereas 'avowed infidels' will be excluded.

Ely's proposal is contrary to the spirit of Article Six of the United States Constitution, which states that 'no religious test shall ever be required as a qualification to any office or public trust under the United States'.

Frances sees a conspiracy here: It is 'an evident attempt through the influence of the clergy over the female mind – until this hour lamentably neglected in the United States – to effect a union of Church and State'. She has good reasons for believing this – more women than men attend church services, and although they do not have a vote, their men folk do, and as such can be influenced by them.

Frances is now 'determined to arouse the whole American people to meet [the threat], at whatever cost to herself'. She picks her battleground carefully: the city of Cincinnati in Ohio.

When Frances Trollope left Nashoba, she eventually arrived in Cincinnati. Deciding to stay there long-term, she will end up here for the next two years. She is thus well placed to provide a snapshot of life in the mid-western city and of its women in particular.

Cincinnati has been expanding fast since it was first settled forty years ago. Not striking the visitor as a particularly attractive place, the streets and buildings are laid out in a grid and block pattern typical of

American cities. Frances, looking around for some feature to praise, in fact any feature at all, decides that the landing place for boats on the bank of the Ohio River is 'noble'. Fifteen steamboats are docked here.

She estimates Cincinnati's population to be over twenty thousand. The main industry is the export of pigs, which are allowed to roam free in large numbers around the city: 'It is not very agreeable to live surrounded by herds of these unsavoury animals, it is well they are so numerous, and so active in their capacity of scavengers, for without them the streets would soon be choked up with all sorts of substances, in every stage of decomposition.'

The men are in total control in Cincinnati, and are motivated by one thing and one thing only: 'every bee in the hive is actively employed in search of that honey of Hybla, vulgarly called money; neither art, science, learning, nor pleasure, can seduce them from its pursuit'.

Pleasure is not a pastime indulged here - the Church has seen to that: 'I never saw any people who appeared to live so much without amusement as the Cincinnatians. The game of billiards is forbidden by law, as are playing cards. To sell a pack of cards in Ohio subjects the seller to a penalty of fifty dollars. They have no public balls, excepting I think, six, during the Christmas holidays. They have no concerts. They have no dinner parties.' A theatre has been built, although: 'Ladies are rarely seen there, and by far the larger proportion of females deem it an offence against religion to witness the representation of a play.'

The men prefer to socialise amongst themselves, leaving the women on their own. Frances comments about what passes for a mixed social occasion in Cincinnati: 'The gentlemen spit, talk of elections and the price of produce, and spit again. The ladies look at each other's dresses till they know every pin by heart; talk of Parson Somebody's last sermon on the day of judgment, on Dr T'otherbody's new pills for dyspepsia, till the 'tea' is announced, when they can all console themselves together for whatever they may have suffered in keeping awake...'

While their men are making money, the married women are kept busy with household duties. They are 'too actively employed in the interior of their houses to permit much parading in full dress for morning visits. There are no public gardens or lounging shops of fashionable resort, and were it not for public worship, and private tea drinkings, all the ladies in Cincinnati would be in danger of becoming perfect recluses.'

The younger women devote themselves to the activities of the church because there is little else to do here, and, in any case, it is expected of them. Once inside the chapel, they will be subjected to what can only be described as extreme psychological manipulation by the pastors.

Frances Trollope tells how. She visits a church, warning her readers that the scenes she saw 'made me shudder'. Three priests will take part in the horror show she now describes in detail. One of them enters the pulpit and starts to speak, describing 'with ghastly minuteness, the last feeble fainting moments of human life, and then the gradual progress of decay after death, which he followed through every process up to the last loathsome stage of decomposition.'

Now changing his tone from 'sober accurate description, into the shrill voice of horror, he bent forward his head, as if to gaze on some object beneath the pulpit'. He appears to see something in the pit below him, a gesture that gives 'effect to his description of hell. No image that fire, flame, brimstone, molten lead, or red-hot pincers could supply, with flesh, nerves, and sinews quivering under them, was omitted. The perspiration ran in streams from the face of the preacher; his eyes rolled, his lips were covered with foam, and every feature had the deep expression of horror it would have borne, had he, in truth, been gazing at the scene he described.'

When the priest sits down, the other two priests stand up to sing a hymn:

> It was some seconds before the congregation could join as usual; every up-turned face looked pale and horror-struck. When the singing ended, another took the centre place, and began in a sort of coaxing affectionate tone, to ask the congregation if what their dear brother had spoken had reached their hearts ? Whether they would avoid the hell he had made them see?
>
> 'Come, then!' he continued, stretching out his arms towards them, 'come to us and tell us so, and we will make you see Jesus, the dear gentle Jesus, who shall save you from it. But you must come to him! You must not be ashamed to come to him! This night you shall tell him that you are not ashamed of him; we will make way for you; we will clear the bench for anxious sinners to sit upon. Come, then! come to the anxious bench, and we will show you Jesus! Come! Come! Come!'

A hymn is sung:

And now in every part of the church a movement was perceptible, slight at first, but by degrees becoming more decided. Young girls arose, and sat down, and rose again; and then the pews opened, and several came tottering out, their hands clasped, their heads hanging on their bosoms, and every limb trembling, and still the hymn went on; but as the poor creatures approached the rail their sobs and groans became audible.

They seated themselves on the 'anxious benches' the hymn ceased, and two of the three priests walked down from the tribune, and going, one to the right, and the other to the left, began whispering to the poor tremblers seated there. These whispers were inaudible to us, but the sobs and groans increased to a frightful excess. Young creatures, with features pale and distorted, fell on their knees on the pavement, and soon sunk forward on their faces; the most violent cries and shrieks followed, while from time to time a voice was heard in convulsive accents, exclaiming, 'Oh Lord! Oh Lord Jesus! Help me, Jesus!' and the like.

The two priests walk around giving the women 'whispered comfortings, and from time to time a mystic caress. More than once I saw a young neck encircled by a reverend arm. Violent hysterics and convulsions seized many of them, and when the tumult was at the highest, the priest who remained above again gave out a hymn as if to drown it.

It was a frightful sight to behold innocent young creatures, in the gay morning of existence, thus seized upon, horror-struck, and rendered feeble and enervated forever.'

Frances Trollope, generalising from what she witnessed here, believes that: 'The influence which the ministers of all the innumerable religious sects throughout America have on the females of their respective congregations, approaches very nearly to what we read of in Spain, or in other strictly Roman Catholic countries.' She suspects that the high rank assigned to the clergy in society has given them 'high importance in the eyes of the ladies'. And something else too: 'I think, also, that it is from the clergy that the women of America receive that sort of attention which is so dearly valued by every female heart throughout the world... and in return for this they seem to give their hearts and souls into their keeping. I never saw, or read, of any country where religion had so strong a hold upon the women, or a slighter hold upon the men.'

Frances Wright is determined to confront the intrusion of the Church into American politics, and now launches a campaign to warn of this impending threat to individual freedom in America. To publicise her case she will go out on a series of lecture tours, but to start with, in June 1828, she takes the role of co-editor of the weekly newspaper, the *New Harmony Gazette*, later renamed the *Free Enquirer*. This is a huge surprise for some, that a woman has taken an active editorial role in a newspaper to comment on political matters (up until then an exclusively man's domain in the United States). She sets out her editorials to counter 'the ineptness and corruption of the public press, ridden by ascendant influences, until it is abandoned alike by the honest and the wise, and left in the hands of individuals too ignorant to distinguish truth, or too timid to venture its utterance'.

And in her lectures, she will highlight 'the neglected state of the female mind, and the consequent dependence of the female condition. This, by placing the most influential half of the nation at the mercy of that worst species of quackery, practised under the name of religion, virtually lays the reins of government, national as well as domestic, in the hands of a priesthood, whose very subsistence depends, of necessity, upon the mental and moral degradation of their fellow creatures.'

Women are oppressed in a nation whose constitution starts with these words: 'We the people of the United States, in order to form a more perfect union, establish justice, insure domestic tranquility, provide for the common defense, promote the general welfare, and secure the blessings of liberty to ourselves and our posterity, do ordain and establish this Constitution for the United States of America.' Let's emphasize those first few words - 'We the people...' – but not 'We the men...' Frances will thus set out how women can be treated fairly in the new republic.

On July 4, 1828, Frances Wright gave the Independence Day lecture in New Harmony. By doing this, her biographer Celia Morris Eckhardt considers Frances Wright *'to have probably been the first women in America to have been the main speaker to have talked in front of a large mixed audience'*.

Not that her independence-day talk in New Harmony would have caused any controversy amongst her community-minded audience - they share her views. Frances may have used this first talk as a dry run to ease herself into what will come later; lectures in front of hostile audiences.

Her public lecture series will start in Cincinnati. Frances writes that 'The city of Cincinnati had stood for some time conspicuous for the enterprise and liberal spirit of her citizens, when last summer, by the sudden combination of the clergy of three orthodox sects, a *revival*, as such scenes of distraction are wont to be styled, was opened in houses, churches, and even on the Ohio river. The victims of this odious experiment on human credibility and nervous weakness, were invariably women...'

Something had to be done about this: 'A circumstantial account of the distress and disturbance on the public mind in the Ohio metropolis led me to visit the afflicted city; and, since all were dumb, to take up the cause of insulted reason and outraged humanity.'

The woman who has arrived here, a place of ambitious males and fearful females, is a *liberated woman*; not that anyone in 1828 would have had the least idea what that is. Frances once wrote that when she gave her lectures she felt like an alien from a strange planet arriving amongst people with senses and perceptions different from hers.

Frances Trollope is in Cincinnati when she hears the news - Frances Wright has arrived to give a series of public lectures in the city. How extraordinary. That a woman 'should present herself as a public lecturer would naturally excite surprise anywhere', including the old world of Europe, 'but in America, where women are guarded by a seven-fold shield of habitual insignificance, it caused an effect that can hardly be described...'

It is a momentous occasion, no less because in Cincinnati, Ohio, on August 10, 1828, *the fabric of society is about to be ripped apart.*

Before August 10, 1828, such was the situation: men ran the show; women were invisible. Men took charge, whereas women were wives, mothers, and domestic servants in the household. Men organised society; women were ignored or scolded should they dare to utter anything about public matters. Such were the unspoken laws of society, and, although not binding on everybody, they were strictly adhered to.

Frances changed that. This was a woman – a woman! - who spoke in public. This was a woman who spoke to an audience of both men and women, an audience given the label of 'promiscuous' at the time - a word used here with its old fashioned meaning of mixed - a scornful word, later used to describe loose sexual behaviour. But not only that, Frances talked about politics in public at a time when few women ever did that in private conversation. And by doing so she broke many of society's taboos – smashed them to pieces. What she did shocked everyone. It shocked absolutely.

Some of the men and the women listening to Frances Wright must have asked themselves, what would the world be like if other women took up her example and public talking became normal behaviour for them? Such an unnatural thing for a woman to do. And what, then, would happen to the nation if women were allowed to interfere with how society is run? Such was beyond thinking about...

Frances Trollope knew what was coming next: 'I shared the surprise, but not the wonder; I knew her extraordinary gift of eloquence, her almost unequalled command of words, and the wonderful power of her rich and thrilling voice; and I doubted not that if it was her will to do it, she had the power of commanding the attention, and enchanting the ear of any audience before whom it was her pleasure to appear.'

Frances was about to demonstrate to the world of 1828 that women could be hyper-articulate, have much of importance to say about society, and to say it convincingly. And perhaps most important of all, she will demonstrate that a woman can summon the courage to get up there on a public stage and then talk in front of a hostile audience. Such set a precedent: if one woman can do this, then others may follow.

August 10, 1828

The three lectures in Cincinnati are to be held in the courthouse and are free of charge to the public. Frances Trollope turns up for her friend's first lecture, which is on the topic of the nature of knowledge. She finds Frances's stage appearance striking: 'Her tall and majestic figure, the deep and almost solemn expression of her eyes, the simple contour of her finely formed head, unadorned, excepting by its own natural ringlets; her garment of lain white muslin, which hung around her in folds that recalled the drapery of a Grecian statue, all contributed to produce an effect, unlike anything I had ever seen before, or ever expect to see again.'

Frances Wright has deliberately chosen this costume: it is the dress of an Ancient Greek woman from the Garden of Epicurus in Athens.

The talk that follows is a relatively uncontroversial introduction to her series, that is, apart for the following excerpt, which without doubt enraged the city's clergy:

Eve puts not forth her hand to gather the fair fruit of knowledge. The wily serpent now hath better learned his lesson; and, to secure his reign in the garden, beguileth *her* not to eat. Promises, entreaties, threats, tales of wonder, and, alas! Tales of horror are all poured into her tender ears. Above, her agitated fancy hears the voice of a god in thunders; below, she sees the yawning pit; and, before, behind, around, a thousand phantoms, conjured from the prolific brain of insatiate priestcraft, confound, alarm, and overwhelm her reason!

Oh! were that worst evil withdrawn which now weighs upon our race, how rapid were its progress in knowledge! Oh! were men and, yet more, women, absolved from fear, how easily and speedily and gloriously would they hold onto their course in improvement! The difficulty is not to convince, it is to win *attention*. Could truth only be heard, the conversion of the ignorant were easy. And well do the hired supporters of error understand this fact. Well do they *know*, that if the daughters of the present, and mothers of the future generation, were to drink of the living waters of knowledge, their reign would be ended 'their occupation gone'. So well do they know it, that, far from obeying to the letter the command of their spiritual leader, 'Be ye fishers of men', we find them everywhere *fishers of women*. Their own sex, old and young, they see with indifference swim by their nets but closely and warily are their meshes laid, to entangle the female of every age.

Father and husbands! Do you not understand this fact? Do you not see how, in the mental bondage of your wives and fair companions, ye yourselves are bound? Will you fondly sport yourselves in your imagined liberty, and say, 'it matters not if our women be mental slaves?' Will ye pleasure yourselves in the varied paths of knowledge, and imagine that women, hoodwinked and unawakened, will make better servants and the easier playthings? They are greatly in error who strike the account...

100

However novel it may appear, I shall venture the assertion, that until women assume the place in society which good sense and good feeling alike assign to them, human improvement must advance but feebly.

The reaction is utterly predictable, 'a kindling of wrath among the clergy'. The pastors label her the 'priestess of infidelity', and tell their congregations not to attend her lectures.

August 17, 1828

A week later Frances gives her second lecture inside a crowded courthouse, this time on the subject of free enquiry. She warms up to her main theme; the absence of education for women in America. She asserts that education must '*embrace the two sexes on a footing of equality*'.

As it stands at the moment, America is a republic where 'we see endowed colleges for the rich, and barely *common schools* for the poor', whereas women are 'sentenced to mental imbecility'. Frances argues that this is not equality as such:

We see men who will aid the instruction of their sons, and condemn only their daughters to ignorance. 'Our sons,' they say, 'will have to exercise political rights, may aspire to public offices, may fill some learned profession, may struggle for wealth and acquire it. It is well that we give them a helping hand; that we assist them to such knowledge as is going, and make them as sharp witted as their neighbours. But for our daughters,' they say – if indeed respecting them they say anything – 'for our daughters, little trouble or expense is necessary. They can never be *anything*; in fact, they are nothing. We had best give them up to their mothers, who may take them to Sunday's preaching; and, with the aid of a little music, a little dancing, and a few fine gowns, fit them out for the market of marriage.'

No! Their duty is plain, evident, decided. In a daughter they have in charge a human being; in a son, the same. Let them train up these *human beings*, under the expanded wings of liberty. Let them seek *for* them and *with* them just knowledge; encouraging, from the cradle upwards, that useful curiosity which will lead them unbidden in the paths

101

of free enquiry; and place them, safe and superior to the storms of life, in the security of well regulated, self-possessed minds, well grounded, well reasoned, conscientous opinions, and self-approved consistent practice.

'Let us enquire!', urges Frances Wright, her Dundee accent soaring across the Cincinnati Courthouse. 'Are we miserable creatures, innately and of necessity; placed on this earth by a being who should have made us for misery here and damnation herafter; or are we born ductile as the gold and speckless as the mirror, capable of all inflection and impression which wise or unwise instruction may impart, or to which good or evil circumstances may incline? Are we helpless sinners, with nought but the anchor of faith to lean on? Or are we the creatures of noblest energies and sublimest capabilities, fitted for every deed of excellence, feeling of charity, and mode of enjoyment?'

Enquiry is needed to settle this problem, a matter not small, 'nor the issues at stake trifling. Every interest dearest to the heart, every prospect most exhilirating to the mind, is involved in the question and trembles on the decision.'

August 24, 1828
The Courthouse for her third lecture 'on knowledge' is jammed full, with 'upwards of five hundred individuals' turned away at the door. When she finishes her lecture, Frances is implored to give additional lectures in Cincinnati, this time in the city's theatre which holds more people than the courtroom.

Eight years later Frances will look back on her lecture series in Cincinnati describing it as a success. She 'had arrested in that city the flood of superstition, at a time when it had well nigh irrecoverably overset the intellect of one half the population... ' The city 'wanted some plain truth; I gave it to her, and the sound part of the population received it.'

Although the aim of her lectures has been to free women's minds from being pounced on by the Church, a much larger vision emerges from them - a vision of a glorious new society run through the cooperation of human beings. It is a vision that makes perfect sense as a way of organising human affairs; a society that you and I might want to live in. But is it practical? Perhaps not if you were to heed the advice of Frances's friend and advisor, James Madison: 'If men were angels, no government would be necessary.'

Frances would probably not agree with this sentiment. She is losing her childhood innocence as witness the following sentiments - there are men, all too common in politics, who 'make their opinions ladders to their ambitions and cloaks to their dishonesty'. And as for political parties, the moment one is formed, 'partisans... attach to it their selfish interests than their honour... and pass themselves off for paragons of virtue and martyrs of principle'.

Perhaps some naivety still lingers, because she believes the world can be improved, and that one day human beings will grasp at a better way of living together, a life where reason supplants base motives. By explaining in her lectures how this could come about, Frances Wright is holding up the blazing torch of the European Enlightenment in what can only be described as a dark corner of the new America.

Perhaps Frances reckons that the driving forces for much in human behaviour - status seeking and self-aggrandisement - are not hardwired into human beings, as many believe them to be. Or maybe she reckons they are for some individuals, but once the message is managed through education, the greater part of our species will be persuaded that a cooperative society provides 'the best means yet discovered for securing the one great end - that of human liberty and equality'.

Human beings must change their ways. The profit motive clearly is not working. It creates a society whereby individuals are led to believe they are superior to others:

> The man possessed of a dollar, feels himself to be, not merely one hundred cents richer, but also one hundred cents *better*, than the man who is pennyless so on through all the gradations of earthly possessions – the estimate of our own moral and political importance swelling in a ratio exactly proportionate to the growth of our purse. The rich man who can leave a clear independence to his children is given to estimate them as he estimates himself, and to imagine something in their nature distinct from that of the less privileged heirs of hard labour and harder fare.

The situation then comes about where values get distorted in society because class divisions have arisen:

> The husbandman who supports us by the fruits of his labour, the artisan to whom we owe all the comforts and

conveniences of life, are banished from what's termed intellectual society, nay, worse, but too often condemned to the most severe physical privations and the grossest mental ignorance, while the soldier, who lives by our crimes, the lawyer by our quarrels and our rapacity, and the priest by our credulity or our hypocrisy, are honoured with public consideration and applause.

A heirachical society creates psychological divisions between people, creating alienation and strife, but not happiness for all:

The existing principle of selfish interest and competition has been carried to its extreme point; and, in its progress, has isolated the heart of man, blunted the edge of his finest sensibilities, and annihilated all his most generous impulse, and sympathies. Need we hesitate to denounce the principle as vicious, which places the interests of each individual in continual opposition to those of his fellows which makes of one man's loss, another's gain, and inspires a spirit of accumulation, that crushes every noble sentiment, features every degrading one, makes of this globe a scene of strife, and the whole human race, idolators of gold? And must we be told that this is the nature of things? It is certainly in the nature of our antisocial institutions, and need we seek any stronger argument to urge against them?

There is a much better way to organise human affairs. Should people gather together as a community they will cooperate to create a society where all are happy. In such a society, everybody will be free and equal, men and women, black and white.

The focus here will be on the acquisition of knowledge and human improvement. By doing so, individual fulfilment can be achieved, '... by developing every useful faculty and amiable feeling, and cultivating the peculiar talent or talents of every child, as discovered in the course of education, all human beings might be rendered useful and happy'. Education will be provided for all, including women.

The newspaper editors of the day - men of course - are appalled by these arguments. One editor inadvertently confirms Frances's point about how it is useful for men that women be subjugated: 'She seemed to want to make the world a universal soup house. She wanted girls to be instructed as boys are, but did not state who was to attend to plain and ornamental sewing, making pies and nursing children.'

104

Education will be universal for all children, and will be paid for by taxes on their parents, by property taxes, and by other means. Frances envisages the transformation of churches into halls of science. Such a hall would act as a community centre capable of holding three to five thousand people, and will be a place where ideas can be shared. It will also contain libraries, museums, and a school of industry run as a technical college for children.

This will be a tolerant society where all views are to be heard. Frances anticipates that there will be no place for religion here, but no matter, in a society dedicated to science it will wither away anyway.

The marriage laws will be fairer, that is, if marriage survives the new society. There is much to change: women are currently denied a legal right to their property, their earnings, and their children. No longer. And free love outside marriage will be a matter for the individuals involved, and of no concern to the rest of the commuity:

> The marriage law existing within the pale of the institution is of no force within that pale. No woman can forfeit her individual rights or independent existence, and no man can exert over her any rights or power whatsoever beyond that he may exercise over her free and voluntary affections....

> The tyranny usurped by the matrimonial law, over the most sacred of human affections, can perhaps only be equalled by that of the unjust public opinion, which so frequently stamps with infamy, or condemns to martyrdom, the best grounded and most generous attachments which ever did honour to the human heart, simply because unlegalised by human ceremonies...

> This tyranny... had probably its source in religious prejudice or priestly rapacity; while it has found its plausible and more philosophically apology in the apparent dependence of children on the union of their parents. To this plea it might perhaps be replied, that the end, how important soever, is not secured by the means that the forcible union of unsuitable and unsuited parents can little promote the happiness of the offspring... But how wide a field does this topic embrace! How much cruelty - how much oppression of the weak and helpless does it not involve!

The newspaper editors are outraged by these ideas. One wrote: 'she recommends the encouragement of early prostitution... contemns and discards altogether the marriage contract and in effect recommends transforming this glorious world... into one vast immeasurable brothel...'

Cincinnati is Frances's first stop in a public lecture tour that will cover many of the big cities and towns in the central and eastern parts of the United States over the next two years.

By doing so, Frances will gain a following amongst the working men of New York. They will go on in 1829 to form one of the earliest labour movements in the United States, the Workingmen's Party. The party manifesto included a provision for free education for all. But then the party broke apart because of factional in-fighting. One of the curious consequences of this was that for a few years after, labour activists were described in the conservative press as Fanny-Wrightists, as if this was some kind of insult.

Frances Wright's crusade to change the world faltered in 1829, and eventually crashed to a halt. She had inadvertently entered the well-trodden and woeful path of many a woman. When she took the blacks from Nashoba to Haiti, where they were to be freed, her companion on that trip, Phiquepal D'Arusmont, got her pregnant. Their daughter Sylvia was the result. Frances married Phiquepal D'Arusmont in 1831, eventually discovering him worthless. He tried to grab her financial estate, and after much acrimony, they divorced. And in the midst of all this, Frances's beloved sister Camilla died.

She started her lectures again in 1835, but thereafter Frances Wright slipped into obscurity. Her vision of a cooperative society was never going to happen in a nation gripped by religious fervour, and where vast areas of land were opening up in the interior for anyone wanting to settle there. This was an America where men could make something of themselves; how society was run bothered them little as long as it did not interfere with their pursuit of riches and status.

Frances became almost forgotten, but not quite... This woman had lit a fire, the embers of which still smouldered, albeit the flames were not yet brightening the darkened sky.

The next women to speak in public before mixed audiences in the United States were the Grimké sisters, Sarah and Angelina. They had been brought up in a slave-owning family in South Carolina, where they were appalled by what they witnessed. Moving to Philadelphia, they became Quakers and joined the American Anti-Slavery Society.

Sarah and Angelina lectured on abolitionist issues to small groups of women in houses and churches; and soon after, a few men joined their audience. Before long, their lectures started to draw very large crowds, both men and women. Predictably, this brought down the wrath of the Church upon them, and the Grimké sisters were criticised much as Frances Wright had been before them: the pastors declaiming them for having usurped 'the place and tone of men as public reformer', and by doing so had lost 'that modesty and delicacy... which constitutes the true influence of women in society'. Enraged by these comments, the sisters now started to campaign for women's rights in addition to pursuing their abolitionist platform.

Of particular note are the letters on women's issues compiled by Sarah Grimké in her 1837 book *Letters on the Equality of Sexes and Condition of Woman*. The following quote gained attention at the time and is still mentioned today: 'But I ask no favours for my sex. I surrender not our claim to equality. All I ask of our brethren is that they will take their feet from our necks...'

Another woman who took up Frances Wright's legacy was Polish-born Ernestine Rose. Ernestine also gave lectures against slavery, on education, and on women's rights. And as Frances Wright had done, Ernestine Rose not only spoke, she also took action. She organised a long-term campaign, which in 1848 resulted in a change in the law in New York State. This allowed married women to keep control of their property. And from then on, 'the individual existence of the wife was recognised, and the old idea that "husband and wife are one, and that one the husband", received its death blow.'

In 1860, Ernestine acknowledged her debt:

Frances Wright was the first woman in this country who spoke on the equality of the sexes. She had indeed a hard task before her. The elements were entirely unprepared. She had to break up the time-hardened soil of conservatism; and her reward was sure – the same reward that is always bestowed upon those who are in the vanguard of any great movement. She was subjected to public odium, slander, and persecution. But these were not the only things she received. Oh, she had her reward! ...the eternal reward of knowing that she had done her duty; the reward springing from consciousness of rights; of endeavouring to benefit

107

unborn generations. How delightful to see the moulding of the minds around you, the infusing of your thoughts and aspirations into others, until one by one they stand by your side, without knowing how they came there! That reward she had, it has been her glory, it is the glory of her memory; and the time will come when society will have outgrown its old prejudices, and stepped with one foot, at least upon the elevated platform on which she took her position.

A defining moment on the path to American women eventually gaining the right to vote in 1920, came with the first women's rights convention held in 1848 in Seneca Falls, New York. Those present drafted a 'Declaration of Sentiments', which echoed the United States Declaration of Independence. Women had by now become much more active in asserting themselves on a public platform.

By 1886, the first three volumes of the *History of Woman Suffrage* had been published. Focussing largely on the United States, it would eventually extend to six volumes. The frontispiece for volume one is an engraving of Frances Wright.

A woman from Dundee had thus done something remarkable. *She made men listen, and having done so, they have been listening to women ever since.*

1. A wreck from the Spanish Armada

2 The tomb of Sir George and Lady Bruce, Culross Abbey Church
(Photo by Mike Shepherd).

3 Culross, Fife. Culross Palace, the home of Sir George Bruce, is in the foreground. The Firth of Forth and the site of the Moat Pit is in the background (Photo by Mike Shepherd).

THE BASS IN ITS FORTIFIED STATE.—1690.

4. The Bass Rock, 1690.

5. Frances Wright. Frontispiece to volume one of the *History of Woman Suffrage* (1886).

6. James Croll

7. Tryggve Gran in the Antarctic, third from the right. From *Scott's Last Expedition*, L. Huxley Smith, 1913.

8. Tryggve Gran's Bleriot ready to take off from Cruden Bay beach for the first aircraft crossing of the North Sea in 1914 (courtesy of Gordon Casely)

9. Mary Pratt (Courtesy of Elizabeth Park)

10. This recently discovered embroidery of men on watch on a U-boat conning tower is believed to have been made by the survivors from U-1206 in an Aberdeen prisoner of war camp. Copyright Colin Johnston.

8. JAMES CROLL

James Croll left school at the age of thirteen because his parents wanted help with their croft, a tiny farm covering between one and two acres of rolling countryside nine miles north of Perth. This left a legacy for his life to come: 'I must say that I was rather a dull scholar, scarcely up to the average of boys of the same age, as far as regards getting up my lessons sharply and correctly. I never succeeded in acquiring an accurate style of reading, and by no amount of labour could I manage to become even a moderately good speller...'

He worked in various jobs, a millwright to start with, until, when almost forty years old, James became the janitor for Anderson's College and Museum in Glasgow. And what he achieved thereafter is recognised today.

For example, the Quaternary Research Association, a professional organisation for scientists investigating the Ice Age, awards the James Croll Medal every year to the association member deemed to have made the most significant contribution to the scientific knowledge of the Ice Age. On the nomination form for the medal are these words:

> This is the highest award of the Quaternary Research Association and is named in honour of James Croll (1821-1890). Croll was effectively self-taught. His work and example demonstrate that any individuals from all backgrounds can rise to national eminence and generate science of lasting and major international impact, that is not who you are or where you came from but what you do that is important. These are the qualities that the Quaternary Research Association seeks to celebrate in the award of the James Croll medal.

Heroic qualities.

1832 - 1835

James Croll's latent genius lay hidden at the age of eleven, the meagre education he gets failing to bring it out. And even those basic lessons are interrupted by James's recurring health problems - a persistent and mysterious headache which takes him out of school for a while. This is experienced as 'a rather troublesome pain on the top or about the opening of the head, which prevented me being able, except in the heat of summer, to remain bareheaded; and, as I could not be persuaded to sit in school with my cap on, my parents had for a considerable time to allow me to remain at home. My first lessons were consequently obtained from my parents, assisted by my eldest brother. The village schoolmaster also now and again gave me private lessons at home.'

His health must have improved, because James later returns to the local school, although by this time he has fallen behind with his lessons, 'scarcely up to the average of boys of the same age'. And it is not as if he is showing any early indication of a life of the mind, preferring to play rather than read books, which disappoints his father somewhat.

The moment that changes James Croll's life arrives on a visit to the town of Perth in the summer of 1832. Here he spots a copy of the *Penny Magazine* in a bookshop window, and attracted by the elaborate wood-engraved illustration on the cover, he enters the shop and buys a copy for the price of a penny.

The *Penny Magazine* is new, and James Croll has bought its first number. Published by The Society for the Diffusion of Useful Knowledge, the society's aim for the magazine is to disseminate knowledge to working class children who would not otherwise get the chance to educate themselves. Stuffed into its eight large pages are articles about the history of Charing Cross in London, the life of the French philosopher René Descartes, and descriptions of the animals in the London Zoological Gardens. James Croll celebrated his discovery of the *Penny Magazine* later in adulthood: 'This incident led to a new epoch in my life.' Having devoured the first number, he buys the subsequent copies as they come out on a weekly basis, reading every page 'with zest'. Progressing from there, his newfound thirst for knowledge leads him to start reading books.

A book that makes a huge impression on him is *The Christian Philosopher, or the Connexion of Science and Philosophy with Religion* by the Reverend Thomas Dick: 'Commencing to read it, I was at once struck with the novelty of the ideas.' The book aims to show how science and philosophy are compatible with the presence of God in the universe. Reverend Dick mixes scientific fact with religious doctrine, and is not afraid to resort to the wilder shores of speculation. In one of his books, he suggests that every planet orbiting the sun is inhabited. And by assuming that the surface of each planet holds the

117

population density of England, he estimates the entire Solar System to be peopled with over 21 trillion human beings.

This book and others by Thomas Dick sparks what will be James Croll's life-long obsession, the relationship between the workings of his mind and the presence of God in the universe. James Croll is thus starting to think about big ideas.

For example, he speculates about whether his actions have been entirely predestined by the will of God. If so, then the belief he has a choice about what he does is an illusion: God has already decided every one of his actions beforehand. Alternatively, could it be that God has allowed him a small amount of leeway, 'free will' so to speak, such that he can take independent action every now and again? This conundrum involves James in hours of unceasing self-absorption, not the least because he cannot decide on an answer.

He also mulls over another big idea:

> I well remember one of the solitary musings of my early days, when I could have been only about twelve or thirteen years of age. It was this. I asked myself, what would there be, if there were no world? The ready answer, of course, was that there would be the sun, moon, and stars. What would there be, if there were no sun, moon, and stars? There would be God. However, what would there be if there were no God? There would be nothing but empty space. However, if there were no space, what would remain? This question staggered me. I could not in thought be quit of space. Why could not I in thought annihilate space?'

These musings by James Croll lie close to the age-old question that many an enquiring mind has asked about the universe: 'Why is there something rather nothing?' Which leads on to the next question, 'What exactly is nothing?' And the most straightforward answer is that it is not as if anyone knows or will ever know for sure.

Something else occupies his waking thoughts. James ponders about how God uses scientific laws to control the operation of the universe. I 'procured one or two other books on physical science, among which was Joyce's famous scientific dialogues [Jeremiah Joyce, 1815. *Scientific Dialogues: Intended for the Instruction of Young People, in which the First Principles of Natural and Experimental Philosophy are Fully Explained*]. At first I became bewildered, but soon the beauty and simplicity of the conceptions filled me with delight and astonishment, and I began then in earnest to study the matter.'

This may have been the book he referred to later in a letter written in 1849: 'When I was about twelve years old, I happened to fall in with a book upon theoretical astronomy which perfectly fascinated me, and in order to get a knowledge of that subject, I commenced the study of mechanics and mathematics, and pursued eagerly this subject for six or seven years, as far as time would permit me, to the neglect of everything else...'

James would like to understand all of astronomy in detail, and to do this means getting to grips with the laws of motion, the principles of mechanics, pneumatics, hydrostatics, light, heat, electricity, and magnetism: 'I obtained assistance from no one. In fact, there were none of my acquaintances who knew anything whatever about these subjects. Notwithstanding all these disadvantages under which I laboured, I managed in the course of four years or so, or by the time I was between fifteen and sixteen years old, to obtain a pretty tolerable knowledge of all the general principles of those branches of physical science.'

His tendency to withdraw from social contact gives James much time for speculation.

Living in a retired country place, after the toils of the day, when the shadows of evening were falling, I generally took a stroll in the fields, or along a quiet road for an hour or two, to meditate and ponder over spiritual things. These hours I enjoyed exceedingly, and I continued the practice for years afterwards, until I went to reside in the city. Nothing in city life did I miss so much as these quiet walks.

And just as his curiosity is stirring in his teenage years, he is removed from school, because without James to help on their croft, his parents will struggle to cope. His father works as a stonemason, a job that takes him away from home for much of the year, and his mother has her hands full managing both the household and the croft on her own. In particular, their cow requires to be looked after, and James can do that.

1837 - 1841

At the age of sixteen and a half, and with adulthood fast approaching, James Croll now has a living to make. A university education is out of the question because there is no money in the family to pay for it. Yet,

119

nothing else looks like an attractive option for him, and he cannot think of any special talents that point him towards any specific job:

> After several days' consideration, I thought I might try the occupation of a millwright. As I was fond of theoretical mechanics, it occurred to me that this occupation might be the most congenial and the one for which I was best adapted. But this I afterwards found to be a mistake; for, although I was familiar with theoretical mechanics, yet, as a working mechanic, I was scarcely up to the average. The strong natural tendency of my mind toward abstract thinking somehow unsuited me for the practical details of daily work.

James becomes apprenticed to a millwright near his home, and on the completion of his term in 1841, starts work for a company based near Coupar Angus: 'The wages received were small, being only eight shillings a week, with food, which was of the poorest description possible... It was on the whole rather a rough life. A very considerable part of our work consisted in the repairing of corn, saw, and threshing-mills.'

Every morning, the millwrights walk to the farms where the mills are located, sometimes covering a distance of thirty or forty miles in one day. James suffers badly from corns on his feet from all that walking. Because the problem has become so severe, he has cut holes in his shoes to allow 'the corns to grow out without cutting them or paring them'.

And once he gets to a farm, the hardships continue: 'We millwrights had generally to go to the ploughman's bothy [small cottage]; and when there was no room there, we had to go to the barn or the stable loft above the horses. Frequently we had to bury ourselves under the clothes to secure protection from the rats.'

After two years working as a millwright James Croll now decides to try something else.

1843 - 1850

In the summer of 1843, James uses the carpentry skills learnt from his millwright experience to work as a joiner on a church which is under construction near his parents' home. He likes this job much more than that of a millwright, even though he is working a twelve-hour day from 6 a.m. to 6 p.m. When the church is completed, James finds there is not much work to be had in the area for a joiner. So he moves to Glasgow, and thereafter Paisley, where his skills are more in demand.

Misfortune continues to dog him. In 1846, a childhood injury to his elbow flares up to the extent that his medical advisers tell him to give up joinery and find an 'easier pursuit'. 'This I felt to be a great blow to my future prospects. But although, as we shall see, it led to years of poverty and hardship, nevertheless, being freed from the long hours of manual labour, I enjoyed a great deal of leisure for reading and study. Strange are the ways of Providence. Had it not been for a mere accident in early life, I should in all likelihood have remained a working joiner till the end of my days.'

James now seeks a new profession, reckoning that the life of a tea merchant might be for him. He returns to Perth and enters the town with the vague notion of finding someone to talk to who could give him advice on the matter. On approaching the bridge leading to the town, he spots a man handing out leaflets to passers-by. A quirky thought comes into his head, 'if these bills should relate to the tea trade, I would be guided by these and would go to the shop to which they referred. What could induce me to come to a conclusion so apparently absurd and incautious, I cannot tell.'

Strange as it turns out, the leaflets do indeed direct their readers to a tea and coffee warehouse, which has recently opened in the High Street. James enters the shop and talks to the owner David Irons, 'an agreeable and intelligent person'. David suggests that James might try travelling around the countryside to sell tea to the public; however, this does not work out for him. James writes that 'I soon found that the attempt to push a sale in the country was a rather disagreeable job for me, and I resolved to give it up.'

Another helpful suggestion comes his way from David Irons - he should find a suitable town to set up a tea merchant's business: 'Unfortunately, I had not the means for any such undertaking; but he, in the most kindly manner, offered to assist me. He agreed to give me a stock to commence with, and that I should repay him in regular instalments as it was sold and that he would in this way keep up my stock. I need hardly say that an offer so generous was readily accepted.'

As an introduction to the work of a tea merchant, he is invited to work in the shop in Perth to 'learn the mechanical art of weighing and parcelling up the tea, serving over the counter, and all the usual routine of shop work. I accordingly came in; and, before the winter was over, I became a thoroughly proficient shopkeeper.'

In the spring of 1847, James Croll opens a shop in Elgin. It is advertised in the local press as a 'genuine tea and coffee warehouse' where the prices are 'hitherto unknown in Elgin; being fully convinced that the principles of ready money, small profit, and large turnover, is best for both buyer and seller.'

A year later he is married to Isabella Macdonald who hails from nearby Forres: 'her care, economy, and kindly attention to my comfort during the years of comparative hardships through which we have passed, have cheered me on during all my trials and sorrows.'

James Campbell Irons, friend and biographer, later expressed the opinion that James Croll's personality made him unsuited to shop work: 'The primary qualification for a shopkeeper is an affable, agreeable, and, as some would say, almost obsequious manner. Croll had, to the day of his death, a modest, shy, dry, and almost speechless manner, except on occasions when he was drawn out by congenial conversation among real friends.'

Another acquaintance, who also knew him from his Elgin days, comments: 'It was something altogether extraordinary to see the man, with his large head, massive forehead, and kindly countenance, with his heavy form of body, hard horny hands and stiff arm, standing behind the counter of a tea-shop. One is accustomed to see rather a small thin man with thin nimble fingers and active arms discharging this duty; and no one, even the most casual observer, could see Croll in the character of shopkeeper at this time without knowing that he was not a shopkeeper to the manner born, and that he was evidently in a new sphere.'

For the time being James is content with life: 'The shop work suited me well, as it afforded intervals now and again for reading and study.' He has become obsessed about God, free will, and the universe, concluding that 'a unity, a plan, and a purpose' pervades 'the whole, which imply thought and intelligence'. Now brought 'under deep religious impressions' he had deliberately avoided his scientific studies for the last seven years, 'knowing the danger I was then in of being led away by them if I commenced again'.

Unfortunately, the problem with his elbow recurs, and a serious inflammation brings about the ossification of the joint. With one arm that cannot be moved at the elbow, this hinders his day-to-day business of running the shop: 'By this illness, however, I was so long unfitted

122

for attendance in my shop, that the trade rapidly fell off; and afterwards I could not manage to get the business raised to a paying condition. I struggled on for some time; but at last, in order to avoid losing money and getting into debt, I resolved to close the shop. I accordingly sold off everything, left Elgin, and came south to Perth. This was about the beginning of the summer of 1850.'

Nothing is working out for him: nothing at all.

1850 - 1853

James Croll finds yet another way of making money to keep life and limb together: 'Owing to the weakly state of my arm, it was a considerable time after coming south before I was able to do any manual work. At that time, the influence of electricity and galvanism as a curative agent was exciting a good deal of attention. As I was familiar with the construction of the machines which were used, I thought I should try the making of an induction apparatus, which I accordingly did. It was soon purchased; and, as others were required, I continued at the making of them for some time.'

James does not mention what exactly his machines were used for, although an educated guess can be made. Recent discoveries in the properties of electricity and magnetism had spun off interest in the construction of new medical devices powered by electricity, which ranged from the serious to the cranky.

Most definitely in the cranky category was the invention made by James Graham from Edinburgh. The 'celestial bed', also referred to as the 'medico-magnetico-musico-electrical bed', comprised a variety of electrical devices supported by forty glass pillars surrounding a bed. James Graham claimed that should a barren woman lie in the bed, pregnancy was guaranteed.

Research of a more serious nature was carried out at Guys Hospital in London, specifically on the technique of 'faradisation'. Named after Michael Faraday, the scientist who made major discoveries in electricity and magnetism, a faradisation apparatus was used to treat patients with convulsions and spasms. The near-naked patient was stood on a copper plate attached to an electric generator. An electrode with a wet sponge at one end completed the electric circuit when touched against the affected part of the patient's body, thereby causing an electric current to surge through it. It is plausible that James Croll had been constructing and selling a similar device to this.

James is keen to find a more permanent way to make a living. A friend is building a hotel in Blairgowrie, Perthshire, and offers him the lease once it is completed. He suggests that James could run it as a 'temperance hotel', that is, one selling no alcohol. James has never touched alcohol, and believes that others should abstain from it.

James Croll lives in an age of heavy drinking. One commentator noted in 1830 that 'Everybody is drunk. Those who are not singing are sprawling. The sovereign people are in a beastly state.' Eyewitness accounts from the time tell of rowdy drunken behaviour in the city of Dundee, nineteen miles from Blairgowrie. Men and women mill workers in Dundee spent most of their wages on drinking to excess, frequently absenting themselves from work for days on end. The women were considered worse than the men, their rowdy behaviour shocking the city's middle class. Looking on with obvious disapproval at the women's drunken gallivanting, the upright and sober people of Dundee were greeted in turn by shrieks of laughter. Such scenes were probably witnessed in Blairgowrie as well.

The temperance movement became active for many a year in Dundee. Its most famous moment came in 1922 when Edwin Scrymgeour, campaigning on a prohibitionist ticket, was jointly elected a Member of Parliament for Dundee: famous because Winston Churchill lost his seat as a consequence. Winston was a sore loser, announcing that he would never return to Dundee. Edwin Scrymgeour's first act in Parliament was to propose a private member's bill demanding that all pubs should be closed at once, a law to be made against trafficking in liquor with five years imprisonment for the guilty, and all medicinal alcohol to be labelled 'poison'.

The idea of running a temperance hotel has its attractions for James Croll: 'After due consideration I made up my mind to try that course. But here was the difficulty: the house required to be furnished, and this would require a considerable sum, which I had not. It occurred to me, however, that, as it would be some six or eight months before the house could be ready for occupation, and as my arm was now much improved, I might try and make a considerable number of the necessary articles of furniture during that time. I accordingly set to work: made chairs, tables, bedsteads, basin-stands, toilet-tables, and other articles; and, with the small sum in our possession, we managed to open the house in the early part of 1852.'

However, 'visitors were few and far between', and only with the strictest of attention to outgoing expenses can the Crolls avoid the business going into debt: 'As we had no family, my wife, anxious to lessen expenses as much as possible, proposed to dispense with a servant, and do all the work herself. The house was kept in the perfection of cleanliness, and every attention was paid to the comfort of visitors, who generally expressed themselves well pleased.'

Even so, the hotel is failing because James had set out with a flawed business plan; the village with 3,500 inhabitants already has a hotel, and not selling alcohol has proved a disadvantage given that drinking is a hugely popular pastime in Blairgowrie; a place with fifteen inns and public houses. Otherwise, there is no railway here to attract visitors from outside the town. 'After a year and a half's trial of the hotel, we found that there was little chance of its ever becoming self supporting; so we gave it up, sold the furniture, and left the place.'

James Croll's struggles continue.

1853 - 1857

After working as a millwright, a joiner, a tea merchant, and a hotelier, James Croll is again in search of a new job. In May 1853 he returns to Glasgow where he finds work selling insurance, first of all in Scotland and then in Leicester.

When his wife becomes seriously ill, it proves necessary to move back to Glasgow so that her sisters can look after her. James gets an insurance job in nearby Paisley, sticking it out for 'six or eight months. I then finally abandoned the insurance business altogether, after spending four and a half years of about the most disagreeable part of my life. To one like me, naturally so fond of retirement and even of solitude, it was painful to be constantly obliged to make up to strangers.'

He finds solace during this time in his philosophical studies, and becomes entranced by the books of the German philosopher Immanuel Kant. He overdoes it: 'At this time I became very much troubled by pain in the eyes, occasioned by looking so much on white paper. When the pain began in the eyes, strange to say, it left the top or opening of the head, the place where it had been seated almost from infancy. I found that, by placing a small piece of plain coloured glass on the page of the book, I could manage to read without feeling much inconvenience. The pain in the eyes continued for several years.'

Now at a loose end once more, James Croll has much time on his hands. He writes a book *The Philosophy of Theism*, which is based on his investigations into religion and metaphysics. The aim of the book is not to prove the existence of God, but rather to highlight the methods that could be used to do so. It is published in 1857 in a small print run of five hundred copies, most of them 'circulated privately', although it fails to gain much public attention.

1858-1859
A new job comes his way. James starts work for a Glasgow weekly newspaper, the *Commonwealth*, whose pages promote temperance, social and political reform. And now: 'After remaining for upwards of a year and a half in the *Commonwealth* office, I learned that a person was required to take charge of Anderson's College and Museum [in Glasgow], and applied for the situation. There were about sixty applicants. Fortunately for me, as it afterwards turned out, I received the appointment, and entered on my duties at the end of the autumn of 1859.'

He is happy there:

> Taking it all in all, I have never been in any place so congenial to me as that institution proved. After upwards of twenty years of an unsettled life, full of hardships and difficulties, it was a relief to get settled down in what might be regarded as a permanent home. My salary was small, it is true, little more than sufficient to enable us to subsist; but this was compensated by advantages for me of another kind. It will naturally be asked why such want of success in life? Why so many changes, trials, and difficulties? There were several causes which conspired to lead to this state of things. The mishap to my elbow joint compelled me to give up the occupation of a joiner when a young man; and the inflammation which destroyed the joint five years afterwards had the effect of blasting my hopes in the way of shop keeping. The main cause, however, and one of which I had been all along conscious, was that strong and almost irresistible propensity towards study, which prevented me devoting my whole energy to business. Study always came first, business second; and the result was that in this age of competition I was left behind in the race.

Anderson's College and Museum, sometimes referred to as Andersons University, was founded in 1796 at the bequest of the will of the late John Anderson, Professor of Natural Philosophy [physics] at the

126

University of Glasgow. His intent had been to set up a second university in Glasgow; one that would concentrate on 'useful learning' (it would later become the University of Strathclyde in 1964). The institution holds the scientific library of the Glasgow Philosophical Society, which James is permitted to use, and use it he does. Besides which, there is also the library of the institution itself numbering four or five thousand books, and yet another collection of two thousand books which had belonged to John Anderson, the founder of the college. 'When I came to Anderson's College, I had been engaged in philosophical and theological studies for a period of fifteen years... I soon found, however, that the attractions offered by the institution for the study of physical science were too strong to allow me to continue my metaphysical studies.'

Something momentous happens, which coincides with James Croll starting work in Anderson's College at the end of autumn. On Thursday, November 24, 1859, Charles Darwin's book *On the Origin of Species* is published. The impact the book makes on human thought is equivalent to a Richter-scale-ten earthquake.

To put the upheaval in context, it should be appreciated that religious misgivings had long been building since the Enlightenment at the end of the eighteenth century. Material views of the universe had been taking hold, which, in Thomas Carlyle's words, is 'all void of Life, of Purpose, of Volition, even of Hostility... one huge, dead, immeasurable Steam-engine, rolling on, in its dead indifference, to grind me limb from limb.'

This outlook had already been discomforting many a human being from before the publication of Darwin's book. *On the Origin of Species* further shook those souls whose anchor in life had already been loosened from its foundations in religion. It created a generation who saw 'the spring sun shine out of an empty heaven, to light up a soulless earth'- human beings 'who felt with utter loneliness that the Great Companion is dead'.

The publication of the *Origin of Species* made people sit up and notice. For the learned men of Anderson's College this must have been the most exciting thing to happen to science for years. James Croll gets caught up in this fervour; because something prompted him to start thinking about scientific subjects again.

Yet, James is comfortable with Darwin's theory of evolution, and accepts it. He regards the laws of science as bearing the fingerprints of

127

God's action in the universe, including Darwin's theory: evolution happens because God has willed it.

Many other subjects in science have also been undergoing a revolution recently: physics, for example, which has been invigorated by the invention of the steam engine, and mention could be made of Michael Faraday's investigations into electricity and magnetism. It is physics that fascinates James Croll, to start with anyway: 'At this time, the then modern principle of the transformation and conservation of energy and the dynamical theory of heat attracted my attention. I read also with much interest the researches of Faraday, Joule, Thomson, Tyndall, Rankine, and others on heat, electricity, and magnetism.'

1864

Four years later, a scientific problem comes James Croll's way: 'At this period the question of the cause of the Glacial epoch [the Ice Age] was being discussed with interest among geologists. In the spring of 1864 I turned my attention to this subject.'

It is not as if he is much interested in geology: 'I had no relish, namely, [for] chemistry and geology, more particularly the latter. The reason was that to me they appeared so full of details and so deficient in rational principles, being so much sciences of observation and experiment.'

Nevertheless, geology comes knocking at James Croll's door. Although geologists have made progress in understanding the Ice Age, many questions remain unanswered. And those questions are being asked in that hot-house arena of nineteenth-century Ice-Age research – Glasgow.

What the geologists do not know yet is that in order to make progress in their understanding of the Ice Age they will require new perspectives from someone who has the ability to step beyond the bounds of geological science. Such a person should have a wide interest in the physical phenomena of the universe, superb recall of many different scientific facts, and should be intimately acquainted with the principles of astronomy, physics, meteorology, and oceanology. It will also help that this someone is perpetually questing to understand how God operates the universe through actions discoverable by science; and who has the mindset to develop a new way of thinking on a grand scale. And having established this framework of thought, to ask the questions which nobody has asked before and to then find the answers for them.

Someone who is the janitor at Anderson's College in Glasgow.

9. THE ICE AGE

1863 - 1864
James Croll's biography mentions that: 'Considerable commotion was caused among geologists by the publication in 1863 of a paper by Dr. Archibald Geikie, read in Glasgow, regarding the Glacial epoch in Scotland. Doubtless Croll must have read the paper; for, in the spring of 1864, he turned his attention to the subject...'

Archibald Geikie is a geologist with the Geological Survey of Great Britain and Ireland, a government body tasked with making geological maps of the nation. The Survey geologists are sent out into the countryside to search for rock outcrops, identify the type of rock found in them, and to record their findings. The information is used to make coloured maps, with each colour representing a rock type or sequence of strata recognised in 'the field'.

The mapping of Scotland's geology started in 1854, with Archibald Geikie joining the project a year later. Although the work was focused on scientific research, it was also recognised that the British economy would benefit should the geologists find new mineral resources. For example, when Geikie investigated the sedimentary strata in Midlothian and West Lothian, he discovered bands of black shale outcropping in several places. These, on sampling, proved 'so bituminous as to be easily kindled into flame'.

Someone took a great interest in Geikie's discovery: 'Mr James Young, afterwards known as "Paraffin Young," consulted me as to the extent of these shales, and accompanied me on the ground. I was able to show him many localities where their outcrop could be seen, and to indicate to him roughly the area under which they extended. He did not say anything about the purport of his enquiry. But in a short while, having secured the right to work these and other shales over a considerable tract of ground, he began active operations for the extraction of mineral oil from them. He thus founded the oil-shale industry of Scotland from which so much wealth has since been obtained.' This Scottish oil boom ended in 1962, only seven years before the first commercial offshore oilfield was discovered on the UK side of the North Sea.

In 1861 Archibald Geikie took an interest in the 'superficial deposits', the loose sediment sandwiched between the soil and the underlying bedrock - deposits found over much of Scotland. The survey geologists had previously ignored them, focussing only on mapping the bedrock underneath.

The typical superficial deposit is boulder clay, a jumble of rock fragments ranging from small pebbles up to huge boulders, all of which is embedded within a clay matrix. Here and there, layers and mounds of sand and gravel interleave with the boulder clay.

The superficial deposits had long excited curiosity amongst geologists because they are most unlike the ancient sediments found in older strata. The older sediments are demonstrably the deposits of ancient rivers, deserts, beaches, and seas. But what agency had been responsible for laying down these mysterious sediments containing huge boulders? The sediments are obviously recent on a geological time scale because they lie immediately below the soil, but what a chaotic jumble they are.

Geikie also pointed out that the boulder clay drapes a distinctive landscape. The present-day highlands and lowlands of Scotland exhibit landforms that are undoubtedly recent in origin. Everyone can see their features - specialist geological knowledge is not required to recognise them. The traveller in the 'glens and mountain-sides of the Highlands, the broad undulating expanse of the central district, and the pastoral uplands of the southern counties' will see 'certain aspects in common... the rounded and worn aspect of many of the hills...' and their 'flowing outlines' (by comparison the scenery found elsewhere in the world, such as the blocky angular mountains and ranges along the Mediterranean shoreline or in the Rocky Mountains of Utah and Arizona, is markedly different).

A traveller in Scotland might also note that 'spread out in thick masses over the Lowlands, and extending even for many hundreds of feet up into the recesses of the mountains, there are deposits of clay and boulders of the most irregular and tumultuous kind. Hummocks and mounds of sand and gravel everywhere abound, sometimes blocking up a Highland valley, or running in wavy ridges among the moors and corn-fields of the lower grounds. Blocks of rock, sometimes of great size, may be seen strewed over the valleys and plains, or perched on the sides and summits of the hills, many leagues from the nearest points from which they could have come.'

Other unusual features are seen: 'Not only do the hills, when looked at from a distance, wear the aspect of having had their crags and knolls shorn down or rounded off, but the crags themselves exhibit the same structure in detail. They have a general undulating form somewhat like

131

that of huge woolsacks or pillows, with smooth hollows and dimples between.' The bare rock on these crags typically exhibit smooth surfaces and are often covered in parallel grooves resembling scratches.

Yet another curiosity is seen: 'Perhaps that feature of river scenery in Scotland, which of all others most forcibly and universally presses itself upon the attention of the observer, is the apparent inadequacy of the present streams to have produced the deep, wide valleys and ravines through which they flow.'

Geikie concludes that: 'When the observer, in his passage through the country, is constantly brought face to face with these and other similar features, he is naturally led to associate them with some powerful agency which has operated on the rocks.' Furthermore, 'the general abrasion of the surface, with the production of vast masses of clay, sand, gravel, and boulders, must be one of the latest of the many geological revolutions which this part of the earth's crust has undergone.'

The geologist Sir James Hall provided an early explanation for such observations in 1815, which he also surmised from geological fieldwork in and around Edinburgh. He recorded, as Geikie would later, the smoothness of the landscape, the chaotic jumble of boulders everywhere, and the polished and scratched surfaces of rock outcrops. Hall suggested that this was evidence that the Edinburgh area had experienced a huge catastrophe at some time in the geological past: one where the landscape had been inundated by a titanic sea wave sweepingt across Scotland in an instant.

Sir James Hall made his hypothesis sound convincing. In keeping with the prevailing school of thought in Scottish geology, he pointed out that the above features could readily be explained by geological processes observable in the present day. He gave accounts of the catastrophic tsunami waves set off by major earthquakes, which then spilled over coastlines to devastate the land. Perhaps in the geological past, mega-tsunamis occurred that were far larger than those observed today: to be able to comprehend this, it is merely a matter of scaling up a known present-day phenomenon.

He wrote that, 'The surface of this district, together with the alluvial part of its mass, bears every mark of the effects which a wave of sufficient magnitude to overwhelm it, might be expected to occasion.' The Edinburgh area had yielded 'numberless points of attack' to a giant water wave. 'Many of the rocks being rent in various ways, the hardest parts being in a shivered state, would easily be carried forward.'

Violent earth tremors under the sea, Hall believed, had been responsible for setting this gigantic wave in motion, which then rampaged across Scotland from west to east before heading out to the North Sea. Picking up enormous quantities of mud and rock on the way, it was 'the passage of a single wave, embracing a period of time that could only be expressed in minutes; but during that short time, I conceive the water to have been urged forward with such force, and to have carried with it so many powerful agents...' The rocks whisked along by the torrents acted as an abrasive, smoothing the underlying bedrock and scratching their surfaces. The chaotic mass of mud and boulders then dropped to the ground only once the waters had subsided.

As the giant wave surged over the west coast, parts of it rebounded off the high ground around Ayr, Kirkcudbright, and Dumfries, thus creating the narrow valleys and gorges to be found here. Further east, the titanic wave encountered huge crags of rock including the crag that Edinburgh Castle now sits on. It overwhelmed them, leaving a trail of debris strung out in the lee of the crags. This action, Hall believed, created the sloping land surface followed by the Royal Mile in Edinburgh (today it is known to be underlain by solid bedrock). The giant tadpole shape created by the mega-tsunami with its tail pointing to the east indicates the direction of travel of the phenomenal wave.

William Buckland, reader in geology at Oxford University, championed a more traditional explanation – the Biblical Flood had been responsible for the chaotic jumble of sediments. In a lecture given in 1820, he announced that 'the universality of a recent deluge, are most satisfactorily confirmed by everything that has been brought to light by Geological investigations; and as far as it goes, [the account in the book of Genesis in the Old Testament] is in perfect harmony with the discoveries of modern science.'

The modern explanation for the unusual sediments and features of the landscape came to prominence when, on July 24, 1837, the Swiss geologist Louis Agassiz gave an address to the Swiss Society of Natural Sciences arguing that Switzerland had been covered by a vast ice sheet during a recent Ice Age. And not only in Switzerland, ice had extended over most of northern Europe, parts of Asia, and North America had similarly been covered by an ice sheet.

Agassiz, familiar with the Swiss landscape and its present-day glaciers nestling high in the Alpine valleys, knew that unusual features could be seen on the lower slopes below the glaciers. Others before Agassiz had commented about the huge granite blocks perched upon limestone bedrock and the trail of similar exotic boulders found strewn along the alpine valleys. Local farmers were known to tell travellers that glaciers, no longer to be seen locally, must have transported these boulders in a past age.

Louis Agassiz's address to the Swiss Society of Natural Sciences came as a huge surprise to the attendees who had been expecting their President to talk about fossil fish - a subject that would have been much more welcome than the talk he gave. Many in the audience angrily disagreed with his conclusions: their president had supported ideas for an extensive Ice Age already decisively rejected by the scientific community in Switzerland. Although the ideas were not new, Agassiz had now restored them to the centre of scientific debate throughout Europe, and, as such, they could not be ignored. To put a further stamp on the matter, Agassiz's book *Studies on Glaciers* was published in 1840.

Agassiz travelled to Scotland in 1840. At a meeting of the British Association for the Advancement of Science in Glasgow, he gave a talk summarising his thoughts on the Ice Age. Afterwards, he toured Scotland and Northern England accompanied by William Buckland, who, having changed his mind about his Biblical Flood hypothesis, now agreed with Agassiz. As they walked around the countryside, they recognised the same features that led Agassiz to believe that ice sheets had once covered his native Switzerland and beyond. The two geologists had no doubts: glaciers had once been here in Scotland.

Agassiz believed that during the Ice Age, the entire Scottish landmass looked much as Greenland does today. A vast sheet of ice covered the land; perhaps not even a mountain peak showing above its surface. What he presented to the public at large was *not* the cosy vision of blue-white valley glaciers similar to those nestling below the majestic Swiss Alps, but a much bleaker vista of ice extending as far as the eye could see: a blizzardy whiteness everywhere. Although he persuaded many geologists in Britain that the Ice Age theory was valid, others reckoned he had gone too far. The idea that vast ice sheets had buried the landmass of Scotland stretched the imagination beyond credibility.

Perhaps a simpler explanation was possible. The brilliant Scottish geologist Charles Lyell, author of *Principles of Geology*, was sceptical about the ice sheet theory, and suggested an alternative hypothesis.

Lyell latched on to observations made by John Smith, an amateur geologist and yachtsman from Glasgow. On his sailing expeditions, some of which took him into Arctic waters, Smith liked to collect shells from the bottom of the sea. He sought help from experts to identify the shellfish species he found. Having then taken an interest in geology, he made the curious discovery that here and there the superficial deposits of Scotland contain the shells of species now found on the shores of Newfoundland, Labrador, Greenland, Iceland, and Spitsbergen, but not living today around the Scottish coast. Scotland had clearly been much colder back then than it is now – compelling evidence that the climate had changed over time. Not only that, the beds he examined lay up to 25 metres above present-day sea level. This demonstrated that the sea had risen above the Scottish coastline at a time when Arctic conditions prevailed.

Lyell expanded on these observations by suggesting that the Scottish landmass had been entirely under water in the recent past. Furthermore, he concluded that the boulder clay had formed at the bottom of this sea, having been sourced from mud and boulders rafted in on top of floating icebergs, which on melting had dropped their sediment load into the sea.

Recorded observations of sediment-laden icebergs in the present-day Arctic gave support to Lyell's hypothesis. He wrote in 1847 that in 'countries situated in high northern latitudes like Spitzbergen... glaciers, loaded with mud and rock, descend to the sea, and there huge fragment of them float off and become icebergs... Many of them were loaded with beds of earth and rock of such thickness, that the weight was conjectured to be from 50,000 to 100,000 tons.'

And the scratches on rock surfaces? 'There can also be little doubt that icebergs must often break off the peaks and projecting points of submarine mountains, and must grate upon and polish their surfaces, furrowing or scratching them in precisely the same way as we have seen that glaciers act on solid rocks over which they are propelled.'

Lyell gave a new name for boulder clay and related sediments – 'drift' – they had drifted into the sea on top of icebergs (although Lyell's idea has long since been rejected by geologists, the term 'drift' survives today as a synonym for superficial sediments). Lyell's iceberg theory eventually fell out of favour when it was pointed out that icebergs laden with sediment are not that common.

Even so, John Smith's discovery of marine Arctic shells in deposits located above the present-day Scottish coastline remained a puzzle. Raised beaches and clifflines were also found stranded inland, and these also lie above present-day sea level (for example, just behind my house on the Aberdeenshire coast is a former cliff dating from 7,000 years ago, which is three metres above the high tide mark). To confuse the issue further, submerged forests are found along the coast of Scotland, showing that in the recent past, sea level had also fallen below where it is now.

Victorian geologist struggled to cope with the contradictory evidence for rising and falling sea level during the Ice Age, and never satisfactorily explained it. As an indication of the huge complexities they faced, it was pointed out in 1841 by Charles Maclaren, editor of the *Scotsman* newspaper and an amateur geologist, that if huge ice sheets had covered much of the northern hemisphere, it followed that they constituted a huge volume of water locked up in frozen form, which otherwise would have flowed from rivers and streams into the sea. Much of the world's surface water had thus disappeared to form solid ice and was now on land. If so, then the sea level must have dropped substantially because of this, and perhaps by as much as 240 metres. This was a good point well made, and one still accepted by science. Today's estimate is that at the last glacial maximum, relative sea level fell by 130 to 135 metres.

OK, so you can explain why sea level fell during the Ice Age. How, then, do you explain why it also rose above the present day level to form raised beaches, cliffs, and shell banks? How can you reconcile a rise in sea level with the idea that a large volume of the world's surface water had been locked up within vast ice sheets on land?

Thomas Jamieson, a Scottish geologist, came up with an explanation. Because a thick ice sheet is heavy, it will press down on the land lying underneath it, much as a mattress will do after a slab of concrete has been placed on top of it. If so, then the edges of the land surface will have been pushed below the sea, making it appear that the sea level is rising, although it is actually the land that is being pushed down relative to the sea. And when the ice melts and the land becomes unburdened from all that weight, it rises again, and the edges of the landmass will rise out of the sea, thus making it appear that sea level is falling relative to the land.

Although Jamieson's idea never gained consensus in Victorian times, geologists accept it today. They estimate that the last ice sheet to cover Scotland was over a kilometre thick at its maximum, and the weight of the ice pushed down the land surface by over 100 metres.

If this surprises, consider that the land beneath our feet is remarkable flexible. Here is an anecdote to illustrate this. When I was a first-year student at the University of Aberdeen, I attended lectures in physics given by Professor R. V. Jones, who had, in his younger days, worked as a World War II scientific boffin. He built an ultra-sensitive tiltmeter in his Aberdeen laboratory that could detect the slightest change in the tilt of the earth's surface. He kindly demonstrated the device to me. Using measurements made by the tiltmeter, he could show that every time the tide came in at Aberdeen beach, the increased weight of water on the shore pushed the earth's crust down by a minute amount, and that this was sufficient to cause the city of Aberdeen to tilt ever so slightly towards the coast. When the tide went out, the city tilted back again.

Once the ice sheets started melting, the position of the shoreline in Scotland moved back and forth in a complex response to not one but two controlling factors: rising sea levels due to the melting of the European and North American ice sheets (which ended 7,000 years ago) and rising landmasses unburdened by the weight of all that ice. The land rose quickly at first, but then slowed to a crawl (and a large area of the Scottish landmass is still rising today by up to a millimetre a year).

We return to Archibald Geikie. He supported Agassiz's idea that ice sheets had covered most of Britain during the Ice Age: 'The present aspect of North Greenland probably affords us a close parallel to the state of Scotland during the earlier stages of the Drift period. The interior of that tract of country is covered with one wide sheet of ice, which, constantly augmented by fresh snowfalls, moves steadily downward from the axis of the continent to the eastern and western seas.'

Concluding his work, which had started in 1861, Archibald Geikie wrote up his research in his 1863 paper, *On the Phenomena of Glacial Drift in Scotland*, describing it as 'the first attempt to present a connected view of the sequence of events in the history of Scotland during what is known as the Glacial period or Ice Age.'

In beautifully written prose, Geikie convincingly explained the origin of the boulder clay. He noted that the boulder clay contained rock fragments obviously ripped up from the underlying bedrock, and then dumped on top of it, or else had jammed up against irregular features on the bedrock surface. A great force had thus torn up the rock fragments - huge boulders included - and then moved them large distances, occasionally hundreds of miles. Geikie concluded that the great force was provided by moving ice.

Furthermore, Geikie laid down hints of a big idea to come; one which when it arrived would vastly improve the understanding of the Ice Age. This was the idea, now accepted, that the Great Ice Age was not a single interval of time when ice sheets covered large areas of land for the duration. Instead, the Ice Age constituted a multiple series of glacial periods when ice sheets spread over land, separated by intervening warm periods when there was much less ice around and the climate was as mild as it is today, occasionally warmer.

Archibald Geikie could demonstrate that the climate varied during the Ice Age: 'It is scarcely likely that one vast and unbroken sheet of ice and snow would continue, year after year, completely to conceal the land.' He points to evidence within the boulder clay of the 'existence of streams and lakes'. 'Moreover, in the deposits left by such streams, we find branches of trees and layers of peat... an indication that such patches of soil must have remained free of ice, not for one summer only, but for a succession of years, so as to admit of the growth of mere seeds into hardwood shrubs or trees.'

Geologists also found mammoth tusks and reindeer bones in these sediments. Geikie mentions that 'The earliest recorded discovery of organic remains in the Scottish boulder-clay' was in 1817. Two mammoth tusks were found in clay lying above sandstone in a quarry in Kilmaurs, Ayrshire. One of the tusks 'measured 3 feet 5 inches in length, and about 13 inches in circumference, and weighed 20 pounds'. He also records that, 'The frequency of [the] association of the bones [with] valleys can hardly be accidental. I believe it will be found to receive its explanation in the probable existence of these valleys during the boulder-clay period, when they were traversed, during at least the summer months, by streams issuing from the adjacent ice-fields, and were thinly covered over with a scanty Arctic flora. In such valleys the herbivorous mammals would naturally congregate, and the remains of these animals would be much more likely to be preserved there than if they were left on the snowy surface of the surrounding uplands.'

Geikie concluded that, 'The occurrence of the stratified deposits in the Scottish [boulder clay] further indicates that although the intervals of quiet and vegetation may have lasted for many years, they were in the end brought to a close by the return of severer winters, when the ice once more crept down the valleys which it had abandoned, and began anew its ancient powers of abrasion and waste.'

Furthermore, 'it appears that the island was covered, as large tracts of Greenland are, with a wide sheet of snow and ice, which, constantly augmented by fresh snowfalls, pushed its way outward from the main mountain chains towards the sea; that there were periods of varying climate; that sometimes many of the valleys glowed with the vegetation of an Arctic summer, rills of water trickled down their sides or dashed over their rocky ledges, and herds of huge mammals pastured in their solitudes ; that again the cold increased, and the ice, once more pushing down the valleys, buried their beauty under one wide pall of cheerless desolation.'

In these passages Geikie is pushing on the boundaries of Victorian science and almost but not quite grasping at a concept which is as yet formless in 1863 – the concept of global climate change. Note that this is global climate change in response to *naturally occurring phenomena*; it is *not* climate change resulting from human activity. Awareness of the latter only arose at the end of the nineteenth century, although the key concept at the heart of man-made climate change, the Greenhouse Effect, had been explained two years earlier in 1861 following measurements made by the Irish physicist John Tyndall.

In the 1860s, the ideas of Charles Lyell dominated the prevailing theory on climate change, although this was a theory for local and not global climate change. Lyell proposed that the local climate changed when the local geography changed in response to earth movements, causing land to either rise from the sea or sink into it. When a larger landmass forms, its interior is hotter in summer and cooler in winter. When a landmass shrinks in size, the milder climate of its coastal margins becomes increasingly influential.

Two places in Archibald Geikie's paper probably caught the attention of James Croll when he read them. Firstly, where Geikie speculates that 'the boulder clay is not the result of one great catastrophe, but of slow and silent, yet mighty forces acting, sometimes with long pauses, throughout a vast cycle of time.' Secondly, where Geikie refers to climate change. He accepts Lyell's idea for local climate change: 'The submergence of a large tract of land would tend to ameliorate the climate.' Nevertheless, he asks: 'Whether this was the main agency concerned, or whether it only coincided with some vast cosmical change affecting the whole planet, and of which as yet we know nothing...' Geikie hints that not all had yet been explained.

Archibald Geikie finishes his paper with stirring words about the 'echoes of ceaseless change with which all the wide domains of Nature are ringing...'.Such change is a sign of 'the law of progress which, alike in the organic and inorganic worlds, has been the supreme law in the past, is the supreme law still, and that the task, as well as the noblest duty of man, is to aid in carrying out that law in the future, taking ever the lead of the wide creation over which he bears rule, and thus, as a fellow-worker with God, advancing to higher and yet higher stages of physical and intellectual development.'

In summary: climate change needs its champion if science is to make progress.

James Croll took up that challenge.

10. JAMES CROLL'S BIG IDEAS

1864

James Croll found plenty of time for research at Anderson's College, janitorial work permitting: 'My duties were regular and steady, requiring little mental labour; and as my brother was staying with me, he gave me a great deal of assistance, which consequently allowed me a good deal of spare time for study. The museum was open from 11 a.m. till 3 p.m. ...and there were but few visitors. I had generally a few hours a day of a quiet time for reading and study.'

Four years into the job and not long after the publication of Geikie's 1863 paper, Croll starts investigating the Ice Age. In particular, he seeks to answer the question hanging over science ever since Agassiz's address to the Swiss Society of Natural Sciences in 1837: 'why had the northern hemisphere been overwhelmed by ice?'

An explanation for this may have something to do with variation in the amount of heat coming from the sun, and then, when that heat arrives at the earth, something to do with the conditions on the earth's surface which influences how much of this heat hangs around to warm up the land, sea, and air. It could be that a natural thermostat exists, which scientists have yet to discover; one that acts to cool down or warm up the earth's surface as time goes by. But what is that thermostat and how does it work?

James Croll now brings his astronomical knowledge to bear on the problem. And in the way that a police detective intuitively knows who committed the crime but does not have the evidence yet, James targets an already established body of astronomical theory, believing the answer to lie there.

The theory contends that both the earth's orbit and the tilt of its axis of rotation varies in predictable cycles over tens of thousands of years: cycles which repeat again and again, and probably have done for millions of years past. Could it be that these eccentricities and wobbles are somehow responsible for the cooling down and heating up of the earth's surface over the long term? That at one moment in time an ice age starts, and then thousands of years later all that ice melts again.

This is what James Croll knew about this astronomical theory before he started searching for an explanation for the Ice Age. Two astronomical cycles act on the earth's orbit around the sun, and a third

141

affects the tilt of the earth's axis of rotation. Let's explain them one by one.

1) *Eccentricity.* The path of the earth's orbit around the sun does not quite form a circle. It resembles the shape of a rugby ball cut along its length - an ellipse. The earth's orbit is not quite circular, because the other planets in the Solar System exert enough pull through gravity to distort its shape. These planets orbit around the sun at different speeds and end up in different places relative to each other at any one particular time, all of which serves to create a varying force field, which squashes and stretches the earth's elliptical orbit accordingly. A long-term pattern emerges from all this such that the shape of the earth's orbit varies from almost circular to a stretched-out ellipse and back again over a cycle that lasts for about 100,000 years. The amount the orbit varies in shape from a perfect circle is described by its eccentricity (an ancient astronomical term).

Something else should be understood about the earth's elliptical orbit: the distance between the earth and the sun will vary along the orbit. And the more elongate the shape of the orbit, the more this distance will vary. Of particular relevance is the fact that a single point exists on the earth's annual orbit where the earth makes its closest approach to the sun, and another single point exists where the sun and earth are at their greatest distance apart from each other.

Although the distance between the earth and the sun varies, this results in only a minor difference in the amount of the sun's heat arriving at the earth's surface. This fact had been established by science before James Croll started taking an interest in the subject. Acknowledging this, James wrote that 'a simple change in the sun's distance would not alone produce a glacial epoch' and that 'physicists were perfectly correct in affirming that no increase of eccentricity of the earth's orbit could account for that epoch'.

2) *Precession.* The fact that we experience seasons of the year is probably the outcome of a freak accident that happened to the earth billions of years ago. Our planet is thought to have collided with a large object, perhaps a small planet, and the wallop knocked the earth over. The earth's axis of rotation, around which the earth spins every day, is now at a tilt. Which means that the axis points to the same point in space all the year round. Today it is 23½ degrees out of true (where true is a line perpendicular to the plane of the earth's orbit).

With the earth stuck on a tilt like this as it moves around the sun, for one half of the year the northern hemisphere is brought to face towards the sun and for the other half of the year it is brought to face away from the sun. Summer comes about in the northern hemisphere because the tilt towards the sun results in the sun's rays falling more directly onto the land and sea at a time went the days are longer: thus heating up the ground and the air above it. In winter, when the northern hemisphere is tilted away from the sun, the sun's rays are more spread out at a time when the days are shorter: thus, everywhere is that bit cooler at ground level. And let's make the trivial but telling remark about how winter in the northern hemisphere coincides with summer in the southern hemisphere, making it a wasted effort for Australians to sing the Christmas song 'Let it Snow!'

What is also important for the reader to appreciate, so that the discussion to follow makes sense, is that the points where spring, summer, autumn, and winter start on the earth's orbit for a particular hemisphere are not fixed. The starting points for the seasons drift very slowly around the earth's orbit on a regular 22,000-year cycle. Scientists call this feature precession (or precession of the equinoxes).

Had the earth's orbit been an unvarying perfect circle, precession would not matter in the least to anyone but a pure scientist. But because the earth's orbit is elliptical, a consequence of precession is that the timing for the onset of the various seasons happens at differing distances from the sun. Take the start of winter for example. If this happens when the earth is at its furthest distance from the sun, then that winter will be a touch colder (and longer) by comparison to those years when winter starts where the earth is at its closest approach to the sun (and the winters are shorter and milder). These observations will provide a crucial part of James Croll's theory to come.

Something else to take into account: because of precession: the seasons differ in length over the years, more so as the earth's orbit becomes increasingly eccentric. The length of the individual seasons will vary depending on the precession cycle. For half the cycle, that is, for 11,000 years, summer will be longer in the northern hemisphere and winter shorter (with the situation reversed in the southern hemisphere). For the remaining half of the cycle, summer will be shorter and winter longer. At the present time, summer in the northern hemisphere is about four and a half days longer than winter, and spring is three days longer than autumn.

143

3) *Tilt.* It has been mentioned that the earth's axis of rotation is tilted at an angle out of true, which is why we experience seasons. This angle also varies on a regular cycle - one that lasts roughly 41,000 years. The earth thus wobbles very slowly over time. The tilt varies between a minimum of about 22 degrees (low tilt) to a maximum of about 24½ degrees from true (high tilt). This does not seem like much, a few degrees of variation only; however, the change in tilt matters a lot to the story.

The degree of tilt influences how much heat the earth receives across its surface; the effect is large in the polar regions, less so at the equator. When the tilt is high, the poles are directed more towards the sun in the summer, and the ground receives more heat. When winter comes around, the polar regions are directed that bit more away from the sun, with the sun's rays more spread out across the surface in this part of the world, and the ground surface getting less heat. Conversely, when the tilt is low, the sun's rays are more spread out across the poles in the summer and the ground receives less heat; the winters are less intense too. In summary: the overall effect is for significantly hotter summers and colder winters when the tilt is high, and milder summers and winters when the tilt is low.

Three systems all act to influence when, where, and how the sun's heat arrives on the various parts of the earth's surface over time. If you want to explain the coming and going of a major Ice Age, then these astronomical cycles deserve investigation.

The French scientist Joseph Alphonse Adhémar was the first to have a go at explaining the Ice Age in terms of the earth's orbital cycles. In his 1842 book, *Revolution of the Sea*, published five years after Agassiz's presentation, he focussed on the 22,000 year cycle of precession, and, in particular, the variation in the length of the seasons.

He knew that Antarctica was covered with ice, but had no more information about the place other than that. Sailors had seen the edge of the ice, although no one had ever clambered over it. Adhémar believed that ice existed in Antarctica for a reason, and that is because the southern hemisphere is currently undergoing an ice age. He estimated the average thickness of the Antarctic ice cap to be more than 1,000 kilometres (the modern estimate is just over two kilometres).

As mentioned, the length of the seasons varies over the precession cycle. On this basis, Adhémar proposed that the hemisphere with the

144

longest winter, that is, with more days when the hours of sunlight are short, would undergo an ice age. And these conditions will persist year after year for thousands of years. In consequence, an ice age will alternate between the southern and northern hemispheres every half-cycle of precession, that is, for the first 11,000 years in one hemisphere and for the next 11,000 years in the other.

Taking his idea to its logical conclusion, Adhémar proposed that when an ice age ends every 11,000 years the consequences are catastrophic. As the sea warms up it melts the 1,000-kilometre thick polar ice sheet starting from its base upwards, and by doing so, creates a humongously tall ice mushroom. Rapidly becoming unstable as the climate warms up and the stalk wastes away, the colossal ice mushroom topples over into the sea, letting loose a mountainous wall of water and ice fragments, which then tear around the globe devastating all in its path.

Nice idea, flawed conception. Scientists pointed out at the time that despite the varying lengths of the seasons, it could readily be demonstrated that both hemispheres of the earth get more or less the same amount of heat from the sun every year nonetheless. Adhémar's Ice Age theory could not be made to work. Although rejected by science, Adhémar's theory was important. It introduced the idea that there might be a link between astronomical cycles and global climate change.

And then James Croll came along.

After investigating the subject for six months, James saw his first scientific paper published in 1864: 'On the Physical Cause of the Change of Climate during Geological Epochs'. He comments, 'The paper excited a considerable amount of attention, and I was repeatedly advised to go more fully into the subject; and, as the path appeared to me a new and interesting one, I resolved to follow it out. But little did I suspect, at the time when I made this resolution, that it would become a path so entangled that fully twenty years would elapse before I could get out of it.'

Why all the fuss? *James Croll spotted something the world's scientists had overlooked.* So what was James Croll's new idea?

Let's go through the steps that led to it. To start with, using astronomical calculations published by others, he drew a graph showing how the shape of the earth's orbit had varied over an interval of time from three million years before now to the present day. He pointed out using this graph that for the last ten thousand years and up

145

to the present day, the earth's orbit has been in a state of low eccentricity. Before then, the orbit had been significantly more elongate over a length of time lasting more than 100,000 years.

James Croll's train of thought ran as follows: the earth's orbit is currently in a state of low eccentricity and we do not have an ice age. Ten thousand years ago, and further back in time before then, the orbit was more eccentric in shape. Could that have been when the Ice Age happened? Perhaps, this hints that ice ages start when the earth's orbit becomes more eccentric, and ends when the orbit becomes more circular.

But then again, scientists had already calculated that variation in the eccentricity of the earth's orbit would only result in minor changes to the amount of heat reaching the Earth's surface every year.

Following a hunch, James Croll began to investigate the possibility that the 100,000-year cycle of eccentricity could be acting in concert with the 22,000-year precessional cycle to create the conditions for an Ice Age. That when the earth's orbit is highly eccentric over a period of 100,000 years or so, it will during this time interval also undergo four complete precessional cycles lasting 22,000 years. What this means is that on at least four occasions when the earth's orbit is highly eccentric, specific conditions arise that make an Ice Age more likely. For each hemisphere of the earth, there will be at least four instances of winter starting when the earth is as far away from the sun as it can possibly get. Not only would this winter be bitter, it will be a long one too. And as James Croll pointed out, 'The lowering of the temperature and the lengthening of the winter would both tend to the same effect: to increase the amount of snow accumulated during the winter...'

Thus, on these occasions, more than enough snow and ice will pile up to survive the short hot summer every year. And over thousands of years, the cumulative effect of a series of long cold winters would favour the progressive build-up of a large amount of snow and ice. During periods of a high-eccentricity orbit, the 22,000-year precessional cycle will produce such conditions every 11,000 years in the northern hemisphere, and then, every 11,000 years in the southern hemisphere.

Could these long cold winters have been responsible for bringing on a glacial epoch? Not directly, because the earth would only have been getting a little bit less heat than normal on these occasions - that much had been established by science already. But what if something else was also happening?

146

What came next was an 'aha' moment for James Croll and science. *The idea is huge.*

In Croll's book *Climate and Time* is to be found a section headlined 'Important Consideration Overlooked': It reads, 'although the glacial epoch could not result *directly* from an increase of eccentricity, it might nevertheless do so *indirectly*.' And what James Croll worked out is that although the earth was only getting a touch less heat than usual under the conditions mentioned above, the slight cooling was sufficient to set off a cascade of physical effects, all of which acted to intensify the initial cooling such that an ice age started.

Croll identified several ways by which the build-up of snow and ice could be intensified. Here are the two features at the top of his list:

Firstly, the shiny surface of snow and ice on the ground acts a powerful reflector of the sun's heat, sending much of it back out into space again. By comparison, land covered with rock or plants will absorb most but not all of the heat, as does water in the open sea. The absorbed heat will then be released, whereby it warms up the air at ground height, and this heat tends to linger close to the earth's surface for a while.

The larger the area of land or sea covered by ice, the more heat will be reflected back to space and lost. Air and ground temperatures will fall in response. The lowered temperatures make it more likely that the snow and ice will last longer year after year, and will create ideal conditions for the snow and ice cover to expand outwards. And as the area of snow and ice increases and the area of ice-free land diminishes, more heat will be reflected out to space, and the more the temperature at ground level will drop, further intensifying the process.

Secondly, oceans are important to climate. They cover almost three-quarters of the earth's surface, and store enormous amounts of heat from the sun. The top three and a half metres of the sea contains as much heat as is in the atmosphere. Furthermore, ocean currents provide the means to transfer this heat as they move around the globe.

Croll mentions the enormous quantity of heat brought north today by the Gulf Stream from tropical waters as it flows across the surface of the Atlantic Ocean. One outcome of this is that Britain is about 5°C warmer than could be expected for its northerly location. James Croll adds that, 'The Gulf Stream does not heat the shores of Europe by direct radiation. The Gulf Stream heats our island indirectly by heating the winds which blow over it to our shores.'

Because the circulation paths of the ocean currents matter to the distribution of heat around the globe, should these change in response to a cooling climate, this also provides a means to intensify the initial cooling tendency induced by variation in the earth's orbital cycles.

James Croll considers this to be 'by far the most important of all these agencies' responsible for triggering the cascade of effects leading to glaciation. He speculates that 'were the Gulf Stream stopped, and the heat conveyed by it deflected into the Southern Ocean, how enormously would this tend to lower the temperature of the northern hemisphere...' Such 'would lower the temperature of northern Europe to an extent that would induce a condition of climate as severe as that of North Greenland.' And harking back to the last chapter – recall that Archibald Geikie compared Ice-Age Scotland to present-day Greenland.

James Croll's new idea not only revived the astronomical theory for the origin of the Ice Age, it also provided a new concept for science in general. James comments: 'It is quite a common thing in physics for the effect to react on the cause.' And in this case where more of 'A' produces proportionally more of 'B', scientists can express the relationship by a mathematical formula. 'But strange to say, in regard to the physical causes concerned in the bringing about of the glacial condition of climate, cause and effect mutually reacted so as to strengthen each other. And this circumstance had a great deal to do with the extraordinary results produced.' Today, scientists call this phenomenon 'positive feedback'. It is an idea that crops up in many modern academic studies, and not only science; for example, it is found in economics and electrical engineering.

A familiar example is the feedback that occurs when a public address system is used. Somebody speaks into the microphone – the sound is amplified by an electronic circuit and sent to a loudspeaker. The microphone then picks up the sound coming out of the loudspeaker as well as the voice of the speaker – the combined signal is then amplified in an ever-intensifying feedback loop until ultimately a deafening screech is heard.

James Croll now made a prediction based on his investigations. The last glacial period of the Ice Age started about 240,000 years ago and ended 80,000 years ago when the earth's orbit changed into low-eccentricity mode.

1865

148

What was so special about James Croll, a man lacking a formal education, which enabled him to generate world-class science? His niece said, 'He had a most wonderful memory. He seemed to me as if he never forgot anything. He was orderly and very correct. He could go to his library at any time for any book, paper, or pamphlet, as the case might be, and without any trouble whatever lay his hand upon it. He used to say he had a place for everything, and everything had to be in its place. Never any confusion.'

She also mentioned that he thought non-stop about his investigations. While out on walks, Croll habitually dictated his thoughts to her 'on any of the subjects he was writing or thinking about' so she could scribble them down, 'and sometimes I would grumble, as it was of no interest to me'. Uncle James would then reply, 'Well, if you don't, it may never occur to me again.' She adds, 'This even happened sometimes in a *tram car*. He always carried paper and pencil when he went away any distance or any time. He could not be idle. While I was chattering about general topics, he was busy all the while at his own theories. Yet I never seemed to disturb him, so intent was he.'

Now that James Croll had at last found the happy road to fulfillment, a mysterious brain disorder threw major obstacles his way:

One evening in July of 1865, after a day's writing, I hurriedly bent down to assist in putting a few tacks into a carpet, when I experienced something like a twitch in a part of the upper and left side of the head. It did not strike me at the time as a matter of much importance; but it afterwards proved to be the severest affliction that has happened to me in life. Had it not been for this mishap to the head, all the private work I have been able to do during the twenty years which followed might have easily been done, and would have been done, in the course of two or three years.

I could think as vigorously as ever, but I dared not 'turn on the full steam'. After this twitch a dull pain settled in that part of the brain, which increased till it became unbearable, if I persisted in doing mental work for any length of time. I was therefore obliged to do mental labour very quietly and slowly, for a short period at a time, and then take a good long rest. If I attempted to do too much in one day, I was generally disabled for a few days to come. Another consequence was this: before this affliction in my

149

head, I could concentrate my thoughts on a single point, and exert my whole mental energy till the difficulty was overcome; but this I never could attempt afterwards. After struggling so many years against difficulties of every sort, and just at the time I had about overcome them all, and was expecting to be able to do some real work, I felt it very hard to be so disabled for the future.

1866 - 1875

James Croll now shows heroic willpower by continuing his research into the origins of the Ice Age, despite these recurring health problems. He is driven by a sense of duty to God, an 'overmastering conviction' that he has 'had a service laid upon him in the way of guiding some of the chief scientific currents of the age'.And with a mind permanently switched on to analytical mode, and one forever mulling over the mysteries of the universe, perhaps it is impossible for him to do anything else.

He is becoming increasingly influential in Victorian science. A reviewer of Croll's book *Climate and Time* even wrote that 'his writings have had the most radical influence on cosmological speculation. In certain directions his influence has been nearly as great as that of Darwin's in biology.'

And with the mention of Charles Darwin, the man himself has become fascinated by Croll's research; that's because it could help Darwin improve his understanding of evolution. Darwin would like to get a better feel for the length of time it took for life to have evolved from when it started to the present day, thus producing the great variety of animals and plants we see around us. Darwin suspects that this must have taken many millions of years.

For example, Charles Darwin would like to be given a realistic estimate of the amount of time that has passed from the start of the Cambrian Period to the present day, because Cambrian rocks contain the earliest fossil organisms then known to geologists. He is also keen to get a time estimate for the origin of the earth. Unfortunately, Victorian science has no reliable methods to date geological events. That is, until James Croll came along to give a hint or two. Using his methods he can provide a believable estimate for the length of the Ice Age; an interval of time that is somewhere between several hundred thousand and a million years (today's figure is about two and a half million years).

150

What intrigued Darwin here was that if the Ice Age had started a million years ago, then this provides a reference marker to calibrate the length of time it takes for evolution to happen. Fossils from sediments laid down directly underneath the earliest Ice Age deposits include many species which are still around today. This demonstrated to Darwin that evolution had not progressed that much over a million years, and is thus a very lengthy process.

Furthermore, an educated guess could be made for the timing of the start of the Cambrian Period and the age of the earth. Croll agreed with the estimate made by Charles Lyell that the start of the Cambrian Period was 240 million years before present (540 million years is today's estimate), and that the age of the earth is at least 500 million years (now estimated to be 4,500 million years).

Even so, these enormous intervals of time are not quite large enough for Charles Darwin. In the later editions of *The Origin of Species,* the landmark book that introduced the world to his theory of evolution, he cites James Croll: 'Mr Croll, in an interesting paper, remarks that we do not err "in forming too great a conception in the length of geological periods...'", and later in the book Darwin encourages him to increase his estimates.

Even more important for science than the help given to Charles Darwin is James Croll's confirmation that the 'long epoch known as the Glacial [Ice Age] was not one of continuous cold, but consisted of a succession of cold and warm periods'. This prompts geologists to look for evidence in the field for alternating cold and warm intervals within the Ice-Age sediments of Scotland, and they quickly find it. The evidence is now accumulating that the climate warmed up and cooled down intermittently during the Ice Age.

That is a huge advance for science. James Geikie, Archibald Geikie's younger brother, wrote in an 1871 paper for the *Geological Magazine* that Croll's theory 'for the first time rendered possible the reconciliation of apparently contradictory facts. Phenomena which had refused to be explained by any number of ingenious hypotheses suddenly seemed to yield their secret, and the great "Age of Ice" appeared all at once in a new light.' Three years later, James summarised what was then known about the subject in his book *The Great Ice Age*, and from there, the existence of glacial and interglacial periods as envisaged by James Croll became accepted scientific fact.

1876

James Croll's big year now arrives. On January 8, 1876, St Andrews University awards him an honorary doctorate, which is officially confirmed in February. He is now Dr Croll, a huge achievement for someone who left school at the age of thirteen.

On June 1, he is elected a Fellow of the Royal Society. Charles Darwin's signature heads one of the two lists of the fellows proposing him. And then international recognition follows the same year when James Croll is made an honorary member of the New York Academy of Sciences.

On September 2, he starts work for the Geological Survey of Scotland in Edinburgh taking up a position as resident surveyor and clerk. To get the job, James Croll had been required to pass a Civil Service exam. Unfortunately, he failed the arithmetic and English tests. It appears that Dr Croll, Fellow of the Royal Society, had got himself into a huge bother about being subjected to the ordeal.

He is given the job anyway because of influence exerted on the senior management of the service to allow him special dispensation. The physicist William Thomson, Baron Kelvin, comments that 'My Lords accepted his great calculations regarding the eccentricity of the earth's orbit, and the precession of the equinoxes during the last 10,000,000 years as sufficient evidence of his arithmetical capacity, his book on *The Philosophy of Theism* and numerous papers published in the scientific journals, as proof of his ability to write good English.'

1878

James Croll's theory of the Ice Age runs into a problem in 1878. Evidence emerges that his timing for the end of the Ice Age, which he gave as 80,000 years before present, is probably wrong. The American geologist Alexander Winchell has published a paper providing plausible evidence that the Ice Age ended only 8,000 years ago.

Winchell had been investigating the St Anthony Falls, the only significant waterfall on the Mississippi river, which today is located within the city boundary of Minneapolis. He pointed out that the current position of the waterfall is 275 metres upriver from where it was recorded in 1680 when discovered by the Belgian explorer Father Louis Hennepin. The 275-metre difference between then and now has come about because the edge of the waterfall had been cut back by the erosive power of the Mississippi.

Erosion by the mighty Mississippi river had been going on for much longer than that. An eight-mile-long gorge marks the progress made by

152

the recession of the waterfall over the centuries. Winchell could prove from geological fieldwork that the gorge had started eroding only once the last ice sheet in the area had melted. He estimated from the rate of erosion of the gorge that this took place 8,000 years ago: a date thus signifying the end of the Ice Age. A similar estimate has also been made from fieldwork on the gorge of the Niagara Falls.

Winchell sends a copy of his investigations to James Croll, writing in his accompanying letter that 'The data there employed are reliable, and they seem to fix the second Glacial Epoch at a comparatively recent date. Several geologists have told me that the result based on the data seems to be the most exact and reliable yet attained.'

What is accepted today is that the last glacial period of the Ice Age reached a maximum 21,000 years ago, and that the ice sheets started to melt immediately afterwards. Because the ice sheets were huge and covered an enormous area, they took thousands of years before they melted completely. The big meltdown accelerated 10,700 years ago when the earth's atmosphere warmed up substantially. Even so, in spite of the much warmer conditions, the ice sheets still took a long time to dwindle to nothing, they had been that big. Doomed they were however: and the European and North American ice sheets had all but disappeared by 7,000 years ago.

Winchell's date of 8,000 years before present became widely accepted in the 1880s as the timing for the end of the ice sheets – and can be considered close enough to today's figure. The new date prompted James Geikie to write in his 1894 book *The Great Ice Age* about the doubts raised over James Croll's theory: 'Some modification of his views will eventually clear up the mystery. But for the present we must be content to work and wait.'

And thereafter, James Croll became the forgotten man of science, his name even disappearing from the later editions of Darwin's *Origin of Species*. Croll's theory had failed to match a reasonably accurate estimate for the end of the Ice Age.

So what had gone wrong?

The answer is that James Croll's theory had been partly right, partly wrong, and partly incomplete. The mismatch between theory and evidence came about for two reasons.

First, Croll made a bad judgment call. The question arose - and was one posed and discussed in his time - which of these factors is more important to the development of large ice sheets? Is growth favoured,

153

as Croll believed, by a series of long cold winters extending over hundreds of years with each winter long enough to ensure a continuous build up of ice and snow? Alternatively, had the build up of ice been favoured by a series of long mild summers which had done little to melt the existing snow and ice cover?

James Croll picked the former, which on the face of it seems reasonable. It is wrong however. Geologists have now demonstrated from fieldwork in polar regions that the summer season is critical for the growth of ice on land. The searing heat of a short intense summer will shrink glaciers and ice sheets big time, whereas the ice is resilient to a long mild summer.

Secondly, James Croll's theory was incomplete and he was aware of this. He knew that the tilt cycle was an important factor governing past climates. Unfortunately, he did not have accurate data available to him to project the tilt cycle back over the last 3 million years as he could do with the other two cycles. This was unfortunate because it was shown later that tilt exerted the strongest influence of the three orbital cycles on Ice Age climate change, whereas eccentricity of orbit was the least influential.

It is understood now that the trigger for the end of the last three glacial periods in the northern hemisphere coincided with the earth's tilt cycle approaching its maximum. More or less coinciding with this each time, the earth made its closest approach to the sun in the precession cycle when it was summer in the northern hemisphere, producing a series of summers that were short but intense. Thus, a double whammy acted to melt the ice. These were the conditions that kicked off the melting of the European and North American ice sheets 21,000 years ago, eventually leading to their ultimate disappearance 7,000 years ago.

In the 1920s, Milutin Milankovitch, Professor of Applied Mathematics at the University of Belgrade, picked up the idea again that astronomical cycles influenced Ice Age climates. He took over from Croll's work the ideas that the three astronomical cycles had influenced Ice Age climates, and that the small decreases or increases in the quantity of heat at the earth's surface had been amplified by a cascade of physical effects.

Milankovitch was advised by a geologist friend that his calculations should focus on the summer conditions rather than winter conditions, thus correcting Croll's mistake. Milutin Milankovitch also had access to detailed information on the long-term variation of the Earth's tilt cycle over time; data that Croll lacked.

He now calculated the variation in the amount of heat building up at ground level at different latitudes on the earth's surface over the last 600,000 years, taking into account the earth's distance from the sun and the angle the sun's rays made as they spread across the surface of the planet. It took the Serb professor many years of hard work to make the calculations. The big slog was beneficial in the end: his output is essentially considered valid and is used by scientists today. The astronomical cycles are now widely referred to as Milankovitch cycles, although a handful of technical papers take pains to refer to them as Croll-Milankovitch cycles.

The conclusion: *science is unforgiving to those who fail to produce a valid answer.*

Although Croll's theory made wrong predictions, it was also partly right; and where it was right, *it changed science.*

In a 2012 paper published in the scientific journal *Polar Record* with the title 'James Croll, a man ahead of his time', two academics from Moscow State University and another from the University of Cambridge wrote that Croll's discovery of positive feedback was the 'main achievement of his theory', and 'the most important discovery in the study' of past climates' (and a major contribution to the study of modern climates as well).

Additionally, the approach he took to problem solving is now an integral part of modern science. James Croll was a generalist in science: someone who is interested in all its aspects. Because of his understanding of astronomy, physics, chemistry, glaciology, meteorology, oceanography, with a dash of geology thrown in, he could readily assemble different facts from different areas of study into a coherent whole to explain the phenomena of ice ages and climate change. Today this is called Earth Systems Science; the study of the earth as a system whereby material and energy are interlinked by complex interactions between the sun, planets, earth, sea, and air.

Recent papers from scientific journals have set out to assess the legacy of James Croll, and all are in praise. Here are two quotes from the many that could have been given:

David Sugden, 2014. *James Croll (1821–1890): ice, ice ages and the Antarctic connection.* 'His paper on the form and behaviour of the Antarctic ice sheet, written before anyone had even landed on the continent, is testament to the power of his approach and made numerous predictions which were clearly testable (and many of them survived!).'

Alastair Dawson, 2021. *The oceanographic contribution of James Croll.* 'In the many writings of James Croll on ocean currents, we encounter, as with other areas of research, numerous remarkable ideas ahead of their time.'

Note that assessment repeated by today's scientists: *James Croll, a man who was ahead of his time.*

11. TRYGGVE GRAN AND CAPTAIN SCOTT

When he made the first aircraft crossing of the North Sea in July 1914, the Norwegian aviator Tryggve Gran was only 26 years old. Remarkably, this was not his first brush with history and would not be his last: by 1914, he had already taken part in the Scott expedition to the Antarctic. And only 48 hours before he set off on his epic North Sea flight, World War I broke out. Two years later, Tryggve was flying in active combat for the British Royal Flying Corps.

Always seeking adventure, Tryggve Gran ended up perceived as a flawed hero, having been tainted by his activities in Nazi-held Norway during World War II. A flawed hero perhaps, although this will not stop the telling of Tryggve Gran's adventures here, even if only part of his tale is relevant to the North Sea. Your author has good reasons for this – I share a connection to Tryggve Gran on account that I live in Cruden Bay, the starting point for his North Sea flight. And as a member of the local heritage group, I helped with the installation in the village of an information board about the flight. Tryggve's son Hermann read the script for the board and made minor corrections to it.

So let's get on with the story.

1908

Tryggve Gran once said that 'the most interesting part of a man's life is when you can do something other people haven't done'. And on July 12, 1908, at the age of 20, he achieves what is many a young man's dream – the Norwegian is picked to play international football for his country. In the friendly match held in Gothenburg, Sweden beat Norway 11-3.

Perhaps not the greatest accolade for a young man who wants to shout to his fellows, 'I did this!' Tryggve will get other chances for glory, and is someone marked out for adventure. He is supremely fit, loves outdoor sports, mountaineering and skiing in particular, and is extremely restless. What's more, a family legacy has left him wealthy: his father, who died when Tryggve was five years old, ran a marine engineering and shipyard business in Bergen.

Tryggve now enters the Norwegian Naval Cadet College, where he talks to a man who had been on an expedition to Arctic Canada onboard the *Fram*, Nansen's polar exploration ship. Tryggve is enthralled by the conversation, and, there and then, decides to become

157

a polar explorer. The Antarctic is where he wants to go. 'I had some means. As soon as I got the chance, I'd take a ship to go south. But I was very young; I was just twenty. But funnily enough, people didn't laugh. No! They thought it kind of wonderful that a young man would try something.'

1909 - 1910

Gran talks to a ship builder and scopes out plans for the sailing ship he intends to take to the Antarctic - one that can sleep eight men. He also seeks advice for his expedition from three Norwegian polar experts: Roald Amundsen, Carsten Borchgrevink, and Fridtjof Nansen. Amundsen is standoffish, Borchgrevink is friendly, and Nansen makes a helpful suggestion: 'Captain Scott is coming to Norway next March to test his new motorised sledges; why not meet up with him and discuss your plans.'

The arrangements are made, and when Scott arrives in Christiana (now Oslo), he meets up with Tryggve at the sports outfitters who are supplying Scott's Antarctic expedition with sledges and skis. Captain Scott likes the young Norwegian, and invites him to the ski resort of Fefor where the motorised sledge trials are taking place. He tells Tryggve that he does not quite trust this motorised sledge contraption with its petrol engine and chain tracks (similar to that of a military tank), but given time, the design could be improved enough to make it useable in the Antarctic.

While Captain Scott is out in the snowy Norwegian mountains trying out the motorised sledge, he notices that Tryggve is an expert skier. Approaching the young man, he asks him to lay aside his plans and join his expedition to the South Pole. 'I believe it would be good to have someone to show my companions how to use skis.' Tryggve is astonished, and waiting until the next day to give his reply, accepts the offer. Scott is grateful, 'I am very glad. I do not think you will regret your decision.'

Scott has set out two objectives for his expedition to the Antarctic: firstly, to gather scientific and geographical data, and secondly, 'to reach the South Pole and to secure for the British Empire the honour of this achievement'.

It is May 1910, and Tryggve Gran has arrived in London where he will board Scott's polar exploration ship, the *Terra Nova*, an ex Dundee whaler. But before doing that, he goes to Buckingham Palace. The

King and Queen of Norway are there for the funeral of King Edward VII, who had died at the start of the month. King Haakon hands him a silk pennant, a gift from Queen Maud, and asks Tryggve to use it as his sledge flag on Scott's expedition. Beautifully embroidered, it displays the Norwegian coat of arms - a golden lion holding a silver axe set against a red background; and above the arms, a golden crown.

The *Terra Nova* sets out for Cardiff where it will pick up coal before heading out on the long voyage south. Christchurch in New Zealand will be the last port of call before setting foot in the Antarctic.

Arriving *en route* in Melbourne, Australia, Captain Scott receives a mysterious telegram from Amundsen: 'Beg leave to inform you that *Fram* proceeding Antarctic. Amundsen.' That is worrying, and Scott is anxious to know more. He eventually discovers that Amundsen had bought Admiralty charts of the Ross Sea area, the place where both he and Ernest Shackleton had previously launched their Antarctic expeditions, and where Scott is heading now. On his first expedition to Antarctica, between 1901 and 1904, the Ross Sea had been a near-enough starting point for the South Pole, although he and his men eventually stopped short of their goal by 530 miles. It looks likely that Amundsen is racing to the South Pole to get there ahead of the Scott Expedition.

November 29, 1910 – January 3, 1911

The *Terra Nova* leaves New Zealand on November 29, destination Antarctica. The ship is taking much longer to get there than anticipated, having been slowed down on the approach by 400 miles of pack ice. All around the ship are ice floes, tens to hundreds of metres across, which drift across the sea in huge numbers. For many a mile around, the men onboard see much more ice than open water.

The ship lurches through the pack ice. Tryggve considers it a marvel that they are still moving forward at all; it sure is slow progress, an average of three miles per hour accompanied by frequent bangs and crashes – the ship sometimes grinding to a halt. At other times, 'leads' open up, wide lanes of water between the ice floes which head in the direction of travel. Putting on a spurt of speed, the *Terra Nova* will hurry along them as far as the leads persist.

Every now and again, they see penguins in groups of four sitting on the ice floes. The men make the curious discovery that penguins are fascinated by music; if they sing to the birds, they will follow the ship.

The occasional stoppages give Tryggve the opportunity to start his ski lessons, or as he is heard to say, to go 'mit dee shee op'. He has not perfected his English yet. The lessons are held on the larger ice floes. On December 11, everyone on the ship has a go, and it is a great success. Captain Scott writes in his diary that 'I'm much pleased with the ski and ski boots, both are very well adapted to our purpose'. And three days later notes that 'Gran is wonderfully good and gives instruction well'.

All this tedious pushing through icy waters day after day provides the time for everyone to get each other's measure and to bond as a group. All come to respect Captain Scott, who commands with a firm but light touch. More than that, Robert Falcon Scott is driven by a determination that never wavers - total determination. Tryggve hugely admires Scott, and for the rest of his life will never say anything bad about him.

Scott has picked his men well; there is an easy camaraderie amongst them: 'Everyone is very cheerful - one hears laughter and song all day - it's delightful to be with such a merry crew,' he writes. There are no quarrels or trouble of any sort. Scott commenting that, 'It is glorious to realise that men can live under conditions of hardship, monotony, and danger in such bountiful good comradeship.'

They call each other by nicknames: Captain Scott is 'the owner', a navy term used for the commander of a war ship; Captain Oates is 'Titus', although Scott calls him 'Soldier'; and Tryggve is 'Triggers'.

January 4, 1911

Today the *Terra Nova* steams into McMurdo Sound, where the men land at Cape Evans on the west side of Ross Island. The Cape is named after Teddy Evans, currently second-in-command of the expedition. Here the men will build a hut next to a beach, beyond which lies the slope of Mount Erebus, an active volcano whose smoky summit reaches a majestic 3,794 metres. She is the 'White Lady of the Antarctic'.

Cape Evans is the dramatic starting point for what will be a dramatic undertaking. Ross Island lies close to the north-west corner of the Ross Ice Shelf, a huge area of sea ice then known as the Barrier on account of its sheer wall of ice facing the open sea; a wall 50 metres high in places and stretching an impressive 370 miles in length. Covering an area comparable to that of a large European country, the ice shelf will have to be crossed to get to the edge of the landmass of the Antarctic continent. The South Pole is located on land beyond this edge.

At six in the morning, the men offload the three motorised sledges, the ponies, and the dogs from the *Terra Nova*. Many penguins have surrounded the landing spot. Enraged by the barking dogs, they attack them. In the unequal fight, the dogs pounce on the penguins and tear them apart.

January 14, 1911

Captain Scott is today organising the next part of the polar campaign, the laying of depots. Food and equipment will be stored at selected locations along the first part of the route to the pole. The last depot in the line will be set up at latitude 80 degrees south, where a large volume of provisions is to be taken and stored in a hut to be built there. Providing staging posts for the journey to the pole and back, the depots will also be used as places of refuge in atrocious weather.

Although it is currently summer in the Southern Hemisphere and will be until March, not enough time is left to get to the South Pole this season. The long trip will have to wait until the end of the following winter. Another practicality comes into play: the sun will soon disappear below the horizon and will not be seen again for four months in this part of the world. All will be dark for the duration.

Scott now tells Tryggve he will be part of the depot-laying team. The plan is to set out in ten days time with twelve men, twenty-six dogs, and eight ponies.

January 20, 1911

Today is Tryggve Gran's twenty-second birthday, which he spends greasing the runners of the expedition sledges with wax. Scott writes about one of the day's meals in his diary, although he does not mention which it is: 'We had seal rissoles today so extraordinarily well cooked that it was impossible to distinguish them from the best beef rissoles.' Gran's birthday is celebrated after supper, when gramophone records are played, including some Norwegian melodies. Tryggve feels strange listening to these here.

January 24, 1911

The depot-laying expedition leaves today.

Tryggve is leading a horse named Weary Willie, who, in turn, drags a sledge loaded with 600 pounds weight of supplies. Although Willie is strongly built, it is a struggle to keep him going. Scott writes in his diary, 'Gran is doing very well. He has a lazy pony and a good deal of work to get him along and he does it very cheerfully.'

Meanwhile, back at base, the *Terra Nova* is being readied for the Eastern Party expedition under the leadership of Victor Campbell. A group of men will depart on the ship from Cape Evans in two days time, and will then proceed eastwards along the edge of the Ross Ice Shelf. The objective is to explore King Edward VII Land.

February 26, 1911

The depot-laying expedition has not gone well. The ponies cannot cope with the cold, and their hooves are sinking deep into snow. With their condition weakening, it is deemed wise to lay the One Ton Depot sooner rather than later, even though this is thirty miles further south than originally planned.

The trudge south has proved a mission of great hardship. There are many hazards down here. The sub-zero temperatures, and it is usually sub-zero, -73° F recorded on one occassion, can bring on hypothermia or frostbite. Many of the men will suffer frostbite on this expedition. The symptoms are these: in very low temperatures, skin and tissues in the fingers, toes, and parts of the face can freeze, turn blue or white, and numbness is experienced. Swelling of the affected parts often occurs, and in extreme cases, amputation of the affected parts may be required. Frostbitten fingers are very painful - the burning sensation making it difficult to get to sleep at night.

Scurvy is another problem due to the scarcity of Vitamin C in the diet (although a small amount is to be had in penguin meat). Teddy Evans experienced scurvy: a series of symptoms that started with the knee joints stiffening, the legs tightening up, before becoming swollen, bruised, and turning green in colour. And that is only the first day. Then his gums became lacerated, his teeth loosened, and the blood vessels ruptured and bled. Teddy Evans survived the ordeal.

Let's also mention snow-blindness, pain in the eyes, sometimes described as 'sunburn' of the eye's surface tissues. Snow is highly reflective to the sun's damaging ultra-violet rays, and to counter ther damaging effects, everyone has been issued with snow goggles made of amber or green glass. They are worn most of the time, but because they fog up, they are removed when traversing dangerous places such as glaciers where deep crevasses lurk for the unwary or the unsighted.

Accidents happen too: men do indeed fall into crevasses despite all precautions - luckily, this happens at the end of a rope; also falling into slushy water and then emerging soaking wet in the sub-zero temperatures; or finding yourself on a sledge speeding out of control towards a precipice and then having to jump for your life.

Today, the party, on their way back from laying the depots, have arrived at Safety Camp, the depot located on the edge of the ice shelf bordering Ross Island. A letter is waiting there in a mailbag, which had been dispatched by Victor Campbell, leader of the Eastern Party, now back at Cape Evans.

The letter contains shocking news. The *Terra Nova* had been sailing along the Barrier, when at midnight on January 31, they approached the Bay of Whales: 'On rounding the eastern point our surprise can be imagined when we saw a ship, which I recognised as the *Fram*, made fast along the sea ice. Standing in, we made fast a little way ahead of her and hoisted our colours, she answering with the Norwegian ensign. There was no doubt it was Captain Amundsen.'

Victor Campbell boarded the *Fram* and talked to the captain, who told him Amundsen was onshore, but would be back at nine in the morning. Campbell returned the next day, met Amundsen, who told him the Norwegians had been there since January 4. Amundsen showed him around: 'The camp presented a very workmanlike appearance, with a good-sized hut containing a kitchen and living room with a double tier of bunks around the walls, while outside several tents were up and 116 fine Greenland dogs picketed around.' By contrast, the Scott expedition had landed with 33 dogs. Amundsen had previously discovered on Arctic expeditions just how useful dogs could be on snow and ice.

Scott records his thoughts on the news: 'Only one thing fixes itself definitely in my mind. The proper, as well as the wiser, course for us is to proceed exactly as though this has not happened. To go forward and do our best for the honour of the country without fear or panic.'

Even so, this does not look good: 'There is no doubt Amundsen's plan is a very serious menace to ours. He has a shorter distance to the Pole by 60 miles – I never thought he could have got so many dogs safely to the ice. His plan for running them seems excellent. But above and beyond all, he can start his journey early in the season – an impossible condition with ponies.'

And neither is Tryggve Gran happy. One of his colleagues told him about Amundsen and his Norwegian expedition by opening the conversation with the words: 'Good news for you Gran', only it was anything but good news for the young Norwegian, who now felt as if a glacier had opened up beneath him. This is now an extremely awkward situation for him. Tryggve records his private thoughts in his diary. Amundsen must have the better chance of getting to the pole because he will start out from a location closer to it, and will get there quicker because he has dogs and will not be held back by second-rate horses. The Scott expedition can only get to the South Pole first should Amundsen suffer an accident - and only if. Gran is well aware that Amundsen is a driven man who lives every moment of his life governed by the motto, 'all or nothing'.

Not in Tryggve Gran's diary as published are what may have been his even more private thoughts at this particular moment. He is now unlikely to be selected for the team to go to the pole next summer. The dreams he held of being one of the first men to reach the South Pole will not now be realised. And the highly awkward situation has come about whereby he is a Norwegian in a British expedition that is likely to be beaten in their efforts by his fellow countrymen: how will his British colleagues treat him after that?

And his colleagues are angry with Amundsen, bitterly angry. Apsley Cherry-Garrard, the expedition's assistant biologist, describes their reaction in his book *The Worst Journey in the World*. For an hour they are overcome with a fit of insane rage; their instinct is to go to the Bay of Whales and 'have it out' with Amundsen and his men (what 'having it out' involves is not explained in the book). They had somehow believed that after all their recent difficulties on the depot-laying mission they deserve the prior right to get to the South Pole first.

March 1, 1911
Scott records in his diary that Weary Willy died overnight: 'It is hard to have got him back so far, only for this.' Reflecting on what Weary Willy's death means for the expedition, Scott writes, 'It is clear that these blizzards are terrible for the poor animals. Their coats are not good, but even with the best of coats it is certain they would lose condition badly if caught in one, and we cannot afford to lose condition at the beginning of a journey. It makes a late start *necessary for next year*.'

164

The men will now over-winter in the hut at Cape Evans for seven months. They keep themselves occupied with games, reading, writing diaries, and scientific research. Football matches are popular; although Tryggve is left wondering why it is with his international experience, he is so often on the losing team. Captain Scott has also organised a lecture series with talks to be given three nights a week from anyone with expertise on any subject. The men learn about parasites, volcanoes, life in Japan, and many other topics.

April 23, 1911
Today the sun dipped below the horizon and will not be seen again until August 22, four months from now. For the duration, it will be twenty-four-hour night time in this part of the Antarctic, albeit with some twilight visible around noon.

May 8, 1911
Captain Scott gives a special lecture today on the 'Plans of the Expedition'. He has not decided how many men will come with him to the Pole; nevertheless, he intends to stick to his original plans as if Amundsen had not turned up. Afterwards, he writes in his diary that 'I could not but hint that the problem in reaching the Pole can best be solved by relying on the ponies and man - haulage... Everyone seems to distrust the dogs when it comes to glacier and summit.' The two remaining motorised sledges will also be used (one was lost when it was unloaded from the *Terra Nova* and fell through the ice into a hundred fathoms of water). Scott writes that the earliest date for setting off to the pole is November 1, with sufficient supplies available for a journey lasting 144 days.

July 14, 1911
Today, Tryggve Gran hears the news he had expected - he will not be going with the Polar party. He is to accompany the geologists on an expedition to the west coast of McMurdo Sound, which is across the water from the hut at Cape Evans. The Norwegian is disappointed, but reckons this outcome had been inevitable.

A second party will also depart on a separate expedition - the Northern Shore party, which will be led by Victor Campbell.

November 1, 1911

Scott sets off at 11 a.m. on the 900-mile journey south to the Pole, the motorised-sledge team having left already. Last night, when the men had packed the sledges with supplies and equipment, allowance had been made to add twenty pounds weight of personal baggage. Scott asks Griffith Taylor what book he should take to read. 'He wanted something fairly filling. I recommended Tyndall's Glaciers—if he wouldn't find it "coolish". He didn't fancy this! So then I said, " Why not take Browning, as I'm doing?" And I believe that he did so.'

And although Scott has taken Browning's poems with him, he has forgotten to pack the Union Jack he intended to raise at the South Pole. Queen Alexandra, the widow of King Edward VII, had given it to him.

Now, it just so happened that the party did not have to turn back to get it, because earlier in the season a telephone wire had been connected between the little hut on Hut Point where they are now and the hut on Cape Evans. So the call comes through to Tryggve Gran, 'bring the flag here', a journey of about fifteen miles.

Tryggve set out the next day, having wrapped the flag around his chest. When he reaches the polar party (at the hut or a bit further on, Gran is not clear about this), Scott tells him, 'It is strange that you as a Norwegian should carry the Union Jack for my South Pole expedition.' Tryggve's private reaction is recorded: 'It was the irony of fate, no doubt about that.'

The last words he would ever hear from Captain Scott are these, 'When you are in the mountains be careful, you are young and have life ahead of you, God Bless you my boy.'

November 15, 1911
Today the Western Geological Expedition sets out. The four men, Tryggve Gran amongst them, undergo the usual thrills, spills, and near-death experiences of an expedition in the Antarctic, and will eventually return home in February. Two incidents are worthy of note.

On December 28, they spot a mountain rising to a summit at seven thousand feet. Initially, they call it Black-Cap because of the black band of igneous rock crossing its peak. It is subsequently renamed Mount Tryggve Gran, 'after our ever-cheerful colleague'.[1]

---

[1] Today it is Mount Gran, to which can be added the Antarctic landmarks of Tryggve Point and Gran Glacier.

166

Tryggve Gran celebrates his 23^d birthday on January 20, 1912. He must have gained a reputation amongst his colleagues as a bit of a playboy, because Griffith Taylor's poem for the occasion hints at this. It also mentions Tryggve's attempts to write a play during the expedition, 'a great nature play full of storms and wrecks'.

ODE TO TRYGGVE
(Chanted at ye Full Pemmican Feast.)[2]
O Tryggve Gran, O Tryggve Gran,
1 would thou wert a moral man,
And yet since we
(The other three)
Are just as moral as can be,
A '*soupçon de diablerie*'
Improves our little company.
O Tryggve Gran, a holy calm
Is most essential in a psalm.
But prose should be a thought less calmer
When elevated into drama.
And yet though we
(The other three)
Are critical to a degree,
We wish success some future day
To the first Polar 'Nature Play'.

O Tryggve Gran, thou art a man
Who hath compressed within a span
Of three and twenty years, such deeds
That hearing which, each man's heart bleeds
Among us three.
And yet though we
Are kind to every girl we see,
1 have no doubt each lovely creature
Would rather help you follow Nietzsche!

Oh, Tryggve Gran, you should be dead
A-many years ago—instead

---

[2] Pemmican is beef extract with 60 per cent fat content, cooked as a soup. The Western Party had taken 11 weeks supply with them.

Of which, he saves you oft,
That 'Little Cherub up Aloft'.
And therefore we
(The other three)
In this new principle agree,
(As with your luck no man can quarrel)
'Twill serve us best to be un-moral!!!

February 15, 1912

The four men from the Western Geological Expedition are picked up today by the *Terra Nova*. The news they hear is that everyone believes Scott's chances to reach the South Pole are excellent. Four men had returned after helping the Polar team with the first part of their journey. They reported that Amundsen had not been spotted, and the horses and motorised sledges were performing well. The not-so-good news is that Victor Campbell and the Northern Shore party have not returned.

Tryggve is much disappointed to discover that he has not received the expected pile of mail from the outside world as his colleagues have done; in fact, only one letter has been sent to him. He opens it, and is disgusted to find a bill requiring payment. He will be grumpy for days afterwards, suspecting that the rest of his mail must have been delivered to the *Fram* by accident. That is plausible: most of his letters will have been dispatched from Norway with an Antarctic address, and as such could easily have been bundled up in the wrong postbag.

February 25, 1912

Tryggve arrives back at the hut on Cape Evans. Meanwhile, two men are to be sent to Hut Point to wait for the return of Scott and his team.

March 7, 1912

It is about now that Scott and the Polar team are expected back. Unfortunately, the telephone connection to Hut Point broke when the cable was washed out to sea during a storm. Arrangements had been made for the two men in the hut to fire rockets once the returning Polar party arrives there.

March 17, 1912

Scott should have been back by now. Gran writes in his diary that it is Captain Oates' birthday today.

March 25, 1912
Rockets have not yet been seen from the direction of Hut Point. No one says anything back in Cape Evans, although anxiety marks every face.

April 11, 1912
The men now believe there is no hope for Captain Scott and the four men with him. It makes no sense to go out to look for them because winter is approaching; the search will have to wait until spring at the earliest.

May 1, 1912
The men of the Antarctic expedition, minus the Polar and the Northern party men, thirteen in number, are currently overwintering in the hut at Cape Evans. Gran finds it painful to see all the empty bunks. No matter, the men take the attitude that it is pointless getting depressed because they have their sanity to preserve. After all, mourning will not bring back the dead.

October 29 – November 11, 1912
Eleven men, Tryggve Gran included, have finally set out south to search for Scott and his team. The weather is excellent. As they approach the 'One Ton Depot' on November 11, the wind picks up and starts blowing hard. They arrive hoping to find the Scott party safe inside, but no. Just large amounts of food and fuel; the fuel having leaked, spoiling much of the food.

November 12, 1912
The search party leaves very early in the morning from the depot. Close to noon, having travelled eleven to twelve miles south, a pyramid shape is spotted half a mile to the west. Tryggve Gran who has a pair of binoculars with him takes a closer look. 'It's rather funny, but it doesn't look like a tent; it looks like a cairn,' he says. Speeding towards it on his skis, he arrives in ten minutes to find that it is indeed a tent, although mostly covered by snow. He will wait until the other men have had a look inside before entering, which he then does.

Scott's body is in the centre of the tent, Henry 'Birdy' Bowers body is to the right and Edward 'Bill' Wright's body is to the left. Only one body is visible, Captain Scott's; the other two are deep inside their sleeping bags. Scott looks frostbitten all over his face and his skin is yellow. He lies with his body twisted out of his sleeping bag - Gran believes this shows he put up a terrific but hopeless fight at the moment of death.

Later, Thomas Crean approaches Gran, shakes his hand and says 'Congratulations.'

'What do you mean congratulations?' Tryggve replies, taken aback.

'Dr Atkinson has just read in the diary of Captain Scott that when they got to the Pole, they found the Norwegian flag there.'

Crean's comment is sincere, and not as mean-spirited as it sounds: the two men now shake hands, look at each other with tears in their eyes, before becoming overwhelmed with emotion.

Later, Tryggve glances through Scott's diary and reads about the tragic events as they unfolded. The following passages are excerpts from it:

> *January 16, 1912.* ...we started off in high spirits in the afternoon, feeling that tomorrow would see us at our destination. About the second hour of the march Bower's sharp eyes detected what he thought was a cairn; he was uneasy about it... Half an hour later, he detected a black speck ahead. Soon we knew that this could not be a natural snow feature. We marched on, found it was a black flag tied to a sledge bearer; near by the remains of a camp; sledge tracks and ski tracks coming and going and the clear trace of dogs' paws – many dogs... Tomorrow we must march on to the Pole and then hasten home with all the speed we can compass. All the day dreams must go; it will be a wearisome return.

> *January 17, 1912.* Great God! This is an awful place and terrible enough for us to have laboured to it without the reward of priority.

> *January 18, 1912.* [They work out that they are not quite at the Pole, it is one mile beyond where they are and three miles to the right.] More or less in this direction Bowers saw a cairn or a tent. In the tent we find a record of five Norwegians having been here [Amundsen's name is at the top and the date given is December 16, 1911. And something else is found.] A note from Amundsen, which I keep, asks me to forward a letter to King Haakon!...We

170

carried the Union Jack about ¾ of a mile north with us and left it on a piece of stick as near as we could fix it.

January 23, 1912. Wilson suddenly discovered that Evans' nose was frostbitten – it was white and hard... There is no doubt Evans is a good deal run-down... he is very much annoyed with himself, which is not a good sign.

February 4, 1912. Just before lunch unexpectedly fell into crevasses, Evans and I together – a second fall for Evans, and I camped... the party is not improving in condition, especially Evans, who is becoming rather dull and incapable.

February 17, 1912. [Evans has fallen behind and they go back to look for him] ...he was on his knees with clothing disarranged, hands uncovered and frostbitten, and a wild look in his eyes... He showed every sign of complete collapse... we got him into the tent quite comatose. He died quietly at 12.30 a.m.

March 2, 1912. Titus Oates disclosed his feet, the toes showing very bad indeed, evidently bitten by the late temperatures.

March 3, 1912. [The crystalline snow causes] impossible friction on the runners [of the sledges]. God help us, we can't keep up this pulling, that is certain. Amongst ourselves we are unendingly cheerful, but what each man feels in his heart I can only guess.

March 4, 1912. For the moment the temperature is on the -20° – an improvement which makes us more comfortable, but a colder snap is bound to come soon. I fear that Oates at least will weather such an event very poorly.

March 6, 1912. Poor Oates is unable to pull, sits on the sledge when we are track-searching – he is wonderfully plucky, as his feet must be giving him great pain. He makes no complaint, but his spirits only come up in spurts now and he grows more silent in the tent.

March 11, 1912. Titus Oates is very near the end, one feels. What we or he will do, God only knows. We discussed the matter after breakfast; he is a brave fine fellow and understands the situation, but he practically asked for advice. Nothing could be said but to urge him to march as long as he could. One satisfactory result to the discussion; I practically ordered Wilson to hand over the means of ending our troubles to us, so that anyone of us may know how to do so. Wilson had no choice between doing so and ransacking our medicine case. We have 30 opium tabloids apiece, and he is left with a tube of morphine.

March 16 or 17, 1912. Lost track of dates, but think the last correct... Should this be found I want these facts recorded. Oates last thoughts were of his Mother... He was a brave soul. This was the end. He slept through the night before last, hoping not to wake; but he woke in the morning yesterday. It was blowing a blizzard. He said, 'I am just going outside and may be some time.' He went out into the blizzard and we have not seen him since.

March 22 and 23, 1912. Blizzard bad as ever – Wilson and Bowers unable to start – tomorrow last chance – no fuel and only one or two of food left – must be near the end. Have decided it shall be natural – we shall march for the depot with or without our effects and die in our tracks.

March 29, 1912. Since the 21st we have had a continuous gale from WSW and SW. We had fuel to make two cups of tea apiece and bare food for two days on the 20th. Every day we have been ready to start for our depot 11 miles away, but outside the door of the tent it remains a scene of whirling drift. I do not think we can hope for any better things now. We shall stick it out to the end, but we are getting weaker, of course, and the end cannot be far.

It seems a pity, but I do not think I can write any more.

R. Scott.

For God's sake look after our people.

Tryggve records his thoughts in his diary: 'When I saw those three poor souls the other day, I just felt that I envied them. They died having done something great. How hard death must be for those who meet it having done nothing.'

A few hours later, with the sun shining down on them, the search team are standing around the tent to give their respects to their dead colleagues. Somebody removes the poles of the tent and the canvas falls on top of the three bodies inside. The men watch this icy burial with their heads bare even though the thermometer is reading -20°F. Tryggve records that 'We built a cairn fifteen feet high, and on top of that we put a cross made with a pair of skis. They were my skis, because I had taken charge of Scott's skis.' These skis had been to the South Pole with Scott, and now they were on Tryggve Gran's feet. He explains why, '*I wanted them to do the trip back again.*'

12. TRYGGVE GRAN FLIES THE NORTH SEA

1913

When Tryggve Gran arrived in New Zealand, his Antarctic adventures over, he decided to return home using passenger ships, because these will get him back quicker than the *Terra Nova*. And now, for the last leg of his journey, he is crossing the Atlantic from New York to Britain on the ocean liner *Lusitania*. Here, he makes the acquaintance of Robert Lorraine, a stage actor and flying enthusiast. Lorraine already has a flying first to his name, when, in September 1910, he flew across the Irish Sea in a flight recorded as the first made from England to Ireland, albeit the plane flopped down in the sea 200 feet from the shore. The achievement is recognised in the record books anyway - it would have been mean-spirited not to.

The chance meeting ushers in a new phase in Tryggve's life. As they chat on the promenade deck, Lorraine tells him, 'I think you ought to take on flying. It must be a damn sight easier to fly than to do all those things on ice.'

'Why not?' Tryggve thinks to himself.

Lorraine tells his new friend that the next big thing in aviation will be a flight across the North Sea. 'And wouldn't it be appropriate for a Norwegian to do that?'

Once the North Sea crossing is in the bag, the Atlantic must surely follow. Whoever makes that first flight over the Atlantic Ocean will be famous.

Tryggve is inspired, deciding then and there that he will be the first aviator to cross the North Sea in an aeroplane. Such a feat would put his name in the headlines, as had happened to Louis Blériot when he flew across the English Channel in 1909. For his efforts, Blériot had won a £1,000 prize from the *Daily Mail* (equivalent to £130,000 today). Tryggve anticipates that should he fly across the North Sea, he will readily attract sufficient funds to make the Atlantic crossing his next target.

Nevertheless, there is one problem with his plans: Tryggve Gran has never seen an aeroplane, never mind that he does not know how to fly one - ski jumping is as close as he has got to flying.

Not long after arriving in Britain, Tryggve meets a Royal Navy officer whose son is a pilot. With a bit of persuasion, he is taken on his first flying trip - one that ends abruptly. The aircraft overturns on landing, leaving Tryggve upside down in his seat. Undeterred by this rude introduction to the hazards of flight, Tryggve now takes lessons at the flying school in Hendon, North West London.

At about this time, the explorer Ernest Shackleton contacts him and asks Tryggve to go with him on his next Antarctic expedition, the aim of which is to make the first land crossing of the southern continent. Shackleton has heard about Tryggve's interest in airplanes, and would like to investigate the feasibility of using them on his expedition. Tryggve does not commit to anything, because his first priority is to make his North Sea flight.

Shackleton's expedition will later become famous for all the wrong reasons. His ship, the *Endurance*, sank in the Weddell Sea leaving twenty-eight men stranded on the pack ice. They eventually reached a rocky island called Elephant Island. Leaving the rest of his men there, Shackleton left with a crew of five in a seven-metre long lifeboat, his intention to get help from a whaling station on the South Atlantic island of South Georgia. After an epic 800-mile journey, they landed on the wrong side of the island, and then made an equally epic journey across mountainous terrain to react the whaling station. All the men were eventually rescued.

1914

Tryggve Gran is taking lessons at the Blériot flying school in Buc, located south-west of Paris and close to Versailles. Here he will gain flying experience with Blériot aircraft.

It is at Buc in June 1914 that Tryggve joins the small list of flyers who have looped the loop; a manoeuvre which starts with the pilot pointing the nose of the aircraft up, and then arching the plane backwards to perform a circle in the air. This is spectacular to see from the ground because at the top of the circle the plane is flying upside down. But watch out should you do this - the wooden boxwork on these early aircraft is known to fail under stress. No matter, this young Norwegian is fearless, bordering on reckless.

Such aerobatic tricks are a novelty in 1914, and provided highlights for a review of the previous year's events in the New Year issue of *Aeroplane* magazine:

March 1913: About the middle of the month M. Chevillard arrived at Hendon from France and proceeded to frighten

175

everybody by his extraordinary trick of turning his Henry Farman biplane on one side and doing half a 'cart-wheel' till quite near the ground. This was really the beginning of the trick flying which culminated in various aviators looping the loop.

September 1913: Abroad, M. Pégoud flew upside down for the first time deliberately, on the 14th, and he looped the loop on the 20th.

Adolphe Pégoud's inspiration for his aerobatic feat came the month before when he took a parachute jump from a plane - one of the earliest recorded. The plane was left pilotless after he jumped out. While descending at the end of his parachute, Pégoud watched with amazement as the out-of-control aircraft made swooping dives and ascents around the sky, before looping the loop all by itself.

Tryggve's loop-the-loop manoeuvre in France has been noticed by the flying world. The Hall Aviation School in Hendon mentions him in their magazine adverts as former pupil 'T. Gran of looping fame'.

Having learned to fly, the Norwegian now needs an aircraft. He buys one from Louis Blériot, who is a big manufacturer. The Blériot XI-2 monoplane had been set aside for the Mexican Government but is offered to Tryggve instead. He hands over 13,000 Francs, half the sale price, which suggests that some hard bargaining had taken place; that, and Blériot probably considered Tryggve Gran's future activities to be good publicity for his aircraft.

The Blériot XI-2 aircraft is a newer version of the plane that crossed the English Channel in 1909, and it will be shipped over to England to be fitted with the latest 7-cylinder Gnome star engine. Revved up to 80 horsepower, the modified aircraft can achieve a cruising speed of 75 miles per hour.

The newly acquired aircraft is given a name, *Ca Flotte* – French for 'it floats', the suggestion of Tryggve's friend Miss Grete Sømme. She gives Tryggve a teddy bear as a lucky mascot for his North Sea crossing.

Following the installation of the engine in the Blériot XI-2, the next step is to get the aircraft from England to Scotland. The wings are removed and boxed up with the rest of the aircraft inside a huge oblong crate. This arrives by ship at Leith, where it is held up because there is no railway wagon large enough to transport it by rail to Aberdeen. As

176

yet, no alternative method of transport has been decided on, so the crate stays in Leith.

July 17, 1914

Tryggve Gran has been in Aberdeenshire for just over two weeks while waiting for his boxed-up aircraft to arrive. He occupies his time with long walks, playing golf, and roaring along the local roads on a motor cycle. He also swims in the sea fully clothed, because this will give him an indication of what to expect should he have to ditch his plane.

Finally, something happens. Yesterday, the large crate was put on board a steamer from Leith, and it arrived today in the city of Aberdeen where Tryggve has gone to get it. He watches as the crate is loaded onto a steam lorry at the docks. And from there, he accompanies the driver on the road north, an anxious journey. His heart skips a beat with every jolt of the lorry as it trundles over the twenty-three miles of bumpy road to Cruden Bay. He fervently hopes that his aircraft will survive the journey without damage.

Cruden Bay has been picked as the departure point because it is only six miles from the most easterly point of the Scottish mainland, As such, it lies close to one end of the shortest line of flight between Scotland and Norway, 285 miles in all.

The village's other claim to fame is that Bram Stoker wrote the early chapters of *Dracula* here while on his summer holiday in 1895, and probably completed the novel when he returned to Aberdeenshire in 1896. Nearby Slains Castle, the seat of the Earl of Erroll, provided part of the floor plan for Castle Dracula. The earl and his family have since moved to England, and are now renting the castle out to wealthy summer visitors.

The lorry arrives at the magnificent Cruden Bay Hotel where Tryggve Gran will be staying. The 55-room hotel, built out of salmon-pink granite, was completed in 1899. It resembles a palace, and deliberately so, because its clientele are the society elite of Britain. They are here to enjoy the outdoor activities provided, such as the magnificent links golf course laid out on the strip of land between the hotel and the beach.

Wasting no time in unpacking the aircraft, two French mechanics put it together under the watchful eye of representatives from both the Blériot and the Gnome Engine Company. Then the engine is run for a while without any problems experienced.

177

Because Tryggve knows that the most common reason for aircraft failure happens when the engine packs in shortly after takeoff, arrangements have been made with James Cruickshank, owner of the nearby Kilmarnock Arms Hotel, to put his motor launch on stand-by on departure day. It will be kept at a distance of one and a half to miles from the shore.

Tryggve Gran is frantic to get going. However, the weather is unfavourable at the moment - a strong breeze blows from the east, which is against his intended flight path.

The locals here in Aberdeenshire are hugely excited and are experiencing airplane mania. A rumour goes around the village today that Tryggve's aircraft had taken off, bringing a large crowd rushing out from their houses to witness the event. Alas, no. Binoculars reveal a large kite fluttering from the roof of nearby Slains Castle, which someone had mistaken for the plane.

July 18, 1914

Tryggve Gran would like to set off today, but is hampered in his ambition by both fog and a strong easterly breeze blowing across the Aberdeenshire coast. Not all is ready yet anyway: some final adjustments to the plane's wings are required and his compass requires checking out. The large crowd gathered to see the takeoff are hugely disappointed.

The unfavourable weather will continue for several days to come.

July 23, 1914

Tryggve Gran gets out of bed and from his hotel window scans the horizon of the sea with his binoculars. A clear day with the wind blowing north-west – it is time to get going. But then, ever-so-annoyingly, the wind veers round and now blows to the west. Caution beckons; he will wait for a weather forecast from Norway to confirm that it is still favourable to set off.

He is taking lunch at the hotel when the coastguard arrives with the wireless report - not good. A freshening wind off the Norway coast is likely to bring on rain showers later. This is so frustrating for the young aviator.

While waiting for the weather to improve, Tryggve looks for a suitable field of grass flat enough to take off from; a task that proves surprisingly difficult. He looks everywhere, but there is always an obstacle of some sort or other, whether stone walls, fences, ditches, or

178

fields covered in crops. The one and a half mile long Cruden Bay beach would have sufficed; however, there is no suitable road to get to it through the long line of fringing high dunes.

A young Australian woman, Inez Currie, meets Tryggve Gran at about this time while on a golfing and bathing holiday in Cruden Bay. While she is there, a cameramen arrives to record film footage of Gran's preparations. It will be used for a newsreel to be shown at an Aberdeen cinema. Inez Currie is asked to join another girl in presenting Tryggve with British and Norwegian flags while the movie camera rolls (the cameraman never kept a copy, and the film is not known to have survived).

For his takeoff, Gran eventually picks a long gently sloping grass field next to the laundry building of the Cruden Bay Hotel. He tries it out and taxies up and down several times before deciding that this field will do. It is not ideal however; an obstacle lies just beyond the end of the field. This is the electrified overhead wires for the trams that carry hotel guests the half of a mile to and from Cruden Bay Railway Station. The copper wires suspended from ornate green wrought iron pillars stretch across his intended takeoff path and are powered to 600 volts. They must be cleared following takeoff, because you would not want to collide with a live electric line while flying a plane laden with enough fuel to get to Norway. *No, not at all.*

Years later, in 1971, when the journalist Gordon Casely drove Tryggve Gran from Aberdeen to Cruden Bay for a commemoration ceremony, the Norwegian kept shouting out during the journey, 'there's a field I could have used!' or 'that flat place, there, is where I could have taken off from!'

July 27, 1914

Tryggve goes to the village post office to send a telegraph to Ernest Shackleton confirming that he will not be going on his Antarctic expedition. That is leaving it very late to tell him, because Shackleton's ship *Endurance* will set sail from London in five days time. While he is in the post office, Tryggve is startled to read a public notice announcing that Britain has decided to shut its airspace to civilian flights at 6 p.m. on July 30, because a war in Europe is looking likely. And should war start before he gets the chance to take off, it could be years before an opportunity to fly across the North Sea presents itself again.

July 30, 1914

Tryggve had previously asked contacts in the British Admiralty, the German Navy, and the Norwegian Navy to send him weather reports for the North Sea. This service has now been withdrawn. All three organisations have other things to worry about on account that Austria declared war on Serbia two days ago in response to the assassination of Archduke Franz Ferdinand of Austria. Tensions have been rising alarmingly ever since (the Austrian declaration on July 28 is now accepted as the start of World War I).

A workaround is arranged to get weather information. A Government wireless station in Aberdeen has been asked to send out a message requesting any ships in the North Sea to radio back with a weather report. Replies come from a German fishing boat and a Liverpool steamship, both advising that the weather over the North Sea is perfect.

So at 9 a.m. with the sun shining on the Aberdeenshire coast, a calm sea, and a slight breeze, Tryggve Gran prepares for takeoff from the grass field next to the laundry house. He wears a close-fitting leather flying helmet with straps for fastening under the chin. His clothes for the flight are a leather jacket, shirt, a thin jersey, blue trousers, and white tennis shoes. With hindsight, because it will be much colder during the flight than he probably anticipated, he should have worn warmer clothes. However, this would have added to the weight carried by the aircraft, and his preference had been to keep this as low as possible.

The navigation equipment to be used for his flight comprises two compasses, one for use, one for backup, a map of the North Sea, and an aneroid barometer on a chain round his neck to indicate flying height. Also around his neck is a waterproof bag containing a copy of the *Daily Mail* and a letter from the newspaper's proprietor, Lord Northcliff. Northcliff has told Tryggve to deliver these in person to Queen Maud of Norway once he arrives at the other end; that's because Lord Northcliff would like to boast that the *Daily Mail* is the first newspaper to have been delivered by air to another country.

Essential supplies are kept in his pocket: a bottle containing a mixture of coffee and brandy, chocolate, and some biscuits. Tryggve might need these should he have to ditch far out to sea where it is unlikely that he will be rescued too soon. And just in case, he had eaten a big breakfast in the hotel this morning.

He will perch a notebook on his knee, intending to use it as a diary during the flight. Tryggve Gran is an obsessive diary writer – it was said of him in the Antarctic that he kept five diaries on the go at any one time. The diary will provide the basis for a book.

Last of all, the teddy-bear mascot, given to him by Grete Sømme, and a small red-painted figure of the Devil are arranged around the cockpit rim. The teddy bear is placed behind and the Devil in front where Tryggve can see him. 'Best to have him in front,' he thinks.

The plane is fully loaded with 55 gallons of petrol, enough for seven hour's flying, although the trip is only expected to take between five and six hours (Tryggve anticipates eating breakfast in Scotland and lunch in Norway). This is more fuel than normal for the aircraft and modifications have been made to allow the extra amount to be carried. The seat in the passenger cockpit behind the pilot has been removed and six extra copper fuel tanks fitted in its place. Also squeezed in are three flotation cushions made from parachute cloth, intended to keep the plane afloat should it have to ditch. Once the weight of the equipment brought on board is added in, the plane is significantly heavier than it would be for a routine flight.

Tryggve makes a thorough inspection of the aircraft, and then climbs into the cockpit, jamming himself into the tight-fitting space. Six men hold down the plane while the engine is started – a necessary precaution because the aircraft is not fitted with brakes. Once the engine starts revving at full speed, Tryggve signals the men to let go of the plane.

Watching all this from the nearby golf course is local man Sandy Cruickshank, who works as a caddy carrying bags for the golfers. Years later, he told the journalist Gordon Casely what happened next: 'The undercarriage was like pram wheels and they bounced up and down as he raced down the grass.'

The recent warm weather and the overnight rain had made the grass in the field grow higher than it had been the day before and it is still wet from the morning dew, all of which has led to more drag exerted on the wheels than anticipated. Disaster now looms, because the aircraft has hardly achieved any lift at all, and is now heading straight towards the electrified tram wires strung out across its path.

Tryggve Gran mutters a prayer, 'asking the good Lord to help me', and yanks at the control stick. The plane 'hedge-hops' over the wire and comes down on the other side just short of the ground. With another sharp tug, the plane curves up into the air.

181

The aircraft circles the hotel at 60 metres above the ground before heading out over the North Sea near the Bullers of Buchan. Twenty miles out to sea, Tryggve flies into a long bank of dense sea fog drifting the way he is going. That, and because his compass is playing up, he decides to turn back. He returns to the coast forty minutes after takeoff, and looking down, judges the sands of Cruden Bay beach to be flat enough to land on.

Sandy Cruickshank, who is still on the golf course, watches the aircraft as it makes a spiral descent. It lands at the southern end of the beach opposite a hill called the Hawklaw, and whizzes along the strand towards the rocks at the far end. Therein lies a problem because the aeroplane has no brakes. Thinking quickly, Tryggve steers into the sea - the seawater will dampen the plane's momentum. That works, but now a new problem arises. The aircraft must be dragged out of the sea before the waves soak the engine. This is a matter of extreme urgency because a wet engine will not start until it dries out, and there is no time to waste: British airspace will be shut to civilian flying after 6 o'clock tonight. Six boys help him to drag the plane back on the beach.

Will the weather conditions be better in the afternoon? More reports come into the Aberdeen wireless station from ships in the North Sea, and are forwarded to Cruden Bay – the fog has lifted out to sea and the wind has died down.

So, Tryggve Gran steels himself to have another go. A small crowd has gathered on the beach to see him leave, including the then-famous opera singer, Dame Clara Butt, who is renting Slains Castle for the summer. A little girl fastens a Scottish thistle onto the cockpit next to the red devil figurine, and everyone wishes him well for the journey.

Several photographs capture the scene on the beach. The aircraft looks light and flimsy - Tryggve Gran later described it as 'an affair of bicycle wheels and piano wire'. The fuselage and wings are built from a framework of wood covered in fabric reinforced with wire. At eight metres in length from propeller to tail, and with a wingspan of just over nine metres, this flying machine will be a plaything for the wind. And the 80 horsepower engine intended to get the plane to Norway is the equivalent today of the engine on a moderately powerful motorbike.

The cockpit is open to the air and has no windshield to protect the flier from the driving wind and rain. You might be happy enough to take this plane for a jolly jaunt over the countryside on a summer's day, but certainly not across 285 miles of open sea at a time when the weather has proved so changeable.

Tryggve Gran's flight to Norway could thus be described as close to reckless, yes. But then again, he is also demonstrating genuine bravery. *Our aviator knows only too well from his Antarctic experience that heroes can die too.*

The Norwegian fixes his compass, shakes hands with the dozen or so onlookers on the beach, and climbs into the cockpit. At 1 p.m., he sets off for a second time, hurtling down the beach for 200 metres before reaching take-off speed. The plane climbs over Port Erroll harbour, turns a little, and then clears the roof of Slains Castle. Tryggve follows the coast for three miles to the north while climbing to a height of somewhere between 180 and 250 metres above the ground. And now he turns away from land and points the nose of the plane in the direction of Norway.

As he flies over the open sea, he reassures himself with the thought that there are plenty of steamship routes between Peterhead and Stavanger, and should he land in the sea the chances are that he will be picked up within a few hours.

The wind is gusting up here, and all that buffeting makes Tryggve queasy. To add to his discomfort, he finds that at his flying altitude of 500 metres over the sea, sometimes higher, it is bitterly cold.

To add to his problems, navigation is proving a tricky affair despite the compass on hand. Following his compass would have done the job had he been able to keep a steady course. But because the craft is so flimsy and the winds are knocking it about, steering in a straight line is difficult in practice. Tryggve is aware that he must take wind drift into account while steering - a wind that is fresh and blowing to the north-west. With his experience onboard ships, he has learnt how to estimate wind strength and direction from the height and motion of the waves on the sea. That information is crucial and is used to double check his compass readings. The initial bearing for his route from Cruden Bay to Norway had been 67°N. Should he have drifted unknowingly onto a flight path bearing 80°N this would take him past the southernmost point of Norway without seeing it. The next landfall would then be Denmark, and he does not have enough fuel to get there.

A man of faith, Gran later said he prayed three times during the flight. The first time when he took off with a full load of fuel and nearly collided with the electric tram wire, and the third time on landing in Norway. That second occasion now arrives when miles out over the North Sea, the plane's engine suddenly cuts out. He had forgotten to pump up the pressure on the reserve fuel tanks, 'but in a plunge down towards the sea he got the engine running again and flattened [out] thirty metres above the waves'. The prayers followed this lucky escape once his plane started climbing again.

Three hours into the flight, he passes through a bank of thick fog and then another fifteen minutes later. This is alarming. If he is disorientated while flying in the fog, he could easily crash into the sea. To add to his problems, the buffeting by the wind makes him air sick. He is suffering from what a modern airline passenger would experience as turbulence – scary enough in a big jet aircraft, but much more terrifying in this flimsy wood and fabric flying machine. He also notices that his petrol supplies are getting low. According to the weekly magazine *Aeroplane* in its edition for August 15, 1914, it is at this point during the flight that the Norwegian aviator started feeling the '*extreme anxiety*' that affected him for the remaining hour of the flight.

To get above the low-lying cloud, Tryggve points the nose of the aircraft up, and climbs to 1,800 metres. He now flies out into glorious sunshine, and not only that, looking ahead of him, he catches a glimpse of the snow-capped mountains on the coast of Norway.

'Hurrah, hurrah' he thinks, and an irrational desire comes over him to celebrate by looping the loop - although this crazy notion quickly passes. So, he now knows that Norway is up ahead. He alters his course a touch, and switching off the engine to save fuel, glides down to a height of 180 metres above the sea.

On approaching the Norwegian coastline, now clearly visible below him, he sees that his choice of a landing spot is limited to a sandy beach along one side of a lake (Lake Orrevatnet, fourteen miles south-west of Stavanger). This patch of sand reminds him of Cruden Bay beach. He adjusts his course to align his aircraft for a landing.

Two boys bathing in the lake spot the aircraft and are alarmed by his approach, believing the aircraft to be the Devil swooping down from the skies. They flee in panic. Tryggve also spots the boys, and assumes they ran because he represents the coming of the war - a death-dealing fighter plane coming their way.

The boys have gone to tell their father Laurits Reve, who is in the farmhouse nearby. Laurits already knows about Tryggve Gran's plan to fly across the North Sea, guessing that this is he. Tryggve lands, having taken four hours and ten minutes for the flight, climbs out of the cockpit, and walks to the farmhouse. The farmer welcomes him with the words, 'you must have been frozen in that thing, come in and have a drink.'

Tryggve asks to use his telephone. He wants to get telegrams sent out: first of all to his mother, then to King Haakon of Norway, and to the *Daily Mail*. He also sends a telegram to his helpers back in Cruden Bay, announcing his safe arrival with the words: 'Perfect landing, horrid crossing, all right'.

He is then driven twenty miles north to the town of Stavanger: his mission is to deliver the copy of the *Daily Mail* to King Haakon and Queen Maud in Christiania (Oslo).

Tryggve Gran has now become a celebrity in his native Norway. He has achieved a new record too: the longest continuous flight out of sight of land. When he leaves Stavanger by night steamer en route to Christiania, 10,000 people are gathered on the quay to cheer him on.

The *Daily Mail* led the next day with a splash on his flight, although the headlines in every other newspaper are dominated by the slide into war. And despite having a reporter in Cruden Bay, *Aeroplane* magazine only provides space for a single paragraph on the North Sea crossing: discussions about the role of the aeroplane in the new war having taken over most of its pages.

Tryggve Gran has picked exactly the wrong moment for his achievement to get much in the way of publicity, yet he can be proud about his feat. With great skill, he has flown his craft across the North Sea, and most impressive of all, he has landed his craft where he said he would, an extraordinary feat of navigation.

In 1967, Tryggve returned to Cruden Bay, when he made a telling and somewhat modest comment during a talk in the parish church. 'I am only half a pioneer,' he told his audience, 'the real pioneers were men like Louis Blériot who had built their own planes and taught themselves how to fly.'

Perhaps; but then again there was plenty of scope for heroes of every sort during the early years of aviation.

13. TRYGGVE GRAN GOES TO WAR

1914

Four days after the North Sea flight, the Norwegian Government buys Tryggve Gran's Bleriot XI-2 aircraft for their air force. With armies mobilising in Europe for war it might be needed, even though Norway has declared itself neutral. Tryggve is made a first lieutenant of the Norwegian Air Force, and asked to fly up and down the Norwegian coast in the Bleriot XI-2 - his task to look for any foreign submarines lurking in the fjords. Not that he finds any – just the occasional fishing boat. It is tedious work for an adventurous soul, especially when the war offers so much potential for action on a grand scale. His chief mechanic, sensing the young man's restlessness, reckons Tryggve will not be happy until he is in 'the thick of it'. First Lieutenant Gran heartedly agrees.

1916

Two years later, Gran contacts the Norwegian Minister of Defence with a request to be seconded to the Royal Flying Corps in Britain. He would like to gain expertise in night flying with them.

Night flying is now at the forefront of military strategy because Germany is waging a new type of warfare over Britain: namely, the aerial bombing of the nation's cities, infrastructure, factories, and military installations. The Germans send across Zeppelins, giant balloons the size of ocean liners, to carry out bombing raids at night. Every now and again, bomber aeroplanes are used, although Zeppelin raids will predominate in the early years of the war. The British counter these night raids with searchlights and anti-aircraft guns located in strategic positions on the ground, although they are not that effective as yet.

The Royal Flying Corps have also set up home-based flight groups of fighter aircraft tasked with defending British skies against the Zeppelins. A long learning curve ensues for the British as they gradually work out the best way for a fighter aircraft to attack and destroy Zeppelins at night.

It is not even clear from the start that an aircraft can safely fly at night. Eventually it is found that night flying is achievable should it not be too cloudy – that's not the problem. The most hazardous aspect of night flying is landing in the dark; less so, when the landing strips are lit up by paraffin lights or flares and are clearly delineated.

Yet, it is extraordinary difficult for an aircraft to find and bring down a Zeppelin. Although the Zeppelins are huge, they are hard to spot at night unless picked out by a searchlight beam, which is a rare event.

There is much discussion within military command about how a plane should attack a Zeppelin. The senior officers stick to the belief that bombing a Zeppelin from above is the most effective procedure, although this is difficult to achieve in practice. The low-powered fighter aircraft struggle to reach the high altitudes the Zeppelins fly at, let alone get above them.

The solution is discovered in combat. On the night of September 3, 1916, William Leefe Robinson flying a B.E.2 aircraft is tracking a German airship on a bombing raid over North London. He approaches the airship, letting loose a round of incendiary bullets along its belly from head to tail, but with no effect. He reloads his gun, and this time strafes one side of the monster balloon, which also has no effect. Loading his third drum of incendiary bullets, he flies to a level 150 metres below the airship, and attacking upwards, concentrates his fire on a single spot under its rear. The bullets tear open a large gash in the airship's fabric, allowing air to mix with the hydrogen gas inside. The incendiary bullets then ignite the explosive hydrogen and air mixture.

No sooner has Robinson stopped firing, than a red glow appears inside the hull, and seconds later the entire back end of the giant balloon is shrouded in flames. Robinson hastily flies out of the way, as the humungous airship transforms into a second sun. It roars like a furnace and lights up the sky, the clouds below glowing pink. The incandescent mass then falls to the ground from a height of 3,700 metres in a huge fiery sheet, which is visible for forty miles around.

Exhibiting sheer exuberance at his feat, the airman fires his signal flares into the air and also drops a lighted parachute flare below. He, William Leefe Robinson, has just discovered how to shoot down a Zeppelin (from now on, five more German airships will be shot down this way by British aircraft before the end of 1916).

Two days after his heroics, Robinson is awarded the Victoria Cross by the King at Windsor Castle. He will also be given the £3,500 in prize money, which was to be awarded to the first airman to bring down an enemy airship over home soil.

Now, all of a sudden, highly vulnerable to attack, the Zeppelin raids wind down in intensity, and the next phase of the air war over Britain sees the Germans sending in fleets of bomber aircraft in their place.

The British are slowly discovering how to defend their country against bombers at night using fighter aircraft, and Tryggve Gran wants to know more (and he is probably in a state of great agitation to get the chance to shoot down a Zeppelin while they are still coming over). His request to be seconded to the Royal Flying Corps is granted, and on October 26, 1916, the Norwegian is told to report to the War Office in London.

There now arises the awkward business of what he should wear on duty – civilian clothes will cause problems; that, and his foreign accent will inevitably excite suspicion should he visit an airfield where he is not known. He is asked to wear a British captain's uniform and to assume the name Teddy Grant, a Canadian by nationality. You cannot be too careful: the German spy network is very active these days, and it would be best if they do not find out that a Norwegian is working with the British military.

On November 7, Tryggve Gran, alias Teddy Grant, reports to Major Moores of the 11th Air Squadron at Northolt, twelve miles west of London. His primary mission is to train advanced pupils at the base, although he will also be allowed to get experience in night flying.

First, he will have to pick up his new aircraft from the Royal Aircraft Factory in Farnborough, 30 miles to the south west of the base. By the time he gets there and takes control of his plane, it is late in the afternoon on November 20, and twilight is setting in. No matter, Tryggve will fly the aircraft back anyway. Half an hour after take-off, it starts to snow and hail. From now on, he is flying 'blind' with only his instruments to help him. He decides to turn off the engine and drift down to see where he is, discovering to his great surprise he is flying over London. Turning west in the hope of reaching Northolt, he flies beyond the outskirts of London, only to notice through the gloom that the entire countryside is flooded. He is also totally lost. Eventually landing on a field, which appeared dry enough compared to the others, the plane trundles along the ground in the darkness before coming to an abrupt halt when it hits a bank of mud - a humiliating start to Tryggve's night-flying ambitions.

Five days later, Tryggve takes the official test to qualify as a night pilot - everything proceeding without mishap this time. Having flown the entire night, the next day he is informed that he passed the test and is now entitled to wear night-flying proficiency badges on his uniform.

The day after, he is transferred to the 37th Squadron at Rochford, and assigned a B. E. 12 fighter plane. The following morning, November 27, 1916, he takes off for a spot of practice shooting at a target in the River Thames. And that evening, the pilots from the base go on a night out to the Westcliffe Hotel in nearby Southend, where they enjoy a spot of dancing. Then the alarm bell rings. The night fliers amongst them, including Tryggve Gran, rush to the aerodrome in a car driven at top speed. They will wait there for further instructions.

At 11.30 p.m., numerous telephone calls to the base are passing on reports of Zeppelin sightings over England, and the pilots are told to ready for action. A telegram arrives from headquarters confirming that Zeppelins are here - one was shot down near Hartlepool.

This is now Tryggve's chance to do his bit in the war. However, it was not to be - no call was ever made that night for the pilots to take off. He is informed why the next day: an 'enemy flier' had arrived over London, and dropped bombs in the area around Victoria Station at 11.30 p.m., the time the base was readied for action. However, the decision was then taken that there had been no point in dispatching the night fliers, because by the time they had taken off and arrived over London, the enemy intruder would most likely have been half-way home.

1917

In March 1917, someone in Norway discovers that Tryggve Gran, a Norwegian officer attached to the British for training purposes, has been wearing a uniform in a foreign country, contrary to Norwegian military regulations. The offence is aggravated because the uniform is that of a British captain. Tryggve is thus ordered to resign his commission from the Norwegian Air Force.

He is happy to do so, because he is keen to fight on the Western Front, and this is not possible for a Norwegian officer whose country is neutral in the war. Tryggve sends in his resignation via the Norwegian Embassy in London, which is accepted. A week later, he joins the Royal Flying Corps where he is commisioned as a captain. By doing so, he has honoured a promise he once made to Captain Oates and Henry Bowers while in the Antarctic that he would fight for the British should a war start with Germany.

189

Tryggve witnesses the war at first-hand in April 1917 when he volunteers to transfer a night-flying aircraft from Britain to St Omer in Northern France - it will be used to drop special agents behind enemy lines. While he is out there, he takes a day tour to see what is going on down below. Flying out of the clouds, Belgium comes into view: Ypres is on his right, and below him is the Yser Canal, 'where hundreds and thousands of small flashes seemed to be running up and down both sides of the waterway'. Having delivered the aircraft, Tryggve returns home to Britain.

His first action with the Royal Flying Corps arrives on the morning of May 24, 1917. Six Zeppelins are approaching Britain for a bombing raid on London, although they could not have picked a worse night for it. A gale is blowing and the rain falls in torrents. The Zeppelins lose their way, arriving over the Suffolk coast many miles north of their objective. They drop their bombs anyway, causing only minor damage.

Tryggve Gran is on duty at the North Weald aerodrome to the north of London when the alarm is sounded. Despite the atrocious weather, and against all advice, he takes off in his B. E. 12 aircraft. *Nothing will hold him back.*

He soon discovers that night flying in a raging storm is a very silly idea. Totally disorientated and with his aircraft thrown about by the rain and hail, he comes to realise he is flying upside down. He knows this because he can see the flares of the airfield landing strip above the plane and not beneath it where it ought to be. Putting the plane into a half-roll, he gets upright again. Tryggve now flies through the murk using his compass and his control instruments to guide him, an alarming experience, described as seemingly taking years. He will not see a Zeppelin tonight or much else besides.

Spending two hours 'going backwards and forwards', he hopes to catch sight of the aerodrome at North Weald. Then the engine stops. His aircraft glides down through thick cloud; whither it is going he has no idea. Eventually, he descends below the clouds, and, with the breaking light of dawn, spots a field of grass he can land on. Once down, he gets out of the aircraft and walks to a nearby road.

Stopping a passing car, he asks the driver, 'Where is the nearest town?'

'Hull', he is told. Hull is 140 miles north of his home base.

After much trouble, he starts the engine and takes off. Because daylight has arrived, he has no problem getting back to the aerodrome, where he receives an ecstatic welcome. No one had expected to see him back in one piece.

Will Tryggve ever face an enemy aircraft in action? His frustrating experiences are typical for a home defence airman – the enemy is hard to pin down. One British pilot had been less fortunate than Tryggve Gran that night. Still missing, it is believed he chased a Zeppelin out beyond the coast and on returning home against gale-force winds, he ran out of fuel, and was forced to ditch in a stormy sea.

On June 13, 1917, Tryggve finally makes contact with the enemy. A daylight-bombing raid by a fleet of German bomber aircraft called Gothas is under way. Fourteen Gothas fly over London and drop 126 bombs on the capital. They fall on the East End of London, the London docks, and around Liverpool Street Station. Sixteen infant children are killed when a fifty kilogram bomb lands on Upper North Street School in Poplar; two more will die later in hospital. Altogether, 162 people are killed and 432 injured in what will turn out to be the deadliest bombing raid on Britain during World War I. The public are outraged, and in response to the anger, the British Royal Family wisely changes their surname from Saxe-Coburg-Gotha to Windsor.

Tryggve wrote a report of the day's events for his commanding officer: Following a spot of shooting practice in his B. E. 12 warplane, an aircraft armed with three guns and nicknamed 'The Fortified Terror', he is flying over Sutton's Farm Air Base when he notices it is displaying ground signals for an enemy air attack under way. He looks around him, and spots dark dots of smoke to the south – these are the airbursts of shells fired at enemy aircraft.

Promptly flying in this direction, Tryggve climbs to 3,300 metres. When he approaches the town of Maidstone, south-east of London, he sees two British fighters attacking an enemy aircraft. He attempts to cut the German bomber off as it flees from the fighters, but is unable to follow through with an attack because the sun is in his eyes. The bomber saves itself by disappearing into the haze.

Next up, Tryggve climbs above the mist to 3,700 metres, and in clear sunshine sees six German bombers near Southend to the north of him. Tryggve flies to intercept, but then loses sight of them. From there, he crosses the Thames Estuary, and is flying over Colchester when he spots four more aeroplanes in the distance and to the south-east of his position. He believes these to be British, but when the airbursts of anti-aircraft shells appear around them, the aircraft are marked out as German bombers.

191

'The Fortified Terror' now flies up behind the Germans and, coming in from the direction of the sun, Tryggve fires his guns at the rearmost bomber from a position 150 metres below and a 100 metres behind. He claims to have hit the rear-gunner in his cockpit behind the tailplane, who then fell over his gun. The German aircraft veers to the left, and disappears under him, lost to sight.

He wrote in his report that bullets fired by the German planes hit his engine leaving it ailing (the official report differs at this point, stating that an anti-aircraft shell burst close to his aircraft, damaging it to the extent that it started vibrating 'alarmingly'). He is now forced to land at the nearby airbase at Rochford, just north of Southend.

The following month, Tryggve's squadron is ordered to Hainault Farm to the north east of London. A new squadron, the 44th, is to be based here and will fly Sopwith Camel aircraft.

While there, Tryggve's daredevil attitude almost gets him killed. He flies out from Hainault accompanied by another aircraft, and the two of them give a display of aerobatics to their friends down below in London. The two aircraft loop the loop, fly upside down, and perform spins for their audience on the ground.

The planes fly back to Hainault. The two pilots, exhilarated by their antics, repeat the show above Hainault aerodrome for the airman watching below. Tryggve unwisely attempts a rolling spin, which causes his plane to dive downwards at great speed. At 300 metres above the ground, he attempts to pull out of the dive by pushing the control stick as far over as it will go. No response. Still hurtling towards the ground and with death approaching, he remembers the advice he had been given on how to get out of a tailspin. He revs the motor at full throttle, and only now does the aircraft respond to the control stick. It's all a bit too late however, because the aircraft smashes into the ground. Remarkably, Tryggve Gran survives the impact and is only slightly concussed. After a few days leave, he is keen to get going again.

On September 1, 1917, he is posted to the Western Front, which is exactly where he wants to be. Not only that, he will be flying one of the 70th Squadron's newly arrived Sopwith Camels. He is proud of his new aircraft, which looks 'beautiful' and works 'to perfection'.

Tryggve goes out on patrol in a team of fighter planes, and is pleasantly surprised that not too many bullets or shells are being aimed at them from the ground. This will be a 'picnic', or so he thinks. Then the leading pilot rocks his wings, starts climbing, and turns sharply.

Tryggve hears the sound of bullets from behind him, and turns to see the British plane attacking two German fighters. The British fighter then latches onto the tailplane of one of the Germans flying an 'Albatross'. Under relentless machine gun fire, the German biplane smokes, catches fire, and falls in a steep dive out of the sky looking as Tryggve describes it 'like a burning torch'.

One down, more to go. The four-man patrol heads towards Ypres where they see seven German fighters up ahead. They launch a surprise attack, to which the German planes respond by dividing and veering off in all directions. Tryggve is given a clear chance for a kill because one of the planes has dived beneath him in a way that makes it highly vulnerable to attack. His Sopwith Camel hurtles after it, and Tryggve, looking through his telescopic sights, sees his bullets drive home for a kill. He reckons his victim to have been a beginner, but then again, he reflects that this would also describe him too.

The Western Front is a dangerous place as Tryggve comes to appreciate. Such as the occassion when he goes on a social visit to another squadron with his fellow pilots. Having gathered for a jolly evening in the mess, fifty men are sitting around a big table, when the whistle of a bomb is heard dropping nearby. The lights go out and the music stops. Somebody cries, 'Hurrah, Huns overhead,' and everyone rushes out the hut door. More bombs fall and explode on the aerodrome, raising huge columns of smoke and flame. The pilots take shelter amongst the trees. A bomb drops amongst them, showering Tryggve with earth and stones.

Huh! Something *must* be done to give these cheeky chaps a lesson. It is a moonlit night and some of the men here are experienced night fliers, Tryggve amongst them. So he takes off in a Sopwith Camel and gives chase. Afterwards, he describes the outcome as 'very successful' but without providing any details.

This episode gets him noticed as an experienced night flier by senior officers in the Royal Flying Corps, and, in consequence, Tryggve is now moved to the 101st Squadron. He will fly seventeen night bombing raids for them, of which thirteen are described as successful and four were aborted due to bad weather or because the bombs failed to release. Strange to say, Tryggve does not provide details about these raids either. What is known is that he is also given special duties. These are carried out using a Sopwith Camel aircraft with a side chair attached. It may have been used to drop spies by parachute behind enemy lines.

His luck runs out on November 30, 1917, when, on a low-level bombing raid at night over Douai in northern France, he is hit by shrapnel in the left leg. With the help of the observer, the plane flies back across the front line, and lands on an emergency landing ground near Arras.

1918

By the middle of January 1918, Tryggve's wounds have healed sufficiently to allow him to walk on crutches, and in March, he takes leave, returning to Norway. He exercises his wounded leg while on a trip to the mountains

Tryggve returns to what is now the Royal Air Force following a reorganisation in April 1918, and is put in charge of a squadron back in Britain. At the end of April, the RAF's only Norwegian officer marries the musical comedy actress Lily St John (Lilian Johnson), a stormy marriage that will end in divorce three years later.

In August 1918, Tryggve Gran is awarded the Military Cross, the citation of which is for 'bombing enemy aerodromes with great success, and engaged enemy searchlights, transport and other targets with machine-gun fire. He invariably showed the greatest determination.' He will later add a Distinguished Flying Cross to his medal collection.

Now a major in the RAF, he is told he will be posted to Archangel, a port in northern Russia on the coast of the White Sea. The allies are intervening in a civil war, which broke out following the Russian Revolution in 1917. They are supporting the White Russians in their struggle to overthrow the Bolsheviks. Tryggve will take control of the British air squadron there.

He departs on a troopship from Dundee on September 20, 1918. The ship, one of three in the convoy, is crammed with several thousand men. Unfortunately, the Spanish Flu is virulent at the time, and runs rampant on board. Tryggve Gran survives a high fever; others are not so lucky. When, at one point, he asks why the ship comes to a halt every now and again, he is told that this is for burials at sea.

Arriving in Russia on October 1, he is ordered to take up headquarters in the village of Bacaritsa, which is on the opposite bank of the River Dvina from Archangel. Not that he sees any flying while he is there. Winter is approaching at the end of the month, and all that can be done is to get the equipment ready for the following spring. Meanwhile, the intense cold has been aggravating his leg wound, and

194

on doctor's advice, he applies to be returned to England, which is granted. Shortly before he leaves Russia on November 8, he is told there will be an Armistice on the Western Front on November 11, 1918, which duly happens. The First World War is now over.

1919
Tryggve Gran had envisaged his North Sea 'jump' as a gateway to an even greater aviation achievement, the crossing of the Atlantic. And now that opportunity beckons for him in June 1919, the *Daily Mail* having announced a prize of £10,000 for the first person to fly across the Atlantic in 72 consecutive hours. He is in one of several competing teams lined up in Newfoundland, having been given leave by the RAF to take part. Major Tryggve Gran is a member of the crew for the enormous Handley Page biplane with its wingspan of 126 feet. It will be loaded with 2,000 gallons of fuel for the journey across the Atlantic.

Fame does not come his way this time. The Handley Page's engines overheat during test flights and will require new radiators to be fitted. These are ordered from Britain. While the Handley Page crew are hanging around waiting for their radiators to turn up, John Alcock and Arthur Whitten Brown take advantage of the delay by sneaking off from Newfoundland in their modified Vickers Vimy bomber to fly across the Atlantic, and then landing in Ireland to win the prize.

1921
In May 1921, Tryggve Gran is hurt in a serious motorcycle accident, whereby the wartime injury to his left leg is further aggravated. He now leaves the RAF and returns to Norway. With Atlantic glory having gone elsewhere, he lines up his next big adventure – he wants to be the first to fly over the North Pole, but fails to get sufficient financial backing to make the trip.

1926 – 1928
In 1926, Roald Amundsen, the Norwegian who beat Captain Scott to the South Pole, shares the glory for the first flight taken over the North Pole, after joining a team flying an airship from Spitsbergen to Alaska via the Pole.

When, in 1928, an airship crashes on its return from the North Pole, Amundsen takes part in the search for survivors, only for his flying boat and five other crew members to go missing in turn. Tryggve Gran heads up the rescue mission and searches for them by ship – a feat giving him the distinction of having searched for both Scott and Amundsen after they had gone missing. No trace is found of Amundsen however.

1930
Tryggve now proposes an expedition to the South Pole by motor cycle. This may be more practical than it sounds. It is common practice in Norway to fit skis either side of each wheel of a motor bike in winter. Again, he is looking for funding to make the trip, but nobody is interested.

1934
For the twentieth anniversary of his North Sea flight in 1914, Tryggve repeats the experience by flying from Dyce Airport, near Aberdeen, to Stavanger. Now a major in the Royal Norwegian Air Force, he is in charge of a team of three military Fokker aircraft made available for the trip. Even though these are much more powerful than his old Bleriot XI-2, the flight still has to be delayed for a day because of bad weather.

Dyce Airport, newly built, had just been opened three days before the trip, but not without controversy. A protestor sneaked in overnight and painted on a wall, 'This aerodrome is being opened in preparation for war. Fight against it'. This is a sign of the tension building up in Europe following Hitler's seizure of power in Germany the year before.

The Aberdeen visit had been part of a round Europe jamboree starting in Oslo, which had taken Tryggve Gran to Copenhagen, Berlin, Paris, London, Aberdeen, and then back to Norway again. When he was in Berlin, Tryggve met Hermann Goering, who would shortly afterwards become commander-in-chief of the Luftwaffe. Gran later claimed that during his conversation with Goering, they had compared notes about their flying exploits in the First World War, and both had agreed that Tryggve shot down Goering's plane on the Western Front in September 1917.

1939
The 25th anniversary of the flight across the North Sea is celebrated in Norway on July 29, 1939. Tryggve Gran is at the centre of attention for the festivities in Stavanger, including sporting events, music concerts, and an official ceremony, which ends with the audience singing in

praise of their hero. A two-ton boulder taken from the vicinity of landing site at Lake Orrevatnet is transported to Stavanger Airport where it is put on display. Meanwhile, the Bleriot XI-2 he flew across the North Sea is installed in the Norwegian Technical Museum in Oslo.

War breaks out in Europe, and Britain declares war with Germany on September 3, 1939. Norway stays neutral again.

In December 1939, Florence Harriman, the United States Minister to Norway, reports to the US Secretary of State that Wilhelm Keilhau, a Norwegian advisor to the Nobel Institute, had told her that 'in an effort to ascertain present opinions in leading German circles' he had recently sent Tryggve Gran to Berlin to meet with Hermann Goering. Tryggve is described as 'a personal, intimate friend of Goering through their common interest in aviation'. He is given a meeting alone with Goering, and then introduced to 'high officials of the Foreign Office'.

Florence Harriman forwards the intelligence gained by Tryggve Gran to Washington, although it states what the Nazis would like Norway and the outside world to believe, and has little value. Tryggve is told this about the recent German non-aggression pact with the Soviet Union: part of the agreement is that Germany will stand by should the Soviet Union invade Finland. Also, that should Norway and Sweden declare war on the Soviets in response to the invasion of Finland, Germany will similarly stand back should both countries then be attacked by the Soviet Union. The situation is embarrassing for the Nazis, because the German people and army are in full sympathy with Finland. The Germans anticipate that should Finland be defeated, the Soviet Union is likely to claim 'those Norwegian ports further north which might be a danger to Murmansk and also Spitsbergen'.

Tryggve Gran tells Keilhau afterwards that he believes Germany to be strong enough to wage a protracted war. The benefit of agreeing peace now is that 'it would spare the world incalculable suffering and would perhaps be the only way of saving Finland and preventing the whole of Scandinavia from being devastated by war'.

1940

Only a matter of months after Gran's mission to Berlin, the Nazis invade Norway and Denmark on April 9, 1940. The Germans claim by doing so, they are protecting the neutrality of both countries.

1941

Tryggve Gran is given a minor post in the pro-German Norwegian Government for six months, one that reports to the Minister of the Interior. By giving him this job, the Norwegian fascists appear to be appealing to Gran's need for recognition, and in return have gained prestige from what they will portray as support from a Norwegian national hero.

1943

The book *Hermann Goering, the Man and His Work* is published in Oslo with a foreword written by Tryggve Gran. It is unclear why the book is then immediately banned after it was printed. Perhaps Tryggve had unwisely repeated the old (and unreliable) story that he had shot down Hermann Goering during World War I while flying a British warplane.

1944

The thirtieth anniversary of Gran's North Sea crossing is celebrated on July 30 in Nazi-occupied Norway. The fascist leader, Vidkun Quisling, gives a speech at a conference honouring Tryggve Gran. Tryggve gives thanks in return.

The Norwegian Post Office has issued a stamp to commemorate the North Sea crossing in 1914. On it is a map showing the flight path from Cruden Bay to Stavanger. Tryggve had been asked if he had any objections to the stamp being issued, and replied, 'my consent is a matter of course'.

It is ironic that three years earlier, the Luftwaffe had flown out from their base in Stavanger to bomb Cruden Bay and then returned home along the exact same route as shown on the stamp. This happened twice. The first time on March 1, 1941, when four bombs were dropped on Fountainbleu Farm near the village, killing the airman in charge of the RAF mobile beacon there. And on April 2, 1941, bombs fell on The Cruden Bay Brick & Tile works, killing the manager and his foreman.

1948

Three years after the end of World War II in Europe, Tryggve Gran is on trial in Norway for his activities during the occupation. Several charges are made against him, although only three will be upheld. He is accused of having joined Quisling's National Assembly, which he denies. He is said to have endorsed the activities of the Quisling

Government, wrote propaganda for them, and had given a radio broadcast about his friend Hermann Goering. He is also accused of having broken the jaw of a ship owner who described him as a mobster and scandal maker.

In his defence, Tryggve argues that he had been afraid of being sent to a German prisoner of war camp because he had been a major in the RAF. He sought help to avoid this, and a minister in the Quisling Government had provided the necessary protection for him.

Tryggve Gran is sentenced to eighteen months in jail, but having already been in custody for thirteen months, he is free to go. There are mitigating circumstances for his offences; he had shown no previous history of involvement with fascism (or politics of any kind) and was only given a token role in the Quisling Government. Nevertheless, Norway's national hero has been tarnished by his association with the fascists. He will rehabilitate himself in the years after the war by giving lectures and writing books.

These days Tryggve Gran is as much celebrated in Cruden Bay as he is in Norway. A monument was erected in the village in 1971 to commemorate his North Sea crossing from the Aberdeenshire village; Tryggve was present to inaugurate it. And every year on the 30th July, Norwegian flags are hung out on the wooden fence next to the monument. That is fitting because Tryggve Gran considered this flight to be his finest moment. He told the reporter Gordon Casely that he celebrated the anniversary every July 30 by firing a cannon from his home in Norway.

Tryggve Gran died at the age of 91 on January 8, 1980. He had been a hero in the classical mould, both bold and daring. Such a hero knows that life seldom ever provides truly exceptional situations for a human being to demonstrate their truly exceptional qualities. *As Tryggve Gran knew only too well, the trick is to spot them immediately and then grab them before anyone else does: a feat he excelled at.*

14. MARY PRATT

It can come about that a man or a woman in the normal routine of their day is suddenly and dramatically confronted by circumstances that compel them to take action. Such happened at the end of World War II to Mary Pratt, a farmer's wife who lived at Whiteshin Farm on the east coast of Aberdeenshire, two miles north of Cruden Bay. Hers was a small act of heroism, although one that made a huge impression on me when I was first told about it.

That had been in March 2018, when the Port Erroll Heritage Group organised a photographic exhibition in Cruden Bay, my home village. As a member of the group, I helped on the day. We had set up tables along one wall where visitors could take a rest from viewing the photographs, and sit down for a chat with their friends over a cup of tea and a cake. John Ross, I think it was, told me that a woman sitting at one of the tables wanted to speak to me. I went over and sat down in front of an older woman who introduced herself as Nora Simpson. She asked me if I would be interested in hearing about Mary Pratt, her aunty. 'Of course,' I replied. And as I listened to her, I became utterly engrossed in the story she told me; the story of a German U-boat that sank near Cruden Bay in 1945. Sometime later, Elizabeth Park, Mary Pratt's granddaughter, gave me more details. Her mother, Isabel Smith, a young girl in 1945, had told her about the events of the time.

Although the following narrative focuses on Mary Pratt and her extraordinary day, also mentioned here are three men caught up by the same events: these are the Peterhead fishermen Alec John Steven, John Smith, and William Robertson.

The first part of the tale is almost famous and appears every now and again in newspaper articles and books written about the more bizarre episodes of World War II. These frequently carry the headline or chapter heading, 'The Toilet that Sank a Nazi U-boat', or something similar.

This U-boat, U-1206, lies on the bed of the North Sea near Cruden Bay, having sunk after its crew abandoned it on April 13, 1945, only 25 days before the end of World War II in Europe.

This, then, is the story.

Thursday, April 6, 1945

The 67-metre long submarine propelled by two twin-screw diesel engines and two electric motors left Kristiansand in Norway on April 6, 1945. The U-boat is armed with five torpedo tubes, four at the bow and one at the stern, and can defend itself on the surface with three anti-aircraft guns. Captain Karl-Adolf Schlitt, who is twenty-six-year-old, has been given orders to attack shipping convoys off the east coast of Scotland. Under his command is a crew of forty-nine men.

These men are embarking on an exceptionally dangerous mission. Although the German U-boat campaign had been successful in the early years of the war when they sank hundreds of merchant ships and naval vessels, by 1945 new detection technology and new weapons have made the submarines highly vulnerable to attack. Should they surface they will quickly be located on radar installed in enemy planes and ships; if they send a radio message, their position can be located by direction-finder equipment; the encrypted messages they send and receive from headquarters using their Enigma coding machines can be read by the British and Americans, although the Germans do not know this. When the submarines are underwater, they can be detected by sonar pulses sent out from warships.

And once found, warships and planes will rapidly converge on a U-boat. Although a U-boat can submerge within ten seconds on being alerted to an attack, once underwater they are still vulnerable when depth charges are launched - steel barrels filled with high explosive, which sink through the sea and are manually set to explode at the depth where the submarine is expected to be. If a depth charge explodes next to a U-boat, the vessel falls apart and all onboard are drowned.

The U-boat hunters are merciless: they will never give up until the U-boat is blown apart by depth charges; confirmation of which arrives when a mixture of oil, debris, and body parts float to the surface. To destroy a U-boat frequently involves the release of dozens of depth charges over several hours - one after the other – an utterly terrifying ordeal for the crew of a submarine to endure. Sometimes they survive, sometimes they do not.

Furthermore, one of the old methods from World War I still works to sink U-boats: mines are laid to ensnare submarines as they cruise underwater. The North Sea is a nest of hidden mines, some laid down by the British to catch German U-boats unaware and others laid down by German U-boats to catch British ships unaware (the mines are ejected by compressed air through the submarine's torpedo tubes). They are also a menace to coastal communities. Shaken loose by

201

currents, the mines drift onshore in shoals, and then explode. The tiny fishing village at the Bullers of Buchan on the Aberdeenshire coast has suffered from this. Even though the houses are perched high on a cliff, those on the front row facing the sea have been badly damaged by exploding mines. This ever-present danger has led to the villagers moving out for the duration of the war.

The North Sea is an even more dangerous area for U-boats than is normal for them. It swarms with naval vessels and planes forever on the lookout. It is safer for a U-boat to be hunting convoys in the wide-open expanse of the mid-Atlantic or the Arctic seas where there is less chance of being found.

Overall, to be a crewmember on a German U-boat in 1945 is tantamount to taking part in a suicide mission. The statistics are grim: by the end of the Second World War, seventy-five per cent of all U-boats built had been sunk or reported missing.

One plus for U-1206 as it slides under the sea on its way from Norway is that it is fitted with a *schnorchell* (snorkel), referred to as a *snort* by the crew. This device, a double-barrelled tube that can be raised and lowered like a periscope, allows the U-boat to stay submerged longer. This matters because the U-boat's propellers are driven by a combination of diesel engines and electric motors: diesel motors are used on the surface and electric motors underwater. It is not possible to expel the fumes from the diesel engines while submerged, so electric motors are used while moving at depth. Once the batteries lose power, the U-boat is obliged to come to the surface where the batteries are recharged by running the diesel engines. To do so is dangerous, because a U-boat on the surface of the sea is liable to be spotted by enemy planes or radar. Once *snorts* started to be fitted to U-Boats from 1943 onwards, that changed. The U-Boat can now rise to a shallow depth, just short of breaking the waves, and by raising the snort device above the sea surface, one barrel emits diesel fumes into the atmosphere, while the other sucks in air to replace the stale air inside the submarine. This lowers the chance that the enemy will spot the submarine.

Thursday, April 12, 1945
Today the submariners spot a convoy moving along the coast near Peterhead, although there is not much they can do about it: U-1206 is experiencing technical problems. One of the diesel engines stopped working, and now the other has conked out. It is essential to repair

202

them to ensure that the batteries for the electric motor can be charged because they are running low on power. Captain Schlitt gives the order to put the U-boat down on the seabed to make repairs. The spot chosen is close to a minefield where the chances of detection by surface patrols and their sonar equipment are lessened. Their location is at a depth of 280 feet below sea level, ten miles east of the village of Collieston on the Aberdeenshire coast.

Friday, April 13, 1945
Repairs continue the next day.

What happened next is not clear because the accounts are contradictory. The story told here is based on the book *The Hunters and the Hunted* by the German writer Jochen Brennecke, a vivid account of U-boat operations in World War II. Although Brennecke provides no source material for the stories in his book, it is known that he had access to archive documents in his role as the Secretary General of the German Society for Shipping and Naval History. He was also the President of the Research Institute and Archive for Shipping and Naval History. Brennecke probably interviewed the crewmen from U-1206 (Captain Schlitt also gave an account elsewhere, although he omits some of the details provided by Brennecke, possibly because he did not want these to become widely known to the public for reasons of personal reputation and embarrassment).

Captain Schlitt needs to use the toilet at the forward end of the boat. A new type of toilet has recently been installed in the U-boat. Its contents can be discharged out to sea when the submarine is deep underwater, whereas previously a toilet could only be flushed near the surface. The benefit provided by the new toilet is that a submarine can spend longer underwater.

After using it, the occupant of the new toilet operates a system of valves which require to be turned in a specific sequence, a procedure that ends with the opening of a vent on the outside of the hull to expel the sewage. Because the water pressure on the outside of the hull is substantial in deep water, the material must first be isolated, and then pressured up to match the water pressure of the sea. Only then can the outside vent be opened, whereby the contents are expelled by a blast of compressed air. Because all of the steps involved in using the toilet must be carried out in the right order, a manual has been provided to ensure the correct operation of the valves by the crew.

203

Captain Schlitt has read the manual twice before engaging the toilet's elaborate plumbing. Nevertheless, it does not flush. An engineer familiar with the new type of toilet is brought in to investigate. He opens a valve on the toilet apparatus, only for a violent inrush of water 'as thick as a man's thigh' to erupt from the toilet, bodily throwing the man backwards.

This part of Brennecke's story is absent from Captain Schlitt's account, which is not altogether surprising. It is only now that the captain's commentary starts. Schlitt is in the engine room at the stern when he is informed of a severe water leak at the front of the boat, which is identified as sourced from the outboard vent of the forward toilet. The captain has 'learned' that the mechanic had been trying to repair the outboard valve connecting to the sea. The inboard valve had probably been removed by this stage. This is a huge blunder of catastrophic proportions. Now open to the sea, the bow end of the boat is flooding rapidly. And if that is not alarming enough, the crew now discovers that the submarine's pumps are defective when they try to use them.

The chief engineer is in the control area, and takes immediate action. The ship's crew are ordered to move to the stern where their weight will restore balance now that the submarine has started to tilt. The contents of the ballast tanks are now blown into the sea by compressed air: this provides the necessary buoyancy to bring the submarine to the surface.

Captain Schlitt climbs the conning tower to have a look around outside. He sees a convoy of ships in the distance with planes flying overhead. Not good. An attempt is made to send a radio signal to U-boat command, but it will not get through because the transmitter is faulty.

Meanwhile, water is filling up the inside of the U-boat, and the batteries have become covered in seawater. A reaction takes place inside the batteries releasing highly toxic chlorine gas corrosive to the human lung. What's more, although the diesel engines have started working again they conk out minutes later. The situation has become hopeless: the submarine is incapable of diving or moving, and is sinking by the bow end. Four out of five of the torpedoes are now fired in attempt to lighten the vessel. Captain Schlitt comments, 'At which point in time British planes and patrols discovered us. I let the boat sink.' What he does not mention in is account is that two RAF planes flew overhead and released two bombs, both of which missed the submarine.

The conning tower of the submarine is spotted seven miles to the south-east by HMT *William Brady*, a trawler requisitioned at the start of the war and converted into a patrol vessel. The ship is providing an escort to minesweepers operating near Aberdeen. They ships arrive just in time for those onboard to see the U-boat roll over and sink.

The Germans had by this time abandoned the U-boat, having climbed into four rubber dinghies. Spotting the light from Buchanness Lighthouse nine and a half miles to the north-west, they paddle towards it. Close to midnight, the British minesweeper HMT *Nodzu* overtakes two of the dinghies; the Germans are captured, and taken onboard. The other two dinghies escape unseen.

Although the toilet story is well established, it is curious that when the survivors from U-1206 were subsequently interviewed by British military intelligence, they gave a different version of events from Brennecke. They told their captors that 'severe leaks had developed after the U-boat had hit the bottom for some unexplained reason'.

A team of amateur divers - 'The Buchan Divers' - discovered the Nazi U-boat on the seabed in 2012, finding it intact. The only obvious damage to the submarine had been caused by the trawl net of a fishing boat, which had caught a much bigger haul than anticipated; the net had become entangled with the U-boat's anti-aircraft guns and periscope.

The Buchan Divers team made a detailed investigation of the circumstances surrounding the sinking. They report on their website that 'Some stories... claim that it was the captain himself who caused the leak. While this may be true, a relative of a crew member has been in touch to state that his father was told, long after the war, by Captain Schlitt himself, that the officers decided to surrender and created the leak as a cover story to protect them from the reprisals they would suffer in prison camp if the truth was known.'

This is plausible, and quite likely in my opinion. By April 1945, the crew would have known that the Nazis had lost the war. With the allies rapidly closing in on Germany from both east and west, the situation was hopeless for the Nazis. These men were in their twenties with their lives ahead of them – *so why should they take any risks now that the war is about to end?*

Saturday, April 14, 1945

The two remaining dinghies, one with the captain onboard, continue on their way towards the lighthouse, which, now that night has arrived, is their only sure indication of where the coast lies.

As it gets darker, the men in the captain's dinghy lose contact with the other boat. It is a bitterly cold night and the men are soaked through - conditions likely to lead to hypothermia should they not be rescued soon. They spot British ships in the distance on several occasions, but because they have no flares or electric torches, they are unable to make their presence known. To keep up morale, the men sing sea shanties and crack jokes.

Captain Schlitt recalled later how their dinghy attracted the attention of large shoals of fish - fish that were thriving at the time because they had found a secure home at the bottom of the sea in ships sunk by German bombs.

They travel north-west for eight miles, and by morning, they discover they are being pulled by strong tidal currents towards the rocks at Dunbuy, a rock arch jutting out from a long line of granite cliffs one mile north of Cruden Bay. The Germans are in trouble because they will have little chance of survival should the waves hurl their rubber dinghy against the granite cliffs. Once in the water, they will be confronted by a sheer line of cliffs with no way to get to the top, that is, if they are not quickly smashed by the waves against the red granite rock. Luck now comes their way.

That Saturday morning, three Peterhead fishermen had set off in the *Reaper*, a 27-foot long fishing boat with the cabin at the stern and a sail in front. They headed south to lift their lobster creels in the rock pools near the cliffs. On board are the skipper of the vessel Alec John Steven, fourteen-year old John Smith who is serving as an apprentice deckhand, and his cousin William Robertson.

At seven a.m., they are half a mile off Dunbuy rock when Alec spots a yellow object in the water, which at first glance he takes for a salmon coble, a single-masted flat-bottomed fishing boat. But then he sees that it is a large yellow dinghy packed full of men. The dinghy is towing two life rafts with a sick man lying prone on each,

The *Reaper* sails alongside the dinghy to take the thirteen Germans on board. They are led down into the hold, except for the two sick men from the life rafts who are carefully laid out flat on the deck of the fishing boat. The two men may have been suffering from hypothermia

– Alec John Steven reckons the Germans had spent ten to twelve hours out in the open by this time.

With all the men on board, the *Reaper* returns to Peterhead. It is only now that the crew discover they have picked up German submariners. Because they spoke no English, the fishermen had assumed the men were Norwegians who had escaped from a ship sunk by enemy action.

When they reach Peterhead, Alec brings the Germans to the harbour master, who invites them into his office. Captain Schlitt puts a briefcase on the table, removes a holster and gun from it, and places them on the table alongside the brief case. 'I have no further use for this,' he says. The police are called, and a sergeant and constable arrive to take them to the police station, where they will spend the rest of the day sleeping off their ordeal.

The second dinghy with eleven Germans in it approaches the shore about a mile further north from where their compatriots had been rescued. They find themselves under some of the highest cliffs on this part of the Aberdeenshire coast: sheer granite cliffs over 60 metres high. Captain Schlitt wrote later that 'In an attempt to negotiate the steep coast in heavy seas, three crew members tragically died.' Their names are given as Hans Berkhauer, Karl Koren, and Ernst Kupper. Captain Schlitt clarified this later: one of the dead men had been taken aboard the dinghy from the U-boat beforehand, whereas only two had died on the cliffs.

They land at the bottom of an inlet known as the Gwight, where there is a 30-metre-wide pebbly beach backed by a steep grassy slope. One of the Germans scrambles up the slope. This must have been a struggle for him given that he had been sitting soaking wet in a dinghy for between ten to twelve hours on a bitterly cold night.

Mary Pratt now enters the story. Her life up until now had been no different from many others in rural Aberdeenshire at the time. Let's mention in passing that it takes a special sort of person to run a farm in the North of Scotland - someone with what the Dutch call a 'farmer's brain'. Through shrewd and hard-headed thinking, extreme competence, and incessant hard work, they can make money from the most marginal of business opportunities.

Two six-year old boys, Jimmy Love and George Young, have been sent by Mary Pratt to the top field at Whiteshin Farm to check on the cattle there. The field is next to the cliffs. On the way there, Jimmy tells George that Mrs Pratt had sent him earlier that morning to the local shop at Tillymaud where the shopkeeper George Ironside told him that a German U-boat had been bombed by RAF planes near Collieston the previous night, but had missed it.

As they approached the field, Jimmy laughed and said to George, 'Wouldn't it be funny if we saw the Germans coming over the cliff!' At which point they spot the German who had come up the Gwight. He then disappeared behind a stone dyke. Jimmy recalls that the German was wearing a uniform, and he had thought him to be the captain or possibly an officer.

The two boys run back in a panic to the farmhouse where they tell Mrs Pratt what they had seen. 'Nonsense!' she says.

That same morning, nine-year-old Sandy Bain, dressed in short trousers and a jersey, sets off from his home next to where the Longhaven quarrymen live. He is carrying a metal flagon, which he will get filled up with milk at Whiteshin Farm. While walking along the farm road, he is given a huge surprise when a man dressed in uniform pops up from behind a stone dyke and speaks to him in German.

Sandy, frightened for his life, runs as fast as he can towards the farmhouse. When he gets there, he tells Mary Pratt in great excitement, 'The Germans have landed! The Germans have landed!'

Mrs Pratt replies, 'Don't speak rubbish Sandy!', only for the German to walk in, having followed the boy into the house.

The German says something to Mary and points towards the cliffs, making it clear from his gestures that there are more Germans in that direction. Mary sends Sandy to call the police from the phone at George Ironside's shop.

When Sandy returns, Mary's husband James ushers the German into his car to take him to Peterhead Police Station. The two boys come too, crowding into the front seat. They had not wanted to share the back seat with the German even though there is plenty of space to sit there. Young Jimmy is watching him nervously in the driver's mirror, when of a sudden he sees the German reaching into the inside pocket of his jacket with his right hand.

'Oh No. He's going for his gun!' thinks Jimmy, only for the German to take out a comb to sweep back the hair from his face.

The police, the coastguard, and several members of the Home Guard now arrive at Whiteshin Farm, where a rescue operation commences to bring the seven remaining Germans up from the Gwight. They are taken to the farm, and lined up outside the farmhouse, wet, frightened, and dejected.

It is now that Mary Pratt did what she did: an act that will cause huge controversy in the neighbourhood.

There in front of Mary Pratt are the hated Germans, not that they look anywhere close to formidable. These men are miserable and haggard looking after their near-death experience. Mary later mentioned to her foster daughter Isabel that the men she saw that day were mere youngsters and very frightened. That figures - the average age of a U-boat crewmember in World War II was in the mid-twenties. Mary took pity on them and now utters the words that will cause so much controversy later, *'Would you like to come in for a cup of tea?'*

One of the Germans, who understands English, flinches in astonishment at her words. His colleagues, not understanding what Mary has just said, also flinch when they see their colleague's reaction, only for her words to be translated for them. It is now their turn to look astonished.

'Yes', the English-speaking German said. 'We would like a cup of tea'.

One of the men guarding the Germans steps forward and says, 'I don't think you want to do that Mrs Pratt.'

To which Mary replies, 'Nobody tells me who or who not is allowed into my house!' and beckons the Germans inside.

She leads them into the dining room, looks out her best china tea set, and makes a pot of tea. Years later, Mary Pratt's niece, Nora, told me that the tea party was very civilised. The Germans brought out their emergency chocolate rations, now no longer required, and shared them out. Mrs Warrander, a neighbour, came in to help. One of the Germans gave her his cap badge (which probably depicted the emblem chosen for U-1206, a stork – all U-boats were painted with a unique emblem and special cap badges were made with the emblem on them).

And then when all the tea had been drunk, the Germans went outside, where they are kept waiting until a bus turned up to take them to the police station at Peterhead. My neighbour Gordon Findlay, who was six at the time, saw the Germans in the bus as it passed by his house - an old bus with a snub nose. He already knew that the Germans had been at Whiteshin Farm, only to be told very forcibly by his mother that on no account was he to go anywhere near the place.

When the Germans arrived at Peterhead police station, word goes around the town that the Germans are being kept there. An angry mob gathers in the street, where they let loose their feelings of utter hatred.

Looking back now, the reaction of the angry mob was not in the least bit surprising. This part of Aberdeenshire had been subjected to a large number of air raids; much more than would be expected given the size of the main towns here: namely Peterhead and Fraserburgh. The area had been given the name 'Hellfire Corner' during the earlier part of the war and aptly so. Les Taylor in his book *Luftwaffe Over Scotland* provides a table of locations where bombs had been dropped in Scotland during World War II, and these are ranked by the total number of air raids experienced. Peterhead is top of the list with 28, Fraserburgh is third (after Aberdeen) with 23 raids. The explanation for this is geographical: this part of Aberdeenshire lay closest to the Luftwaffe's air base in Norway.

One raid in particular was devastating for Peterhead. On September 29, 1941, a two tonne parachute mine was dropped onto James Street near the harbour. It blew apart two tenement blocks killing thirty people. The shockwave from this monster bomb caused damage to half the buildings in Peterhead.

Enemy planes frequently opened fire with machine-guns on the public out in the open. Nobody was safe. One boy, who later became Mary Pratt's son-in-law, tells how he was in the school playground at Port Erroll School in Cruden Bay when a German plane flew overhead and opened fire on the children there. He had to jump for cover. Luckily, no one was hurt, although one of the boys, who had been laughing off the incident afterwards, was told by his friend that smoke was coming out of his school bag. It had been hit by a bullet, probably a ricochet, and had embedded in one of his schoolbooks.

Such atrocities had become commonplace by the end of the war. Machine-gunning a school playground is an unforgivable act of great evil, although it has to be remembered that the Germans who did this may have had relatives in cities subjected to saturation bombing by the British; cities where wives, daughters, sons, sisters, and grandmothers were all at great risk of suffering a violent death or severe injury.

It had been much more civilised near the start of the war five years earlier. Back in April 1940 when a Heinkel bomber crashed in East Anglia killing all four of the crew, they were given a funeral with full military honours courtesy of the RAF. Their coffins were covered with flowers bought by local people - one wreath bearing the words 'With Heartfelt Sympathy From a Mother'. But now in 1945, it was total war.

In the early days of the war, that is, before most of the enemy planes were diverted to the Eastern Front following the invasion of the Soviet Union in 1941, the coastal convoys sailing up the east coast were regularly attacked by the Luftwaffe. Their planes turned up every two or three days. The ships were easy targets in those parts of the North Sea where they passed through the narrow channels swept through enemy minefields. A system was in operation whereby northbound convoys were separated from southbound convoys by a distance of a quarter of a mile, leaving them with no room to manoeuvre should they be attacked. It was a common and distressing sight at the time to see a bombed ship shrouded in flames only a short distance offshore from the Aberdeenshire coast.

Isabel, Mary Pratt's foster daughter, remembers standing on the cliff top at Longhaven watching the convoy ships as they passed by. When she started to count them, Mary stopped her. 'Don't do that, it's unlucky,' she was told. 'Some of them might never come back.'

Although towards the end of war there were no more bombing raids in Scotland, fighting continued in continental Europe as the Allies and the Soviet army closed in on Germany. Many of the locals were anxious about their menfolk on active duty in Europe and SE Asia, or sailing on ships with the Atlantic or Russian convoys. Every morning the local newspaper published yet another list of those killed or lost in action. Those with menfolk overseas grabbed the paper when it arrived and would anxiously scan down the list.

By April 1945, details were starting to emerge about the Nazi concentration camps. The war correspondent for the *Aberdeen Press and Journal* reported on April 14 about the Belsen death camp. The report reflects how little was known about these camps at the time. As the tanks of the British 11th Armoured Division approached the camp, 'which covered six square miles and contained 60,000 political prisoners and criminals', much concern was expressed about the rampant disease which had taken hold inside the concentration camp - 1,500 cases of typhus, 900 cases of typhoid, and 9,000 other prisoners were ill from unknown causes. The guards had abandoned the camp a few days earlier and German soldiers had taken their place. Should the German soldiers retreat, it would leave the prisoners free to escape and spread their disease amongst the troops.

Bracketing the *Press and Journal* article were reports of Japanese suicide planes and an article headlined 'Most Gruesome Sight of War'. The German concentration camp of Nordhausen had been relieved with the discovery of 500 Allied prisoners so weakened from starvation they could not stand up. They lay amongst the bodies of 600 prisoners who had starved to death. The 'Most Gruesome Sight of War' was a record that would not even last beyond the next day. It was then that the British soldiers entered Belsen.

The Nazis were hated in Aberdeenshire in April 1945.

When the news got out that Mrs Pratt had invited the Germans in for a cup of tea, her neighbours were horrified.

'How could you do that?' she was asked in outraged tones.

And she always gave this reply. 'If it had been your son or brother over there you would have expected the same.' And should Mary be pressed further on the matter, she would angrily retort, 'They are a' somebody's loons' – *They are all somebody's boys.* Which is indeed the case.

Mary Pratt is one of my North Sea heroes. Although under normal circumstances an act of kindness would not normally be considered exceptional behaviour – there are times when it can be. That is when the stronger emotion of hate obliterates it. The prevailing mood in Aberdeenshire at the end of the war was one of hatred and revulsion at the Nazis, and understandably so. Yet, Mary Pratt ignored all that was expected of her by her neighbours. Seeing past all the hate, she could sense individual suffering for what it was, and then did something about it.

She had intuitively grasped a lesson that life teaches the enlightened. Hatred comes readily when you lump individuals into an amorphous group and then give that group a label, such as 'the Nazis'. By doing so, it is easy to inflict suffering without having to think about the consequences. Individual persons lumped together like this have become abstractions.

Situations that deserve the ultimate in human fellow feeling can thus be trivialised. One *must* always avoid thinking and talking about suffering in the abstract. It demeans and obscures the true horror of individual misery. The abstract words are war, famine, and plague; the details lie with the suffering of fathers, mothers, children, and lovers - Viktor Frankl and his wife in the Holocaust, Mrs Hatsuyo Nakamura and her children at Hiroshima; real people, suffering people. Sheer awfulness happened to them.

Kindness is heroic.

June 1987

In June 1987, Karl-Adolf Schlitt returned to Aberdeenshire to meet the men who rescued him. Two were still alive, the third, William Robertson, had died by that time. Captain Schlitt was there to thank these men. As a thank-you present, he gave his surviving rescuers a wooden plaque inset with a metal U-boat brought out in relief.

Some time before, perhaps in the early sixties, maybe before, it is not clear when, one of the Germans who had been at Whiteshin Farm made a big effort to find Mary Pratt. The man never went back home to Germany at the end of the war. After spending several years in a Prisoner of War camp in England, he settled down in the country, married, and brought up a family there. Eventually locating Mary, he visited her at her home in Cults in the suburbs of Aberdeen. *He had wanted to say thank you for a cup of tea.*

ABOUT THE AUTHOR

Mike Shepherd writes books about dramatic episodes of Scottish history untouched by other authors, including the history of North Sea oil (*Oil Strike North Sea*) and the Scottish origins of the novel Dracula (*When Brave Men Shudder*). His last book, *Slains Castle's Secret History*, was co-written with Dacre Stoker, great-grand nephew of Bram Stoker, author of *Dracula*.

REFERENCES

CHAPTER 1. THE MEN OF THE ARMADA

James Melville. *The Autobiography and Diary.* Edited by Robert Pitcairn. Woodrow Society, Edinburgh. 1842.

C.F. Duro *La Armada Invencible.* Volume 2. Madrid. 1885. W. P. Ker., 1920. *The Spanish Story of the Armada.* The Scottish Historical Review. Vol. 17, p. 165-176.

Calendar of Letters and State Papers (Simancas). Volume 4. Elizabeth 1587-1603. Edited by M. A. S. Hume, 1899. Public Records Office, London.

Robert Hutchinson. *The Spanish Armada.* Weidenfeld & Nicholson, London. 2013.

J. K. Leighton (editor). *State Papers Relating to the Defeat of the Spanish Armada.* Two volumes. Naval Records Society. 1894.

J. K. Leighton (editor). *State Papers Relating to the Defeat of the Spanish Armada.* Two volumes. Naval Records Society. 1894.

Colin John Mackenzie Martin, 1984. *The Equipment And Fighting Potential of the Spanish Armada.* PhD thesis, University of St Andrews.

Calendar of State Papers, Scotland: Volume 9, 1586-88. Ed. William K Boyd. London: His Majesty's Stationery Office, 1915. British History Online. Web. 8 March 2021. http://www.british-history.ac.uk/cal-state-papers/scotland/vol9.

J. Brand. A *Brief Description of Orkney, Zetland, Pightland Firth & Caithness.* 1701. Reprinted from the original. William Brown, Edinburgh. 1883.

David Calderwood. *The History of the Church of Scotland.* Volume 4. Printed for the Woodrow Society, Edinburgh. 1843.

CHAPTER 2. SIR GEORGE BRUCE

The Scottish Engineering Hall of Fame. http://www.engineeringhalloffame.org/ Accessed 16/2/2021

R. L. Galloway. *A History of Coal Mining in Great Britain.* MacMillan and Co., London, 1882.

Donald Adamson, 2008. A Coal Mine in the Sea: Culross and the Moat Pit. *Scottish Archaeological Journal* Vol. 30 (1–2) 161–199.

John Taylor, 1618. *The Pennyless Pilgrimage, or the Moneylesse Perambulation of John Taylor, Alias, The King's Majesties Water-Poet : How he Travailed on Foot From London to Edenborough in Scotland, Not Carrying Any Money to or Fro, Neither Begging, Borrowing, or Asking Meate, Drinke, or Lodging.*

Slavery In The Coal-Mines of Scotland. James Barrowman, Presented at the Annual General Meeting of the Federated Institution of Mining Engineers, 1897. http://www.scottishmining.co.uk/429

Daniel Defoe, 1726. *A Tour Through the Whole Island of Great Britain.*

Robert Bald. *A General View of the Coal Trade of Scotland.* Oliphant and Brown. Glasgow. 1808.

Dundonald, Archibald, 9th Earl of, 1793. *Description of the Estate and Abbey of Culross.* Edinburgh.

Dundonald, Archibald, 9th Earl of, 1793, as above.

CHAPTER 3. JACOBITES IN REBELLION

The Old Scots Navy: from 1689-1710. Edited by James Grant. Navy Records Society. 1912.

Bruce Lenman, 1980. *The Jacobite Risings in Britain 1689-1746.* Eyre Methuen Ltd. London.

P. Hume Brown, 1911. *History of Scotland Vol. 3. From the Revolution of 1689 to the Disruption, 1843.* Cambridge: At The University Press.

Hugh Mackay, 1833. *Memoirs of the War Carried on in Scotland And Ireland, 1689-1691.* Edinburgh.

A. H. Millar, 1905. *Killiecrankie Described by an Eye-Witness.* The Scottish Historical Review, V3, No. 9, p 63-70; *Orain le Iain Lom Mac-Dhomhnuill,* 1895. Antigonish, Nova Scotia.

Charles Sanford Terry, 1905. *John Graham of Claverhouse, Viscount of Dundee, 1648-1689.* Constable, London.

Sir Ewen Cameron of Locheill, 1842. *Memoirs.* Edinburgh.

Colin Lindsay, Earl of Balcarres. *Memoirs Touching the Revolution in Scotland 1688-1690.* Bannatyne Club, Edinburgh 1841.

David Chandler, 1976. *The Art of Warfare in the Age of Marlborough.* Spellmount Limited, Staplehurst.

C. Field, 1922. Notes upon Uniform Dress as Worn by the Scots Brigade in the Dutch Service – circa 1700-10. *Journal of the Society for Army Historical Research.* Vol. 1, No. 3, p.93-97.

James Grant, 1878. *British Battles on Land and Sea*, Vol. 1. Cassell, Petter & Galpin.

Donald McBane, 1728. *The Expert Sword-Man's Companion.* James Duncan, Glasgow. Quoted in Sir Ewen Cameron of Locheill, 1842. *Memoirs.* Edinburgh.

Livingstone, T. 1690. *A true and real account of the defeat of General Buchan and Brigadeer Cannon, their High-land Army, at the Battel of Crombdell upon the 1st of May; 1690.* Edinburgh: Printed by the Heir of Andrew Anderson.

George Carleton, 1811. *Memoirs of Captain George Carleton.* Vol. 2. J. Davis. London

CHAPTER 4. THE MEN OF THE BASS

Andrew Crichton. *Memoirs Of The Rev. John Blackader; Compiled Chiefly From Unpublished Manuscripts, and Memoirs of His While Prisoner on the Bass.* Second Edition, Edinburgh: William and Charles Tait, London, 1826 .

A Complete Collection of State Trials and Proceedings for High Treason and Other Crimes and Misdemeanors from the Earliest Period to the Present Time. Volume 8. Compiled by T. B. Howell, 1812. London.

The Old Scots Navy: from 1689-1710. Edited by James Grant. Navy Records Society. 1912.

Calendar of the Stuart Papers Belonging to His Majesty the King, Preserved at Windsor Castle. Volume 1. His Majesty's Stationary Office. London. 1902.

The small and rarer collection of Jacobitical tracts (memoirs of Lord Viscount Dundee & co.) published in London, 1714'

CHAPTER 5. THE GLORIOUS FRANCES WRIGHT

Biography, Notes and Political Letters by Frances Wright D'Arusmont. J. Myles. Dundee. 1844.

Horace Traubel, 1888. *With Walt Whitman in Camden*, Volume 2.

Henry Cockburn, 1856. *Memorials of his Own Time*.

James Myles, 1850. *Rambles in Forfarshire*. James Myles, Edinburgh.

William Cobbett, 1830. *Rural Rides*; Eric Hobsbawm, 1962. *The Age of Revolution, 1789 - 1848*. Weidenfeld and Nicholson Ltd.

Helen Heineman, 1983. *Restless Angels: The Friendship of Six Victorian Women - Frances Wright, Camilla Wright, Harriet Garnett, Frances Garnett, Julia Garnett Pertz, Frances Trollope*. Ohio University Press.

Frances Wright, 1822. *A Few Days in Athens: Being the Translation of a Greek Manuscript Discovered in Herculaneum*. London: Longman, Hurst, Rees, Orme, and Brown.

Robert Dale Owen, 1874. *Threading My Way*. G. W. Carleton and Company. New York.

Frances Wright, 1835. *Course of Popular Lectures*.

Thomas Jefferson, 1830. *Memoir, Correspondence, and Miscellanies, from the Papers of Thomas Jefferson*. Volume 4. Gray and Bowen.

Goodale, D., 1938. Some of Walt Whitman's Borrowings. *American Literature*, *10*(2), pp.202-213.

Francis Wright, 1821. *Views on Society and Manners in America*.

Frances Wright, 1835. *Course of Popular Lectures*.

C. H. Payne-Gaposchkin, 1975. *The Nashoba Plan for removing the evil of slavery: letters of Francis and Camilla Wright, 1820-1829*. Harvard Library Bulletin XXIII.

Celia Morris Eckhart, 1984. *Fanny Wright: Rebel in America*. Harvard University Press.

Robert Owen, 1825. *Discourses on a New System of Society, as Delivered in the Hall of Representatives of the United States*.

CHAPTER 6. NASHOBA

Frances Trollope, 1832. *Domestic Manners of the Americans.* Whittaker, Treacher & Co., London.

Frances Wright. A plan for the gradual abolition of slavery in the United States, without danger or loss to the citizens of the south. *Genius of Universal Emancipation.* October 15, 1825.

Thomas Jefferson, 1830. *Memoir, Correspondence, and Miscellanies, from the Papers of Thomas Jefferson.* Volume 4. Gray and Bowen.

Madison, James. *Letters and Other Writings of James Madison.* Philadelphia: Lippincott's, 1865.

Biography, Notes and Political Letters by Frances Wright D'Arusmont. J. Myles. Dundee. 1844.

Genius of Universal Emancipation. December 17, 1825.

C. H. Payne-Gaposchkin, 1975. *The Nashoba Plan for removing the evil of slavery: letters of Francis and Camilla Wright, 1820-1829.* Harvard Library Bulletin XXIII.

Robert Dale Owen, 1874. *Threading My Way.* G. W. Carleton and Company. New York.

Genius of Universal Emancipation. June 10, 1826.

The Life and Letters of Mary Wollstonecraft Shelley. Volume 2. Edited by Mrs Julian Marshall, 1889. Richard Bentley and Son, London.

CHAPTER 7. CINCINNATI

Frances Trollope, 1832. *Domestic Manners of the Americans.* Whittaker, Treacher & Co., London.

Frances Wright, 1835. *Course of Popular Lectures.*

Celia Morris Eckhart, 1984. *Fanny Wright: Rebel in America.* Harvard University Press.

C. H. Payne-Gaposchkin, 1975. *The Nashoba Plan for removing the evil of slavery: letters of Francis and Camilla Wright, 1820-1829.* Harvard Library Bulletin XXIII.

Frances Wright, 1828. *Explanatory Notes, Respecting the Nature and Objects of the Institution of Nashoba.*

New York Commercial Advertiser, January 12, 1829. Quoted in Eckhardt, Celia Morris. *Fanny Wright: Rebel in America.* Cambridge, Mass.: Harvard UP, 1984.

Nancy Woloch, 2000. *Women and the American Experience.* Third edition. McGraw Hill.

Stanton, E. C., Anthony, S. B., Gage, M. J., & Harper, I. H. (1881). *History of Woman Suffrage.* New York, N.Y.

CHAPTER 8. JAMES CROLL

James Campbell Irons, 1896. *Autobiographical Sketch Of James Croll: with memoir of his life and work.* Edward Stanford, London.

Quaternary Research Association website: https://www.qra.org.uk/

The Diary of John Sturrock: Millwright, Dundee 1864 – 1865. Edited by C. A. Whatley. Studies in Local History.

Dundee fetes the MP who beat Churchill. Kenny Farquharson. The Times. November 3 2002.

W. E. Houghton, 1957. *The Victorian Frame of Mind, 1830-1870.* Yale University Press.

T. Carlyle, *Sartor Resartus*, 1834. Book 2.

Walter Pater, 1873. *The Renaissance.*

CHAPTER 9. THE ICE AGE

James Campbell Irons, 1896. *Autobiographical Sketch Of James Croll: with memoir of his life and work.* Edward Stanford, London.

Mike Shepherd, 2015. *Oil Strike North Sea.* Luath Press, Edinburgh.

Archibald Geikie, 1863. *On The Phenomena of the Glacial Drift Of Scotland.* John Gray. Glasgow.

James Hall, 1815. *On the Revolutions of the Earth's Surface.* Transactions of the Royal Society of Edinburgh, V. 7

J. Imbrie and K. P. Imbrie, 1979. Ice *Ages: solving the mystery.* Harvard University Press.

Hoffman, P. F. (2015). *The Tooth of Time:: James Smith of Jordanhill.* Geoscience Canada, 42(1), 7–26.

Charles Lyell, 1847. *Principles of Geology.* J. Murray, London.

Archibald Geikie, 1924. *A Long Life's Work: an autobiography.* Macmillan and Co, London.

A brief history of the astronomical theories of paleoclimates. André Berger in: Milutin Milankovitch 130th Anniversary Symposium: *Climate Change at the Eve of the second Decade of the Century, Inferences from Paleoclimate and Regional Aspects.* André Berger, Fedor Mesinger and Djordje Šijački, Editors. Springer. 2012.

C. Hamlin, 1982. *James Geikie, James Croll, and the Eventful Ice Age.* Annals of Science, V.39, P.565-583.

CHAPTER 10. JAMES CROLL'S BIG IDEAS

Berger, A., 2012. A brief history of the astronomical theories of paleoclimates. In *Climate Change* (pp. 107-129). Springer, Vienna.
J. Imbrie and K. P. Imbrie, 1979. Ice *Ages: solving the mystery.* Harvard University Press.

James Croll, 1864. XIII. On the physical cause of the change of climate during geological epochs. *The London, Edinburgh, and Dublin Philosophical Magazine and Journal of Science,* 28(187), pp.121-137.

James Croll, 1875. *Climate and Time in Their Geological Relations: A theory of secular changes of the earth's climate.* Edward Stanford, London.

Colin P. Summerhayes, 2015. *Earth's Climate Revolution.* Wiley Blackwell. P.79

James Campbell Irons, 1896. *Autobiographical Sketch Of James Croll: with memoir of his life and work.* Edward Stanford, London.

The Saturday Review, October 1887.

Charles Darwin, 1883. *On The Origin of Species by Means of Natural Selection.* 6th Edition. Charles Murray. London.

Geikie, J., 1871. IV.—On Changes of Climate during the Glacial Epoch. *Geological Magazine,* 8(90), pp. 545-553.

J. Geikie, 1874. *The Great Ice Age*

221

Winchell, N. H., 1878, The recession of the Falls of Saint Anthony: Quarterly Journal of the Geological Society of London, p. 886-901.

Bol'shakov, V.A., Kapitsa, A. P. and Rees, W. G., 2012. James Croll: a scientist ahead of his time. *Polar Record, 48* (2), pp.201-205.

David E. Sugden, 2014. James Croll (1821–1890): ice, ice ages and the Antarctic connection. *Antarctic Science* 26(6), 604–613 (2014).

Dawson, A., 2021. The oceanographic contribution of James Croll. *Earth and Environmental Science Transactions of the Royal Society of Edinburgh, 112*(3-4), pp.253-260.

CHAPTER 11. TRYGGVE GRAN AND CAPTAIN SCOTT

Gordon Casely interview of Tryggve Gran, 1970.

David Crane, 2005. *Scott of the Antarctic: a life of courage and tragedy in the extreme south.* Harper Collins Publishers, London.

The Norwegian with Scott: Tryggve Gran's Antarctic Diary 1910-1913. Edited by Geoffrey Hattersley-Smith, Her Majesty's Stationery Office, 1984.

T. Griffith Taylor, 1916. *With Scott: the silver lining.* Smith, Elder, and Co., London.

Scott's Last Expedition, arranged by L. Huxley. Smith, Volume 1, Being the journals of Captain R. F. Scott Elder & Co., London, 1913.

T. Griffith Taylor, 1916. *With Scott: the silver lining.* Smith, Elder, and Co., London.

Evans, E. R. G. R., 1921. *South with Scott.* W, Collins Sons and Co., Ltd. London.

Scott's Last Expedition, arranged by L. Huxley. Smith, Volume II, Being the Reports of the Journeys & the Scientific Work Undertaken by Dr E. A. Wilson and the Surviving Members of the Expedition. Elder & Co., London, 1913.

Apsley Cherry-Garrard, 1951. *The Worst Journey in the World.* Chatto and Windus. London.

Roland Huntford. The Man Who Remembers Scott's Last Journey (The Observer, 31 March 1974)

CHAPTER 12. TRYGGVE GRAN FLIES THE NORTH SEA

Roland Huntford. The Man Who Remembers Scott's Last Journey (The Observer, 31 March 1974)

Roland Huntford, 1985. *Shackleton.* Hodder & Stoughton Ltd.

The Aeroplane. January 1, 1914.

The Aeroplane. June 18, 1914.

Tryggve Gran – Norges første flygerhelt. *Tidsskriftet* 30th June 2000.

Anne Hege Simonsen, 2013. *Tryggve Gran Is, Luft og Krig (Tryggve Gran, Ice, Air and War).* Cappelan Damm.

Lieut. Gran's Flight to Norway. *Aberdeen Press and Journal* 18/7/14

The Story and Tales of the Buchan Line. Compiled by Alan Sangster. 1983. Oxford Publishing Co.

Cameron Hazlehurst, 2013. *Ten Journeys to Camerons Farm.* ANU E Press.

Gordon Casely, 2003. Flying Scots – a century of flight. *Leopard, the magazine for NE Scotland.*

Erik Knut Hagen, 2007. Tryggve Gran. Newsletter for Warbirds of Norway Vol. 22, No.1 2007.

From *Cruden Bay: Only a dream away.* Cruden Bay Community Association pamphlet.

Lieut. Gran's Flight to Norway. *Flight.* August 1914.

The North Sea Crossed. *Aeroplane* August 1914

CHAPTER 13. TRYGGVE GRAN GOES TO WAR

John Barfoot, 1993. The Notes of a Norwegian Warbird. *Cross & Cockade International Journal*: The First World War Aviation Historical Society. Volume 24. No.1.

Christopher Cole and A. F. Cheesman, 1984. *The Air Defence of Britain 1914 - 1918.* Bodley Head, London.

Anne Strathie, 2015. *From Ice Floes to Battlefields: Scott's Antarctics in the First World War*. The History Press.

Kagohl 3 War Diary
http://www.airhistory.org.uk/rfc/Kagohl3-diary.html

Aberdeen Press and Journal, July 30, 1934.

Carl Severin Albretsen. Tryggve Gran – Norges første flygerhelt [Norway's First Pilot Hero]. *Tidsskriftet*. 30th June 2000

United States Department of State, 1956. *Foreign Relations of the United States: Diplomatic Papers 1939*. Volume 1 – General.
News of Norway. 1944. Volume 3. Norwegian Information Service. Washington.

CHAPTER 14. MARY PRATT

Nora Simpson interview 24/3/2018

Elizabeth Park interview 11/11/2021

www.buchandivers.com

Gordon Findlay interviews 28/3/2021, 28/6/2021.

Clay Blair, 1999. *Hitler's U-Boat War: The hunted 1942-1945*. Weidenfeld & Nicolson.

Norman Adams, 1990. The Reaper's Strangest Catch. *Scots Magazine*.

Jochen Brennecke, 1960. *The Hunters and The Hunted*. Corgi Books.

John White, 2016. *Endgame: The U-boats In-shore Campaign 1944-1945*. History Press.

John Ross Interview 4/11/2021.

Gordon Williamson, 2005. *Wolf Pack: The Story of the U-Boat in World War II*. Osprey Publishing.

Les Taylor, 2010. *Luftwaffe Over Scotland*. Whittles Publishing. Caithness.

Paul Fussell, 1989. *Wartime: Understanding and Behaviour in the Second World War*. Oxford University Press; Derek E. Johnson, 1978. *East Anglia at War, 1939-1945*.

BBC History website – A Fateful Voyage: Convoy under Attack in the Atlantic - Tale of Unexploded Bombs and Heroism by Bernard de Neumann 15 October 2014.

BBC - WW2 People's War - A Fateful Voyage: Convoy under Attack in the Atlantic - Tale of Unexploded Bombs and Heroism

Victor Frankl, 2004. *Man's Search for Meaning.* Rider.

John Hersey, 1946. *Hiroshima.* Alfred A. Knopf Inc.

Printed in Great Britain
by Amazon

86617506R00129